# Georgiana's World

# Georgiana's World

THE ILLUSTRATED *Georgiana, Duchess of Devonshire*

AMANDA FOREMAN

HarperCollins*Publishers*

First published in 2001 by
HarperCollins*Publishers*
77–85 Fulham Palace Road
London W6 8JB

The HarperCollins website address is:
www.**fire**and**water.**com



A CIP catalogue record for this book is available from the British Library.

ISBN: 0 00 712276 4

05 04 03 02 01
9 8 7 6 5 4 3 2 1

Text abridgment by Phyllis Richardson
Picture research by Julia Brown

Typeset in New Baskerville. The dies of the original version
of this typeface were engraved by the English printer and
typographer John Baskerville in about 1768.

Calligraphy by Rachel Yallop

Colour origination by Digital Imaging
Printed and bound in Great Britain by Bath Press Colourbooks

# *Débutante*

## 1757–1782

1757–1774

# Débutante

'I KNOW I WAS HANDSOME . . . and have always been fashionable, but I do assure you,' Georgiana, Duchess of Devonshire, wrote to her daughter at the end of her life, 'our negligence and ommissions have been forgiven and we have been loved, more from our being free from airs than from any other circumstance.' Lacking airs was only part of her charm. She had always fascinated people. According to the retired French diplomat Louis Dutens, who wrote a memoir of English society in the 1780s and 1790s, 'When she appeared, every eye was turned towards her; when absent, she was the subject of universal conversation.' Georgiana was not classically pretty, but she was tall, arresting, sexually attractive and extremely stylish. Indeed, the newspapers dubbed her the 'Empress of Fashion'. The famous Gainsborough portrait of Georgiana succeeds in capturing something of the enigmatic charm which her contemporaries found so compelling. However, it is not an accurate depiction of her features: her eyes were heavier, her mouth larger.

Georgiana Spencer was born at Althorp, outside Northampton, on 7 June 1757, the eldest child of the Earl and Countess Spencer. (She became Lady Georgiana Spencer at the age of eight, when her father, John Spencer, was created the first Earl Spencer in 1765.) She was a precocious and affectionate baby and the birth of her brother George, a year later, failed to diminish Lady Spencer's infatuation with her daughter. Georgiana would always have first place in her heart, she confessed: 'I will own I feel so partial to my Dear little Gee, that I think I never shall love another so well.' The arrival of a second daughter, Harriet, in 1761 did not alter Lady Spencer's feelings. They loved each other with a rare intensity. 'You are my best and dearest friend,' Georgiana told her when she was seventeen. 'You have my heart and may do what you will with it.'

Georgiana's father was only eleven when his own father died of alcoholism, leaving behind an estate worth £750,000 – roughly equivalent to £45 million today. (The usual method for estimating equivalent values is to multiply by sixty.) It was one of the largest fortunes in England and included 100,000 acres in twenty-seven different counties, five substantial residences, and a sumptuous collection of plate, jewels and old master paintings. Lord Spencer had an income of £700 a week in an era when a gentleman could live off £300 a year.

Georgiana's earliest memories were of travelling between the five houses. She learnt to associate the change in seasons with her family's move to a different location. During the 'season', when society took up residence 'in town' and parliament was in session, they lived in a draughty, old-fashioned house in Grosvenor Street. In the summer, when the stench of the cesspool next to the house and the clouds of dust generated by passing traffic became unbearable, they took refuge at Wimbledon Park, a Palladian villa on the outskirts of London. In the autumn they went north to their hunting lodge in Pytchley outside Kettering, and in the winter months, from November to March, they stayed at Althorp, the country seat of the Spencers for over 300 years. Georgiana was seven when the family moved their London residence to the newly built Spencer House in St James's, overlooking Green Park.

The Spencers entertained constantly and were generous patrons. Spencer House was often used for plays and concerts and Georgiana grew up in an extraordinarily sophisticated milieu of writers, politicians and artists. After dinner the guests would sometimes be entertained by a soliloquy delivered by the actor David Garrick or a reading by the writer Laurence Sterne, who

*Previous pages: Lady Spencer with Lady Georgiana Spencer, by Joshua Reynolds, 1760. Lady Spencer loved her first child with a rare intensity, writing to a friend that 'I will own I feel so partial to my Dear little Gee, that I think I never shall love another so well.'*

*A view of Green Park, 1760, from Devonshire House, with Buckingham House to the right and Spencer House to the left. Georgiana was seven when they moved into the newly built house that took seven years to build at a cost of almost £50,000. The travel writer and economist Arthur Young wrote, 'I know not in England a more beautiful piece of architecture. [It is] superior to any house I have seen.'*

*Above: John, first Earl Spencer, by Thomas Gainsborough, 1763. When Lady Spencer first knew him he loved to parade in the flamboyant fashions of the French aristocracy.*

*Above right: Georgiana, Countess Spencer, by Pompeo Batoni, 1764. The Duke of Queensberry declared that the Spencers were 'really the happiest people I ever saw in the marriage system'.*

dedicated a section of *Tristram Shandy* to the Spencers. The house had been built not to attract artists, however, but to consolidate the political prestige and influence of the family. The urban palaces of the nobility encircled Westminster like satellite courts. They were deliberately designed to combine informal politics with a formal social life. A ball might fill the vast public rooms one night, a secret political meeting the next. This was the age of the Whig oligarchy, when a handful of great landowning families sat in the cabinet, and owned or had a controlling interest in more than half the country's electoral boroughs. Land conferred wealth, wealth conferred power.

Ironically, there was one condition attached to Lord Spencer's inheritance: although he could sit in parliament he could not embark on a political career. However, he retained great influence because he could use his wealth to support or oppose the government. Margaret Georgiana Poyntz, known as Georgiana, met John Spencer in 1754 when she was seventeen, and immediately fell in love with him. 'I will own it,' she confided to a friend, 'and never deny it that I do love Spencer above all men upon Earth.' He was a handsome man then. His daughter inherited from him her unusual height and russet-coloured hair.

Georgiana's mother was intelligent, exceptionally well read and, unusually for women of her day, she could read and write Greek as well as French and Italian. Her father, Stephen Poyntz, had died when she was thirteen, leaving the family in comfortable but not rich circumstances. As a Privy Councillor to King George II, he brought up his children to be little courtiers like himself: charming, discreet and socially adept in all situations.

*Spencer House reflected Lord Spencer's taste as a connoisseur and passionate collector of rare books and Italian art. Each time he went abroad he returned with a cargo of paintings and statues for the house. This design for a room at Spencer House reveals something of the atmosphere of the Painted Room, the first complete neo-classical interior in Europe.*

The Spencers delighted in each other's company and were affectionate in public as well as in private. In middle age, Lady Spencer proudly told David Garrick, 'I verily believe that we have neither of us for one instant repented our lot from that time to this.' They had 'modern' attitudes both in their taste and in their attitude to social mores. They were also demonstrative and affectionate parents. 'I think I have experienced a thousand times,' Lady Spencer mused, 'that commendation does much more good than reproof.' She preferred to obtain obedience through indirect methods of persuasion, as this letter to eleven-year-old Georgiana shows: 'I would have neither of you go to the Ball on Tuesday, tho' I think I need not have mentioned this, as I flatter myself you would both chose rather to go with me, than when I am not there . . .' It was a sentiment typical of an age influenced by the ideas of John Locke and Jean Jacques Rousseau, whose books had helped to popularize the cult of 'sensibility'.

Georgiana's education reflected her parents' idea of a sound upbringing. During the week a succession of experts trooped up and down the grand staircase to instruct Georgiana in a range of subjects, both feminine (deportment and harp-playing) and practical (geography and languages). The aim was to make her polished but not overly educated. The royal drawing-master and miniaturist John Gresse taught her drawing. The composer Thomas Linley gave her singing lessons. The distinguished orientalist Sir William Jones, who was preparing her brother George for Harrow, taught her writing. She also learned French, Latin, Italian, dancing and horsemanship. Everything came easily to her, but what delighted Georgiana's mother in particular was her quick grasp of etiquette. Lady Spencer's own upbringing as a courtier's daughter made her keenly critical of Georgiana's comportment in public; it was almost the only basis, apart from religion, on which she judged her, praised her and directed her training.

Lady Spencer's emphasis on acquiring social skills encouraged the performer in Georgiana. In quiet moments she would compose little poems and stories to be recited after dinner. She loved to put on an 'evening' and entertain her family with dramatic playlets featuring heroines in need of rescue. While Georgiana bathed in the limelight, George concentrated on being the dependable, sensible child who could be relied upon to remember instructions. Harriet, despite being the youngest, enjoyed the least attention of all. She attached herself to Georgiana, content to worship her and perform the duties of a faithful lieutenant. George was proud of Georgiana's talent and at Harrow would show round the verse letters he had received from her. 'By this time there is not an old Dowager in or about Richmond that has not a copy of them; there's honour for you!' he informed her.

Despite being the clear favourite of the family, Georgiana was anxious and attention-seeking, constantly concerned about disappointing her parents. 'Although I can't write as well as my brother,' she told them plaintively when she was seven, 'I love you very much and him just as much.' Adults never failed to be charmed by Georgiana's lively and perceptive conversation and yet she valued their praise only if it made an impression on her mother and father.

In 1763, when Georgiana was six, the stability she had enjoyed came to an abrupt end when the Spencers embarked on a grand tour. Lord Spencer had trouble with his lungs and his invalid condition made him bad tempered. Lady Spencer, worn down by his moods, urged him to rest and heal in the warmer climate of the Continent. Most of their friends were going abroad. Britain had been at war with France for the previous seven years, but with the advent of peace, travel became possible again, and the English aristocracy could indulge in its favourite pastime: visiting 'the sights'.

Georgiana accompanied her parents while George and Harriet, both considered too young to undertake such a long journey, stayed behind. The Spencers' first stop was Spa, in what is now Belgium, in the Ardennes forest. Its natural warm springs and pastoral scenery made it a fashionable watering place among the European nobility. But the gentle atmosphere failed to soothe Lord Spencer's nerves, so Lady Spencer decided they should try Italy.

Lady Spencer wrote to her mother in July and asked her to come out to Spa to look after Georgiana while they were away. She admitted that she was leaving Georgiana behind 'with some difficulty', but she had always placed her role as a wife before that of motherhood. For Georgiana, already missing her siblings, her mother's sudden and inexplicable abandonment was a profound shock. For the next twelve months Georgiana lived in Antwerp with her grandmother. Believing, perhaps, that her parents had left her behind as a punishment for some unnamed misdeed, Georgiana became acutely self-conscious and anxious to please.

When her daughter and son-in-law returned Mrs Poyntz was amazed at the intensity of Georgiana's reaction: 'I never saw a child so overjoy'd, she could hardly speak or eat her dinner.' Lady Spencer immediately noticed that there was something different about her daughter but she decided she liked the change. Although Lady Spencer did not realize it, the improvement was at the cost of Georgiana's self-confidence. Without the inner resources which normally develop in childhood, she grew up depending far too much on other people. As a child it made her obedient; as an adult it made her susceptible to manipulation.

Lady Spencer had become pregnant with her fourth child and, in the autumn of 1765, gave birth to a daughter named Charlotte. She engrossed Lady Spencer's attention just as Georgiana had done nine years before. 'She is a sweet little poppet,' she wrote. This time Lady Spencer even breastfed the baby herself instead of hiring a wet nurse. But infant mortality, although improved since the seventeenth century, was still high. Charlotte died shortly after her first birthday.

Lord and Lady Spencer were shattered by the loss. 'You know the perhaps uncommon tenderness I have for my children,' Lady Spencer explained to her friend Thea Cowper. Three years later, in 1769, Charlotte was still very much in her heart when she had another daughter, whom they called Louise. But she too died after only a few weeks. After this the Spencers travelled obsessively, sometimes with and sometimes without the children, never spending more than a few months in England at a stretch. Seeking an answer for their 'heavy affliction', they turned to religion for comfort.

At night, however, religion was far from their thoughts as they sought distraction in more worldly pursuits. They set up gaming tables at Spencer House and Althorp and played incessantly with their friends until the small hours. Lady Spencer tried to control herself: 'Played at billiards and bowls and cards all evening and a part of the night,' she wrote in her diary. 'Enable me O God to persevere in my endeavour to conquer this habit as far as it is a vice,' she prayed on another

*Fireworks in Green Park to celebrate the signing of the Treaty of Paris, 1763. Now that the war was over, the Spencers, like the rest of the British aristocracy, could resume their travels abroad, and they soon embarked on a grand tour.*

Hamilton delin 1771
10

occasion. The more hours she spent at the gaming table, the more she punished herself with acts of self-denial, tying herself to a harsh regimen that involved rising at 5.30 every morning for prayers.

The children were silent witnesses to their parents' troubled life. Sometimes Georgiana and Harriet would creep downstairs to watch the noisy scenes taking place around the gaming table. 'I staid till one hour past twelve, but mama remained till six next morning,' Harriet wrote in her diary. When the children were older they were allowed to participate. Harriet recorded on a trip to Paris: 'A man came today to papa to teach him how he might always win at Pharo . . . for that his secret was infallible. Everybody has given him something to play for them, and papa gave him a louis d'or for my sister and me.'

Georgiana reacted to the loss of Charlotte and Louise by worrying excessively about her two younger siblings. She also became highly sensitive to criticism and the smallest remonstrance produced hysterical screams and protracted crying. Lady Spencer tried many different experiments to calm Georgiana, forcing her to spend hours in prayer and confining her to her room – to little effect. From this time forward Lady Spencer left nothing in Georgiana's development to chance. Even her thoughts were subject to scrutiny. 'Pray sincerely to God,' Lady Spencer ordered her, 'that he would for Jesus Christ's sake give his assistance without which you must not hope to do anything.'

Georgiana was only fourteen when people began to speculate on her choice of husband. Lady Spencer thought it would be a dreadful mistake if she married too young. 'I hope not to part with her till 18 at the soonest,' she told a friend in 1771. Her daughter's outward sophistication led many to think that she was more mature than her years. In 1772 the family embarked upon another grand tour, this time with all three children in tow, and in Paris Georgiana was greeted with a rapturous reception. According to a fellow English traveller, Georgiana was 'very highly admired. She has, I believe, an exceedingly good disposition of her own, and is happy in an education which it is to be hoped will counteract any ill effect from what may too naturally turn her head.'

Georgiana combined a perfect mastery of etiquette with a mischievous grace and ease which met with approval in the artificial and mannered atmosphere of the French court. People marvelled at the way in which she seemed so natural and yet also conscious of being on show. Many were daunted by the complex and highly choreographed set-pieces of the French salons. 'It was no ordinary science,' reminisced a retired courtier, 'to know how to enter with grace and assurance a salon where thirty men and women were seated in a circle round the fire, to penetrate this circle while bowing slightly to everyone, to advance straight to the mistress of the house, and to retire with honour, without clumsily disarranging one's fine clothes, lace ruffles, [and] head-dress of thirty-six curls powdered like rime . . .'

The family travelled around France for a few months and then moved on to Spa in the summer of 1773, where Georgiana celebrated her sixteenth birthday. They found many friends already there, including the twenty-four-year-old Duke of Devonshire. The Devonshires ranked among the first families of England and had been involved in politics since the reign of Henry VIII, when Sir William Cavendish oversaw the dissolution of the monasteries. Sir William was the second husband of four to the redoubtable Bess of Hardwick, the richest woman in England after Elizabeth I and the most prolific builder of her age. He was the only one whom she married for love, and when she died all her accumulated wealth went to her Cavendish sons. The eldest, William, used his mother's fortune to purchase the earldom of Devonshire from James I for £10,000.

*A rare portrait of the young Georgiana. She was an extremely sensitive child, and her mother worried that though she had 'a charming sensibility . . . when I reflect upon it . . . it gives me concern as I know by painful experience how much such a disposition will make her suffer hereafter'.*

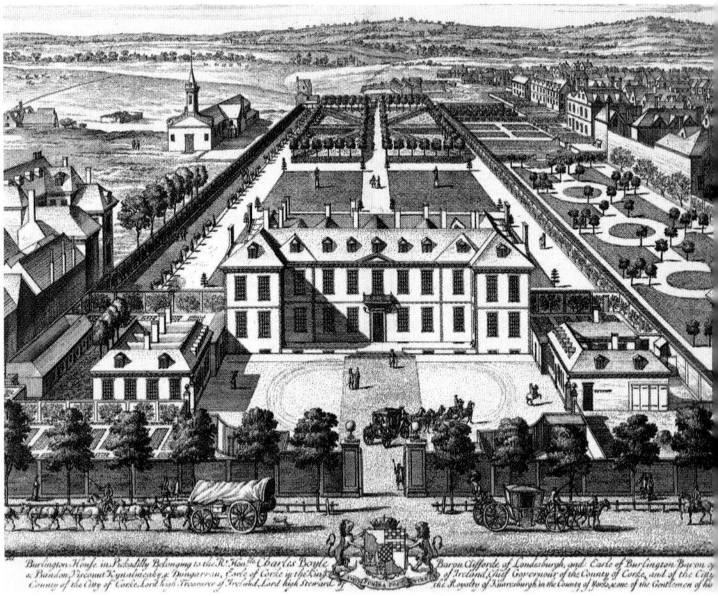

*This page: Bolton Abbey, left, and Burlington House, right, were among the grand estates that the fifth Duke of Devonshire inherited at the age of sixteen when his father, the fourth Duke, died in 1764.*

*Opposite: The fifth Duke of Devonshire, by Pompeo Batoni. Though he was one of the most sought-after bachelors in London, his social awkwardness caused many to think him unsuitable for Georgiana. 'Had he fallen under the tuition of the late Lord Chesterfield he might have possessed* les graces,*' wrote Mrs Delany, 'but at present only that of his dukedom belongs to him.'*

When the fourth Duke of Devonshire died in 1764 aged forty-four, his sixteen-year-old son William (who was never referred to as anything except 'the Duke') automatically became heir-presumptive to the leadership of the Whig party. But a contemporary politician, Nathaniel Wraxall, who knew him well, bemoaned the fact that the Whigs had to rely on a man so ill-suited to public life: 'Constitutional apathy formed his distinguishing characteristic. His figure was tall and manly, though not animated or graceful, his manners, always calm and unruffled. He seemed to be incapable of any strong emotion, and destitute of all energy or activity of mind.'

However, behind the Duke's wooden façade was an intelligent and well-educated mind. According to Wraxall,' his friends regarded him as an expert on Shakespeare and the classics.The Duke had barely known his mother, Lady Charlotte Boyle, who died when he was six. The fourth Duke had married her against his own mother's wishes and so the Duchess would have nothing more to do with her son; when he died she made no attempt to see her grandchildren. The fifth Duke, his two brothers Lords Richard and George, and sister Lady Dorothy, were brought up in cold splendour in the care of their Cavendish uncles. His lonely upbringing was reflected in his almost pathological reserve.

Georgiana's future husband was only sixteen when he came into an income that was twice Lord Spencer's; by one account it amounted to more than £60,000 a year. His property included not only the magnificent Chatsworth in Derbyshire and Devonshire House in London, but five other estates of comparable grandeur: Lismore Castle in Ireland, Hardwick House and Bolton Abbey in Yorkshire, and Chiswick House and Burlington House in London. He was one of the most sought-after bachelors in London – although the prolific diarist Mrs Delany found him boring and gauche: 'To be sure the jewell has *not been well polished.*'

Superficially, the Duke's character seemed not unlike Lord Spencer's: however, behind a shy exterior Georgiana's father concealed strong feelings. One of his few surviving letters to Georgiana, written after her marriage, bears eloquent witness to his warm heart: 'But indeed my

P. BATONI
ANNO

Dearest Georgiana, I did not know till lately how much I loved you; I miss you every day and every hour.' The twenty-four-year-old Duke had no such hidden sweetness, although Georgiana thought he did. The Spencers were extremely gratified by the interest he showed in their eldest daughter, and it did not escape Georgiana's notice that she was being watched; she knew that her parents wanted her to succeed.

By the end of summer, having danced with the Duke on several occasions and sat near him at numerous dinners, Georgiana had fallen in love with the idea of marrying him. His departure from Spa in the autumn of 1772 upset her greatly; she feared that he would make his choice before she was grown up. Lady Spencer, on the other hand, was relieved that the Duke had not made a formal offer. Even though there could be no more illustrious a match, she felt a 'dread . . . that she will be snatched from me before her age and experience make her by any means fit for the serious duties of a wife, a mother, or the mistress of a family'.

In fact the Duke had already made up his mind to marry Georgiana. She was an obvious choice: socially the Spencers were almost equal to the Cavendishes, she had a large dowry, she seemed likely to be popular and, most important, she was young and malleable. Despite Lady Spencer's reservations, discussions between the two families began in earnest while the Spencers were still abroad, and were concluded after they returned to England in the spring of 1774. By now Georgiana was almost seventeen and preparing to make her entrance into society. Hers was not to be an arranged marriage in the sense of those common a generation before. She was not exchanged in lieu of gambling debts, nor thrown in as part of a political alliance. However, it cannot be said that Georgiana had been free to make a proper choice. Unlike her mother she had not been out for several seasons before her marriage, and she had not accepted the Duke because she loved him 'above all men upon Earth'. She would go to any lengths to please her parents, and that included thinking herself in love with a man she hardly knew.

*Georgiana, Harriet and George Spencer, 1774. Clever, amusing and attractive Georgiana always outshone her siblings, though they were a close and affectionate family. George was an eminently sensible and responsible brother and son, and Harriet was unambitious for herself, content to worship Georgiana and perform the duties of a faithful lieutenant.*

As the marriage approached Georgiana's faults became an obsession with her mother, who feared that her daughter did not understand the responsibilities which would come with her new role: 'She is amiable, innocent and benevolent, but she is giddy, idle and fond of dissipation.' Whenever they were apart, Lady Spencer criticized Georgiana's behaviour in long letters filled with 'hints to form your own conduct . . . when you are so near entering into a world abounding with dissipation, vice and folly'.

Most observers shared Lady Spencer's disquiet, although not for the same reason.

> We drank tea in the Spring Gardens [recorded Mary Hamilton in her diary]: Lady Spencer and daughter, Lady Georgiana, and the Duke of Devonshire joined us: he walked between Lady Georgiana and I, we were very Chatty, but not one word spoke the Duke to his betrothed nor did one smile grace his dull visage. – Notwithstanding his rank and fortune I wd not marry him – they say he is sensible and has good qualities – it is a pity he is not more ostensibly agreeable, dear charming Lady Georgiana will not be well matched.

Meanwhile the Spencers assembled a lavish trousseau. In three months they spent a total of £1,486 on hundreds of items: sixty-five pairs of shoes filled one trunk, forty-eight pairs of stockings and twenty-six 'and a half' pairs of gloves filled another. They bought hats, feathers and trimmings; morning dresses, walking dresses, riding habits and ball gowns. There was her wedding dress to be made, her court dress, her first visiting dress, as well as cloaks, shawls and wraps. The prospect of a

union between two such wealthy and powerful families naturally caught the attention of the press – there had been no Duchess of Devonshire for over two decades. People described the marriage as the wedding of the year and anticipated that the new Duchess of Devonshire would revive the former splendour of Devonshire House. The Whig grandees also looked upon the match with favour, hoping that the married state would have a beneficial effect on the Duke.

The wedding took place on 7 June 1774, two days earlier than the official date. There had been so much publicity about the marriage that the Spencers feared the church would be mobbed with curious onlookers. They persuaded the Duke to accompany them to Wimbledon Park and have the service conducted in the parish church there. According to Mrs Delany, Georgiana knew nothing of their plans until the morning of the ceremony. She did not mind at all; a secret marriage appealed to her. 'She is so peculiarly happy as to think his Grace *very agreeable*' and, to Mrs Delany's surprise, 'had not the least regret' about anything. She wore a white and gold dress, with silver slippers on her feet and pearl drops in her hair. There were only five people present: the Duke's brother, Lord Richard Cavendish, and his sister Dorothy, who was now the Duchess of Portland, and on Georgiana's side only her parents and grandmother, Lady Cowper. Georgiana's feelings clearly showed on her face, while the Duke appeared inscrutable. His new wife may have occupied his thoughts, although they may well have turned to another Spencer. Not very far away in a rented villa, on a discreet road where a carriage could come and go unseen, Charlotte Spencer, formerly a milliner and no relation to the Spencers, was nursing a newborn baby: his – their – daughter Charlotte.

# 1774–1776 Fashion's Favourite

*The excess to which pleasure and dissipation are now carried amongst the* ton *exceeds all bounds, particularly among women of quality. The duchess of D—e has almost ruined her constitution by the hurrying life which she has led for some time; her mother, Lady S—r has mentioned it with concern to the Duke, who only answers, 'Let her alone – she is but a girl.'*

MORNING POST, MONDAY 11 MARCH 1776

THREE DAYS AFTER THE WEDDING the Duke was spotted with his drinking companions trawling the pleasure gardens of Ranelagh at Chelsea. He provoked more gossip when he turned up four hours late for his presentation at court with Georgiana. All newly married couples were required to present themselves to the Queen at one of her twice-weekly public audiences at St James's Palace, known as 'Drawing Rooms'. 'The Drawing-room was fuller than ever I saw it,' a witness recorded, 'excepting that of a Birthday [of the King or Queen], owing, as I suppose, to the curiosity to see the Duchess of Devonshire.' Georgiana was wearing her wedding dress and 'look'd very pretty . . . happiness was never more marked in a countenance than hers'. The formidable Lady Mary Coke wondered why the Duke ambled in on his own several hours after Georgiana.

Protocol demanded that Georgiana should pay a call on every notable person in society. For the next three weeks she went from house to house, making polite conversation for fifteen minutes

*Right: A Drawing Room at St James's Palace. Though protocol in the London court was complicated and highly charged, it was much more relaxed than the French salons, which were more rigorous and contrived. Georgiana won praise in both arenas.*

*Below: The interior of the rotunda at Ranelagh Gardens, by Canaletto. Georgiana and her friends often attended entertainments at the gardens. Once she was almost attacked by a crowd because 'she was dressed in a stile so whimsically singular as quickly collected the company round her, they behaved with great rudeness, in so much that she was necessitated to take shelter in one of the boxes, and there remained prisoner for some time, until the motley crew had retired.'*

*Chatsworth. The original Elizabethan house was transformed by successive generations of Cavendishes. The traveller and diarist Joseph Torrington thought the grounds lacked taste, even though they were the work of Capability Brown, and the house itself 'vile and uncomfortable'. He disliked the heavy use of gilt and the combination of unpainted wainscoting and inlaid wood floors which made the rooms so dark even during the day.*

while her hosts scrutinized the new Duchess of Devonshire. Georgiana's visits were highly prized. Lady Mary Coke was not among the 500 whom Georgiana managed to see, which soured her feelings towards her cousin for ever after.

In early July Georgiana set off with the Duke on the three-day journey from London to Derbyshire, to stay at Chatsworth for the summer. The long hours on the road, with no amusement save the view from the window, were the first she had spent alone with her husband. He had hardly addressed a word to her since the day of their marriage. His taciturnity made her nervous and she overcompensated by being excessively lively.

Georgiana's first glimpse of Chatsworth revealed a rectangular stone box, some 172 feet long and three storeys high, with the Cavendish symbol of interlocking serpents carved along the length of the cornice. As a whole the house and parkland was far more imposing than Althorp. The original Elizabethan design had been transformed by successive generations of Cavendishes, and by the 1770s Chatsworth had an old-fashioned feel; its layout, which followed the seventeenth-century practice of linking public and private rooms along a single axis, was inconvenient and impractical; newer houses had their family apartments entirely separate from their entertaining rooms. But Chatsworth was meant to be more than a family home. Its sumptuous rooms, with their classical wall paintings and triumphant gods staring down from the ceilings, were meant to inspire awe among the lower orders who trooped round on Public Days, and respect – as well as envy – among the aristocracy. Comfort was a secondary consideration. The dining room could easily accommodate over a hundred but – as Georgiana discovered – there were only three water closets in the entire house.

She was not alone with the Duke for long. The Spencers came to stay for an extended visit, bringing with them her sister Harriet and an assortment of pets, favourite horses and servants. They came in part to provide Georgiana with the support and guidance she desperately needed. The Duke's brothers and uncles were already there to check on her behaviour as the new Duchess and chatelaine of Chatsworth. Georgiana was on show from the moment she stepped out of her carriage. Aristocratic life in the eighteenth century had little in the way of privacy: almost every activity took place before an audience of servants. The social pressure on Georgiana was intense. She was now the wife of one of the most powerful men in the country. Everyone – from the staff, to the neighbours, to the people who met her at public functions or read about her in the papers – expected her to know precisely how to perform.

The Duke's agent, Heaton, had prepared a list of the household expenses for her, which included the names of the parishioners and tenants who received charity from the estate and whose welfare was now in her trust. Some received food, others alms. Georgiana's first task was to fulfil her social obligations and, with the importance of the Cavendish name in mind, to establish goodwill between herself and the Duke's many dependants.

These duties gave a rhythm to Georgiana's first days and weeks at Chatsworth. In the morning the men went out riding or shooting, while she made exploratory visits to the neighbourhood accompanied by Lady Spencer, who was pregnant again. She quickly made friends with the Duke's tenants, displaying the charm and sympathy for which she would become renowned. They would return at mid-day, rest, and prepare for dinner at three. It was the most important meal of the day and could last up to four hours. Instead of one course following another, there were two 'covers', or servings, of fifteen or so sweet and savoury dishes, artfully arranged in geometric patterns and decorated with flowers. Georgiana self-consciously practised being the hostess in front of her

*Establishing goodwill between herself and the Duke's tenants was one of Georgiana's first duties at Chatsworth. Her friendly nature quickly won people over. As Mrs Delany commented after meeting Georgiana, 'I can't tell you all the civil things she said, and really they deserve a better name, which is* kindness *embellished by* politeness.'

parents and the Duke, giving orders to footmen and displaying a command which she did not necessarily feel. Not only did Georgiana have to keep up a lively flow of conversation, she also had to watch the servants for neglect, the guests for boredom, and the Cavendishes for signs of displeasure.

In the evening she played cards with some of the guests or listened to music performed by Felix Giardini, the violinist and director of the London Opera. At her request he composed pieces which Georgiana and some of her musical guests performed. As more of the Duke's friends and relatives came to inspect his bride, Georgiana did her best to appear composed and friendly towards the sophisticated strangers who often arrived at short notice and expected to be entertained. Since Georgiana had little acquaintance with her husband or with his world, she depended upon the presence of Lady Spencer by her side for guidance through the first few months.

But in late September Lady Spencer returned to Althorp, having suffered another miscarriage. Georgiana was distraught. Her days were lonely now. 'As soon as I am up and have breakfasted I ride,' she wrote. 'I then come in and write and or do anything of employment, I then walk, dress for Dinner and after Dinner I take a short walk if it is fine and I have time 'till the Gentlemen come out, and then spend the remainder of the evening in Playing at Whist, or writing if I have an opportunity and reading.' Not caring for his wife's after-dinner concerts, the Duke usually took his friends off to drink and play billiards. Georgiana would not see him until much later when, already in bed, she would be woken up – he was impatient for her to become pregnant. She often rose full of dread at what lay ahead in the day. Sometimes she stayed in bed as long as possible, but this evasive measure brought its own problems, such as when she awoke late to find

> another Coachful arrived – of People I had never seen before. As I could not have much to say for myself, and some of the Company were talking about things I knew nothing of, I made the silliest figure you can conceive, and *J* [Lord John Cavendish] says I broke all the rules of Hospitality in forgetting to offer them some breakfast.

She also had to preside over the Public Days which had resumed after Lady Spencer's departure. Chatsworth still maintained the tradition of holding a weekly Public Day when the house was open to all the Duke's tenants, as well as to any respectable stranger who wished to see the house and have dinner with its owners. Georgiana and the Duke stood in the hall wearing their finest clothes, and personally greeted each visitor. They had to remain gracious and sober while their guests helped themselves to the free food and drink. 'Some of the men got extremely drunk,' Georgiana recorded after one dinner, and her friends, 'if they had not made a sudden retreat, would have been the victims of a drunken clergyman, who very nearly fell on them.'

That year the Public Days had a particular purpose; a general election was scheduled in October and the Cavendishes were defending their electoral interests in Derbyshire. The Cavendish influence in parliament depended on the number of MPs who sat in the family's 'interest'. Since peers were barred from personally campaigning in parliamentary elections, their wives and relatives had to look after their interests for them. On 8 October Georgiana went to her first election ball in Derby, dressed in fashionable London clothes for the benefit of the locals. The Duke's brothers were already drunk by the time she arrived and an open-door policy had drawn a crowd. Despite the heat and the sweat, as well as the appalling noise of the amateur musicians, Georgiana kept her poise. The next ball she attended revealed the Derbyshire voters' opinion of the new Duchess: 'we were received there by a great huzza,' she recorded. 'The room was very much crowded but they were so good as to split in 2 to make room for us.'

Despite the fact that people responded favourably to her youth and enthusiasm, Georgiana was constantly terrified of forgetting herself and committing some *faux pas.* The Cavendishes sternly demanded that she conform to their ways. Their manner stamped itself on all members of the family, from the relentless self-control they exerted on their emotions to the peculiar drawl which marred their speech – they pronounced her name 'George-ayna'. In her eagerness to be accepted Georgiana adopted all their mannerisms, even vigorously applying the Cavendish drawl.

By now, three months into her marriage, Georgiana could not help but suspect the true nature of the Duke's feelings towards her. He was kind in a distant sort of way, but he was naturally reticent and she soon realized that they had little in common. Her innocence bored him and Georgiana was too acute not to notice his lack of interest in her. She told her mother that she was secretly making an effort to be more attractive to him. Since he was so much more worldly than her, she read Lord Chesterfield's *Letters to His Son*; and knowing of his interest in history and the classics she began several books on ancient Greece and on the reign of Louis XIV, 'for as those two periods are so distant there will be no danger of their interfering so as to puzzle me'.

At first Lady Spencer tried to reassure her that the Duke 'was no less happy than herself'. She also supplied her daughter with advice on how to please him, suggesting that she should curb any thoughts of independence and show her submission by anticipating his desires. 'A wife must use all possible delicacy and ingenuity,' she instructed, 'in trying to find out his inclinations, and the utmost readiness in conforming to them.'

Georgiana had entered into marriage thinking that, like her mother, she would be a wife and companion. She soon discovered that her chief role was to produce children and carry out her social obligations. The Duke was used to his bachelor life: love he received from his mistress, companionship from his friends; from his wife he expected loyalty, support and commitment to the family's interests. Never having experienced tenderness himself he was incapable of showing it to Georgiana. He did not mean to hurt her, but there was a nine-year age difference between them and a gulf of misunderstanding and misplaced expectations.

They left Chatsworth in January, much to Georgiana's relief. In London she would be surrounded by her own family and friends and no longer reliant on the monosyllabic Duke or his critical relations. Devonshire House lay in London's western end, known as the 'polite' end, encompassing Piccadilly, St James's and Hyde Park. The court resided at St James's Palace when parliament was in session but the aristocracy had to be in London for much longer periods of time, and in a location convenient for both Westminster and St James's. The concentration of so much wealth and power transformed the city. There was a frenzy of building as the capital spread out westwards. By the 1770s modern London was envied throughout Europe for its glass-fronted shops and spacious roads that easily accommodated two lanes of traffic.

*After the Glorious Revolution, parliament met according to a set calendar, during which the aristocratic 'season' took place and the nobility moved from the country to London. The accumulation of so much wealth in one area of the capital caused a frenzy of building activity. By the 1770s, London was envied throughout Europe for its glass-fronted shops and spacious, two-lane roads.*

The aristocratic 'season' came into existence not only to further the marriage market but to entertain the upper classes while they carried out their political duties. The season began in late October with the opening of the new session of parliament, and ended in June with the summer recess. Coffee houses – where men of all classes gathered during the day to read newspapers and discuss politics – had begun to spring up. White's, the first of the London clubs, opened in St James's in 1697; Almack's, Boodles and Brooks's followed half a century later.

Situated opposite what is now the Ritz Hotel, Devonshire House commanded magnificent views over Green Park. The chief attraction of Devonshire House was the public rooms, which were larger and more ornate than almost anything to be seen in London. A crowd of 1,200 could easily sweep through the house during a ball. Guests entered the house by an outer staircase which took them directly to the first floor. Inside was a hall two storeys high – flanked on either side by two drawing rooms of identical size. Beyond the hall was another, even larger drawing room, several anterooms and the dining room. Some of the finest paintings in England adorned the walls, including Rembrandt's *Old Man in Turkish Dress*, and Poussin's *Et in Arcadia Ego*.

Georgiana and the Duke were naturally placed to become the leaders of society's most select group, known as the *ton* or 'the World' – the ultra-fashionable people who decided whether a play was a success, an artist a genius, or what colour would be 'in' that season. The social tyrants who made up the *ton* also considered it deeply unfashionable for a wife and husband to be seen too much in each other's company. The Duke escorted Georgiana to the opera once and then resumed his habit of visiting Brooks's, where he always ordered the same supper – a broiled blade-bone of mutton – and played cards until five or six in the morning. Occasionally they went to a party together but Georgiana was expected to make her own social arrangements. There was no shortage of invitations and she accepted everything – routs, assemblies, card parties, promenades in the park – in an effort to avoid sitting alone in Devonshire House.

With her instinctive ability to make an impression, Georgiana immediately caused a sensation. She was 'so handsome, so agreeable, so obliging in her manner, that I am *quite* in love with her', Mrs Delany burbled to a friend. 'I can't tell you all the civil things she said, and really they deserve a better name, which is *kindness* embellished by *politeness*. I hope she will *illumine* and *reform* her

ERLAND.
Grocer.
No. 32
COLEMAN.

*Devonshire House, London. Situated opposite what is now the Ritz Hotel, Devonshire House was rebuilt after a fire in 1733. The new house was stark and devoid of architectural detail. The building was enclosed behind a brick wall which hid the ground floor from view. One contemporary complained, 'The Duke of Devonshire's is one of those which present a horrid blank of wall, cheerless and unsociable by day, and terrible by night.'*

contemporaries!' Even cynics like Horace Walpole found their resistance worn down by Georgiana's unforced charm and directness. Observing her transformation into a society figure, Walpole marvelled that 'The Duchess of Devonshire effaces all . . . without being a beauty; but her youth, figure, flowing good nature, sense and lively modesty, and modest familiarity, make her a phenomenon.'

Occasionally Georgiana drank too much, especially when she was nervous, and showed off as a result: 'nothing is talked of but the Duchess of Devonshire: and I am sorry to say not much in her favour,' wrote a society lady after Georgiana upset a dignified matron by pulling out her hair feathers. Lady Mary Coke went to Ranelagh and was disgusted to see Georgiana and her new friends amusing themselves by puffing out their cheeks and popping them.

Lady Spencer could see that Georgiana was falling in with the fast set. The gambling in particular worried her: 'let me entreat you to beware of it, and if [gambling] is mention'd to you any more, to decline the taking any part in it,' she begged. Gaming was to the aristocracy what gin was to the working classes: it caused the ruin of families and corrupted lives. 'A thousand meadows and cornfields are staked at every throw, and as many villages lost as in the earthquake that overwhelmed Herculaneum and Pompeii,' wrote Horace Walpole, who had seen men lose an entire estate in a single night. 'Play at whist, commerce, backgammon, trictrac or chess,' Lady

Spencer urged, 'but never at quinze, lou, brag, faro, hazard or any games of chance . . .' Georgiana – as dependent on parental approval as ever – felt guilty and went to even greater lengths to distract herself with frivolity.

Her recklessness entranced society even as it caused disapproval. Whatever she wore became instantly fashionable. 'The Duchess of Devonshire is the most envied woman of the day in the *Ton*,' the newspapers reported. After the three-foot 'hair tower', another of Georgiana's fashion innovations was the drooping ostrich feather, which she attached in a wide arch across the front of her hair. Overnight it became the most important accessory in a lady's wardrobe, even though the tall nodding plumes were difficult to find and extremely expensive. The *ton* wore them with a smug arrogance which infuriated the less fortunate and caused the Queen to ban ostrich feathers from court.

Newspaper editors noticed that any report on the Duchess of Devonshire increased their sales. By the end of the 1770s there were nine daily newspapers, all based in London, and hundreds of bi- and tri-weekly provincial papers which reprinted the London news. For the first time national figures emerged, Georgiana among them, which the whole country read about and discussed, and with whom they could feel some sort of connection. In less than a year Georgiana had eclipsed her husband and become a popular figure in her own right.

*Brooks's was a Whig club, where men gathered to read newspapers, discuss politics and gamble. One contemporary described the gamesters' unusual attire: they put on 'frieze greatcoats, or turned their coats inside outwards for good luck. They put on pieces of leather . . . to save their laced ruffles; to shield their eyes from the light and hold up curls, etc., they wore high-crowned straw hats with broad brims, adorned with flowers and ribbons.'*

Parrures des Dames.
Cœffure à l'Indépendance ou le Triomphe de la liberté

TOILETTE DE LA DUCHESSE DES PLUMES OU LE TRIOMPHE DE LA FOLIE DU SIECLE


During that year Georgiana had also brought herself to a state of nervous and physical exhaustion. She had suffered at least one miscarriage, which convinced Lady Spencer that her daughter should leave England, if only to remain quiet for a while. In July the Spencers and the Devonshires set off for a holiday in Spa. After a few weeks Georgiana's health returned and her unnatural pallor disappeared. On their return they stopped at Versailles to pay their respects to Louis XVI. Georgiana already had more than a passing acquaintance with Marie Antoinette, having met her during previous trips to France. On this visit a close friendship developed which lasted until the Queen's execution in 1793. They discovered they had much in common, not only in having married a position rather than a lover, but also in their intense relations with their mothers.

Similar words have often been used to describe both Georgiana and Marie Antoinette. Horace Walpole thought Marie Antoinette grace itself, and called her a 'statue of beauty'. She had immense charm, which at first endeared her to the court and the people, but she shared Georgiana's tendency to take everything to excess. Her addiction to trivial amusements has also been attributed to her frustration with her marriage.

It was on this visit, too, that Georgiana formed lifelong friendships with members of Marie Antoinette's set, particularly with the ambitious Polignacs. The Austrian ambassador to France complained to the Empress Marie Thérèse that Marie Antoinette was infatuated with the Duchesse de Polignac. The 'Little Po', as she was nicknamed, was a sweet-natured, elegant brunette who exerted a powerful attraction on both Marie Antoinette and Georgiana. Throughout Georgiana's stay the three women went everywhere together, wore each other's favours on their bosoms, and

*Opposite: Women's hair was already arranged high above the head, but Georgiana created the three-foot hair tower. She stuck pads of horse hair to her own hair using scented pomade and decorated the top with miniature ornaments. Sometimes she carried a ship in full sail, or an exotic arrangement of stuffed birds and waxed fruit. The extravagance was, of course, mocked in the press.*

*This page: Ostrich feathers, which were difficult to find and extremely expensive, became the focus of another of Georgiana's trendsetting styles. But the excess generated resentment: according to Lady Louisa Stuart, 'the unfortunate feathers were insulted, mobbed, hissed, almost pelted wherever they appeared.'*

exchanged locks of hair as keepsakes. Georgiana's passionate nature, thwarted in her marriage to the Duke, found fulfilment in such an atmosphere.

On her return to England Georgiana made a renewed effort to please her husband. Initially he responded with unaccustomed sensitivity. 'The Duke is in very good spirits,' she wrote in September 1775. 'I sincerely hope he is contented with me, tho' if he is not he hides it very well, for it is impossible to say how good and attentive he is to me, and how much he seems to make it his business to see me happy and pleas'd.'

But they had so little in common that their efforts to establish a deeper intimacy had petered out by Christmas. It was not a question of dislike; neither understood the other. The Duke was used to being flattered and cosseted by his mistress Charlotte Spencer and resented the emotional demands that Georgiana made upon him. Georgiana, on the other hand, treated him as if he were part of her audience and then wondered why her reserved and shy husband failed to respond. A family tale reveals the misunderstanding between them. The Duke was drinking a dish of tea with Lady Spencer and Harriet when Georgiana walked into the room and sat on his lap with her arms around his neck. Without saying a word he pushed her off and left the company.

Rejected by the Duke, Georgiana once more sought consolation in the fashionable world as soon as the season began. Newspapers speculated on how long she could keep up the frantic pace of her life before her health collapsed. They only had to wait a couple of months. In April 1776 Georgiana went into premature labour. No one was surprised by her miscarriage. The *Morning Post* claimed with gloomy pleasure that the physicians had given up and her death was imminent.

Georgiana denied the prophets of doom their satisfaction, but her recovery was much slower than it should have been. She was harbouring a secret: she was deeply in debt. She had placed all hope of repaying her gambling dues in the birth of the lost child, positive that the Duke would forgive her in the general glow of happiness. Now that her plans had gone awry she had no idea what to do and the worry affected her health. She was not the first woman to find herself in such a predicament; it was a popular theme in the press. Georgiana could not even bring herself to think how she might tell the Duke or her mother that her gambling debts amounted to at least £3,000 (£180,000 in today's money) when her pin money came to £4,000 a year. Like everyone else, the Duke blamed the miscarriage on her reckless living.

In July Georgiana's creditors threatened to apply directly to the Duke, which frightened her into confessing the truth to her parents. They were so angry that Lady Clermont, who had known the Spencer family for many years, felt obliged to intercede on her behalf:

> The conversation you had with the Duchess made so great an impression on her that it made her quite ill. She has not seen anybody since she came to town, except myself, not one of the set. I am convinced she will be very different in everything . . . I do beg you will not say any more to her.

The Spencers listened to Lady Clermont's plea for calm. They paid Georgiana's debts but insisted that she reveal everything to the Duke. When she told him, falteringly and with many tears, he hardly said a word. He promptly repaid her parents and then never referred to the matter again. This unnerved Georgiana more than a display of anger. After a measured period of silence Lady Spencer began writing to her again, but for the first time Lady Spencer sensed that she was losing her hold over her daughter and she feared for the future.

*Marie Antoinette, 1775. Georgiana developed a close relationship with the French Queen, which lasted until the latter's execution in 1793. They had much in common, both being married to men who were not in love with them and having mothers who were dominating and interfering.*

1776–1778

# *The Vortex of Dissipation*

*Gaming among the females at Chatsworth has been carried to such a pitch that the phlegmatic Duke has been provoked to express at it and he has spoken to the Duchess in the severest terms against a conduct which has driven many from the house who could not afford to partake of amusements carried on at the expense of £500 or £1000 a night.*

MORNING POST AND DAILY ADVERTISER, WEDNESDAY 4 SEPTEMBER 1776

'COMING HERE HAS MADE a strong impression on me,' Georgiana wrote during a visit to the Devonshires' Londesborough estate in October 1776. 'Alas,' she continued, 'I can't help but make an unhappy comparison between the emotions I experienced two years ago during my first visit, and what I feel now.' She was suffering from a profound sense of disillusionment, not only with her marriage but also with fashionable life.

For those who could moderate their pursuit of pleasure, Whig society was sophisticated, tolerant and cosmopolitan. Whigs prided themselves on their patronage of the arts as much as they venerated their contribution to statecraft. They were the oligarchs of taste, proselytizers of their superior cultivation. But the *ton*, by definition, inhabited the realm of the extreme. 'You must expect to be class'd with the company you keep,' was Lady Spencer's constant warning to Georgiana. Embarrassed by her own previous association with the *ton*, Lady Spencer regarded it as a magnet for the least respectable elements of her class, and Georgiana's friends as the worst among the bad.

The people who gathered around Georgiana and the Duke shared an attachment to the Whig party, a worldly attitude, a passion for the theatre and a love of scandal. Fashion was the only 'career' open to aristocratic women; politics the only 'trade' that a man of rank might pursue. It was not long before society labelled the *habitués* of Devonshire House the 'Devonshire House Circle'. All Whigs were welcome, of course, but the older, staider members felt ill at ease among the more rakish elements.

*Georgiana emerged as a leader of the* ton, *the small circle of aristocratic men and women who set the trends in fashion and culture and were given to excess. Henry Fielding wrote of the* ton *that 'Nobody' was 'all the people in Great Britain, except about 1200'. Fanny Burney wrote in* Cecilia: *'There's nothing in the world so fashionable as taking no notice of things, and never seeing people, and saying nothing at all . . . and always finding fault; all the ton do so.'*

Serious Devonshire House acolytes identified themselves by their imitation of the Cavendish drawl. By now Georgiana never spoke in any other way and the more it became one of her personal mannerisms, the more compelling it was to her admirers. The 'Devonshire House Drawl' has been characterized as part baby-talk, part refined affectation: hope was written and pronounced as 'whop'; you became 'oo'. Vowels were compressed and extended so that cucumber became 'cowcumber', yellow 'yaller', gold 'goold', and spoil rhymed with mile. Stresses fell on unexpected syllables, such as bal-*cony* instead of *bal*-cony and con-*tem*plate. By the middle of the next century all Whigs would speak in the Drawl, transforming a family tradition into a symbol of political allegiance, but in Georgiana's time it remained the Circle's own *patois*.

At its broadest the Circle numbered more than a hundred people; at its most intimate, thirty. In modern terms they were London's 'café society': the racier members of the aristocracy mixed with professional artists and actors, scroungers, libertines and wits. The playwright and arch-scrounger Richard Brinsley Sheridan was one of its stars. An incorrigible drinker, womanizer and plotter, he embodied the best and worst of the Circle. He was brilliant yet lazy. He was introduced to Georgiana through his wife, the beautiful and talented singer Elizabeth Linley, and worked

feverishly to ingratiate himself into the Circle. He made it his business to be entertaining, to be useful, to know every secret and to have a hand in every intrigue.

David Garrick was another celebrated theatrical member of the Circle. After watching him give a pre-supper performance, Georgiana wrote: 'I have no terms to express the horror of Mr Garrick's reading *Macbeth.* I have not recovered yet, it is the finest and most dreadful thing I ever saw or heard . . .' Second to Garrick in celebrity was the sculptress Mrs Damer, whose heads of Father Thames and the goddess Isis still adorn Henley Bridge. Her husband, the Hon. John Damer, was a pathetic drunk and gamester. In August 1775 he shot himself through the head in a room above the Bedford Arms at Covent Garden after having ruined them both in a single night.

The famous wit James Hare was a member, and was Georgiana's particular favourite, being discreet and trustworthy – rare attributes in the Devonshire House world. Georgiana also felt a special affection for the Whig politician and bibliophile Thomas Grenville, who reputedly never married because of his hopeless love for her.

The women, who were no less extraordinary, divided into those who were received by polite society and those who were not, and included 'beauties' and celebrated hostesses such as Lady Clermont, a great favourite at Versailles, Lady Derby, who had once hoped to marry the Duke of Devonshire, and Lady Jersey, who used her 'irresistible seduction and fascination' to wreck the marriages of her friends. The women were highly competitive and spent much of their time putting one another down.

Lady Spencer loathed one woman in particular: Lady Melbourne. Beautiful, clever and ruthless, Lady Melbourne epitomized the decadence of Georgiana's friends. The incurable gossip Lord Glenbervie recorded in his diary, 'it was a very general report and belief that . . . Lord Coleraine sold Lady Melbourne to Lord Egremont for £13,000, that both Lady and Lord Melbourne were parties to this contract and had each a share of the money.'

Before Georgiana's entry into the *ton* Lady Melbourne had reigned as its leading hostess. People naturally assumed that they would become rivals, but Lady Melbourne had no intention of setting herself up in opposition to Georgiana. She befriended her and adopted the role of benign older counsel instead. Lady Melbourne was a natural manager of people. She had a firm grasp of the recondite laws which governed life within the *ton*, and an unsentimental, even cynical view of humanity. 'Never trust a man with another's secret,' she is reputed to have said, 'never trust a woman with her own.'

Georgiana's activities had become an obsession with the press. Her clothes, her movements, her friends – in short anything new or unusual about her – was considered newsworthy. Rarely did a week go by without a snippet of gossip appearing somewhere. The scandal sheets embroiled her in fictitious escapades with numerous lovers, and there were enough stories of licentious behaviour attached to members of the Circle to give any allegation the veneer of plausibility.

Audiences flocked to Drury Lane in May 1777 to see Sheridan's new play, *The School for Scandal,* partly because it was known to be a satire on the Devonshire House Circle. Sheridan pandered to the audience's expectations by portraying Georgiana's friends as a set of louche aristocrats whose moral sensibilities had been blunted by a life of wealth without responsibility. Georgiana is Lady Teazle: young, easily influenced, possessed of a good heart but needing a firm husband to manage her properly. Members of the Circle thought it was a tremendous joke to see themselves caricatured on stage, and helped to publicize the play by ostentatiously arriving *en masse* to watch the first night.

*David Garrick, opposite, and Mrs Damer, above, were among the celebrity members of the Devonshire House Circle. Georgiana had known the actor since she was a child as he was often a guest in their house. The sculptress Mrs Damer was unhappily married to the Hon. John Damer, a pathetic drunk and gamester.*

Georgiana's thoughts on being portrayed as Lady Teazle have not survived, but the play almost certainly made her uneasy. She told Lady Spencer in August, 'I am afraid that the minute I think seriously of my conduct I shall be so shocked, especially with regard to all that has happened this year . . .' Georgiana was being drawn into a life of heavy drinking and compulsive gambling. She often found herself acting against her own judgement but she felt unable to resist the pressures on her to conform.

In November 1777 Lady Sarah Lennox observed that Georgiana seemed to have no ballast. 'The Pretty Duchess of Devonshire who by all accounts has no faults but delicate health in my mind, dines at seven, summer as well as winter, goes to bed at three, and lies in bed till four: she has hysteric fits in the morning and dances in the evening; she bathes, rides, dances for ten days and lies in bed the next ten.' Georgiana made periodic attempts to reform. She would adopt a starvation diet, lock herself away in her room and see no one for a week, but as soon as she emerged she compensated with all-night drinking and eating binges until she was too exhausted to get out of bed. Her weight fluctuated wildly as a consequence. The effect on Georgiana's general health was catastrophic: she had one miscarriage after another, leading the Duke and the Cavendishes to accuse her of deliberately sabotaging their hopes for an heir. Only Lady Sarah Lennox questioned whether the Duke might not be to blame for neglecting Georgiana when she was young and so vulnerable to suggestion. 'Indeed,' she concluded, 'I can't forgive her or rather her husband, the fault of ruining her health.'

Also in 1777, Georgiana met two quite different people, Charles James Fox and Mary Graham, whose impact on her would have far-reaching consequences. She was introduced to Mary in October while taking the sea air in Brighton. Mary was there with her husband, Thomas, and was recuperating from a bout of pneumonia. Georgiana was there in the hope of improving her fertility. Medical opinion cited a weak placenta as the cause of serial miscarriages like Georgiana's; the only remedy was to take water cures, either bathing in sea water or drinking warm spa water.

Georgiana was immediately captivated by her. 'The Dss likes her of all things,' reported Lady Clermont to Lady Spencer, 'they are inseparable, which is no bad thing. I wish she had half a dozen more such favourites.' Georgiana and Mary were the same age and had married in the same year, but Mary lived a very different, sheltered life. She was quiet, serious and gentle – Georgiana might not have noticed her were it not for her breathtaking beauty: she was known as 'the beautiful Mrs Graham'.

The obvious mutual attachment between the two women was remarked upon at Brighton, and the letters Georgiana wrote to Mary after they had left show that their feelings for each other had grown into infatuation. Both of them were frightened that the intensity of their friendship would become the subject of gossip. It was almost impossible to keep such things hidden. Maids and footmen were not above reading their employers' mail, and there was always the danger of letters going astray or falling into the wrong hands. In one fragment Georgiana wrote: 'I have been reading over this curious letter and I am almost sorry I put so much about what vex'd me when I began writing, I must tell you I am quite easy about it now and if I was sure you would get this letter safe, I would tell you all about it – but I don't dare.'

Almost nothing else survives from their lengthy correspondence except a couple of later fragments. Discouraged by the Duke's freezing civility, Georgiana longed for the tenderness, companionship and affection she experienced with Mary – and also something else, equally if not

*After Mrs Damer's husband ruined them both in a single night of gambling in August 1775, he shot himself through the head in a room above the Bedford Arms at Covent Garden, above. The area was also the theatre district, where the drama played out as much in the stalls as it did on stage.*

more important: relief from having to perform for her relatives or the *ton*. Lady Spencer, her friends, the Duke and his family all placed expectations on her, often forcing her to play roles which made her feel uncomfortable or inadequate. Only with Mary could Georgiana unburden herself and talk about her confusion and dismay.

> The hurry I live here distracts me [she wrote in 1778], when I first came into the world the novelty of the scene made me like everything but my heart now feels only an emptiness in the beau monde which cannot be filled – I don't have the liberty to think or occupy myself with the things I like as much as I would wish and all my desires are turned upside down – you are the only person to whom I would say this, anybody else would only laugh at me and call it an affectation – I seem to enjoy every thing so much at the minute that nobody can think how much I am tired sometimes with the dissipation I live in.

*The 'beautiful Mrs Graham', by Gainsborough. Georgiana developed an intense friendship with Mary Graham after they met in Brighton in 1777. Quiet, serious and gentle, she became a much-needed confidante for Georgiana, and the two exchanged passionate letters. 'Her goodness, her sense, her sweetness have left a strong impression on my mind,' Georgiana wrote after Mary's early death.*

Georgiana's intimacy with Mary helped her to gain a perspective on her situation, particularly on the limitations of her marriage. It was unthinkable, however, for a woman to take a lover before she had supplied her husband with a son. Convention allowed aristocratic women a *cicisbeo* – a term borrowed from the Italian to mean a platonic lover who provided escort duties and other practical services in place of the husband. But, despite a large crowd of suitors eager to comply, Georgiana was the exception in lacking even this. In 1779 her cousin Lady Pembroke remarked to Lord Herbert: 'You wrote some time ago terrible things you had heard about the poor Dss of Devonshire, which made me laugh, they were so totally without foundation, and I forgot to answer it. She has never been even talked for any body in the flirting way yet . . .'

Whether and to what extent physical intimacy played a part in Georgiana's relationship with Mary is impossible to determine. Several of her friendships contained an element of flirtatiousness: it was a French habit she had acquired from Madame de Polignac and Marie Antoinette. However, there were rumours that Marie Antoinette and the Little Po were more than simply friends, which their displays of physical affection encouraged.

Georgiana already lived on a plane of heightened feeling which her English friends found alluring but also disturbing; her passionate imprecations went far beyond the ordinary endearments written between women friends. However, even taking hyperbole into account, Georgiana's letters to Mary were more personal, more intense, clearly separating them from her other correspondence. However, in 1781 the doctors ordered Mr Graham to take Mary to a warmer climate: it was the only hope for her weak lungs. They had diagnosed her as consumptive. Georgiana was bereft and searched without success for a replacement.

Charles James Fox, her second new acquaintance, made a great impression on Georgiana, not in a romantic way – that would emerge later – but intellectually. It was Fox, more than anyone else, who led Georgiana to her life's vocation – politics. Fox was a brilliant though flawed politician. Short and corpulent, with shaggy eyebrows and a permanent five o'clock shadow, he was already at twenty-eight marked down as a future leader of the Whig party when the Marquess of Rockingham retired. Georgiana became friends with him when he came to stay at Chatsworth in 1777. His career until then had veered between political success and failure, between unimaginable wealth and bankruptcy. He confounded his critics with his irrepressible confidence, and exasperated his friends by his incontinent lifestyle. Eighteenth-century England was full of wits, connoisseurs, orators, historians, drinkers, gamblers, rakes and pranksters, but only Fox embodied all these

*Left: Georgiana met and befriended the Whig politician Charles James Fox in 1777. A compulsive gambler, Fox squandered his family fortune at the gaming tables. He and Georgiana remained steadfast friends and political allies.*

*Right: A cartoon depicting the ultra-fashionable 'macaroni'. As a young man, Fox indulged in the foppish style, using the added flourish of coloured hair powder.*

things. He spent so many hours at Brooks's that he was rarely out of his gambling clothes. However, he could always count on friends like the Duke to support him financially and politically.

Fox displayed a sense of fun and theatre that equalled Georgiana's. The term 'macaroni' was coined to describe the fashionable young fops of the 1770s who wore exaggerated clothes about town. The *Oxford Magazine* complained: 'There is indeed a kind of animal, neither male nor female, a thing of the neuter gender, lately started up amongst us. It is called a Macaroni. It talks without meaning, it smiles without pleasantry, it eats without appetite, it rides without exercise, it wenches without passion.' Until his gambling debts made him poor, Fox was one of its most visible exemplars. Like Georgiana, he had an eye for colour and a talent for whimsy.

He went to stay at Chatsworth in August 1777, joining a large house party that included the Jerseys, the Clermonts, the Duke of Dorset, all the Cavendishes as well as their cousins the Ponsonbys, and the violinist Giardini. Fox's presence wrought an immediate change in Georgiana; he intrigued and stimulated her. For the first time since her initial attempts to educate herself two years before, she had found someone to emulate.

> The great merit of C. Fox is his amazing quickness in seazing any subject [she wrote to her mother in August]. He seems to have the particular talent of knowing more about what he is saying and with less pains than anyone else. His conversation is like a brilliant player at billiards, the strokes follow one another piff puff . . .

Fox's ardour moved Georgiana. He talked to her as no one else did, treating her as his equal, discussing his ideas and encouraging her participation. She had once visited the House of Commons out of curiosity with Lady Jersey (women were banned from the gallery in 1778), but

*Cockburn's Theatre on fire, by Thomas Rowlandson. A fire in the theatre is only one of several near-tragic moments in Georgiana's thinly disguised autobiographical novel,* The Sylph.

had not repeated the experiment. Fox awakened in her a sense of loyalty and commitment to the Whig party, which in the 1770s meant opposition to George III, a mistrust of the powers of the crown and a vigilance over civil liberties. By the time Fox left Chatsworth Georgiana was his devoted follower.

Fox and Mary's belief in Georgiana persuaded her that she could make something more of herself. In April 1778 she wrote of her desire to begin afresh. 'I have the strongest sense of having many things to repent of and my heart is fully determined to mend,' she told Lady Spencer; she planned to take Holy Communion (a rite less commonly performed in the eighteenth century) after her trip to Derby. But the same letter also hints at entanglements – gambling debts – which she regretted and feared. 'By going there I break off many unpleasant embarrassments I am in with regard to others and the quiet life I shall lead there will give me time to think . . .'

The result was a thinly disguised autobiographical novel called *The Sylph.* The story follows the misadventures of Julia Stanley, a naive country girl married to the dissipated Sir William Stanley, a rake whose only interests are fashion and gambling. Julia is slowly seduced by the *ton,* learning how to live *à la mode*, how to talk, sing, dance and think like a fashionable person. She realizes that her soul is being corrupted by cynicism and heartlessness but sees no hope of escape. Sir William is cruel, even brutal towards her. He flaunts his mistress in front of her, punishes her when she suffers a miscarriage, and is not above assaulting her when angered. As his creditors close in, Sir William forces Julia to sign over all her personal property. But an anonymous protector, calling himself 'the Sylph', begins sending her letters of advice. When Sir William becomes so desperate for money that he sells the rights to Julia's body to his chief creditor, she runs away, and he shoots himself. The Sylph reveals himself to be Julia's childhood sweetheart. They marry and live happily ever after.

Georgiana wrote *The Sylph* in secret and published it anonymously as 'a young lady'. The novel was a creditable success, and it was not long before people guessed the identity of the author, as there were plenty of clues pointing in her direction. The story's significance lies in the rare insider's glimpse it provides of the *ton*. Georgiana describes a competitive, unfriendly world peopled by opportunists, liars and bullies; a world which encourages hypocrisy and values pretence. The irony did not escape her that even as she hated it she was also its creature. However, in publishing *The Sylph* she was also claiming her independence.

# A Popular Patriot 1778–1781

*One day last week, her Grace the Duchess of Devonshire appeared on the hustings at Covent Garden. She immediately saluted her favourite Candidate, the Hon. Charles Fox.*

MORNING POST, 25 SEPTEMBER 1780

GEORGIANA'S POLITICAL AWAKENING coincided with a disastrous year for the Whigs. The Declaration of Independence of 4 July 1776 proclaimed the American colonies 'Free and Independent States . . . absolved from all allegiance to the British crown'. The Whigs supported the colonists against the government but their rousing talk of safeguarding the liberty of the people had signally failed to impress the country. The public rejected their contention that the government was at fault for having tried to force an unjust system of taxation on the colonists, and the press accused the party of conniving with Britain's enemies to break up the empire. However, the Whigs viewed the American conflict as part of the struggle between the people and the crown and privately hoped that the Americans would win.

In February 1778 France entered the war on the side of the Americans, transforming what had hitherto been a set of military skirmishes in New England into a trans-continental war. Britain now had to fight on several fronts. The debates in parliament became bitter as Whig and government MPs accused each other of betraying the country's interests.

Having enjoyed two years of a distant war, the country now began to mobilize its defences against the threat of a French invasion. As Lord Lieutenant of Derbyshire the Duke of Devonshire returned to the country to organize a voluntary militia. Most able-bodied men were either already in the army or in stable employment; those available to join the home defence force made unpromising material. This did not deter the aristocracy, who threw themselves into the task of training their corps with almost childish enthusiasm. Many of them proudly wore their regimental uniforms to the King's birthday celebrations at St James's.

Since the French were likely to target London first, the government set up two campsites for its protection: Coxheath in Kent and Warley in Essex. So many sightseers flocked to the camps that a London–Coxheath coach service started. Georgiana accompanied the Duke to Coxheath, where they were joined by many of their friends. She was enthralled by the spectacle of thousands of men mobilizing for war. The Duke rented a large house for her nearby, but she persuaded him to allow her to live in the camp with him. Their 'tent' was made up of several marquees, arranged into a compound of sleeping quarters, entertaining rooms, kitchens and a servants' hall. Refusing to equate a state of readiness with austerity, Georgiana decorated it with travelling tables, oriental rugs and silver candlesticks from Chatsworth. Nevertheless conditions in the camp were primitive and sanitary arrangements non-existent.

By mid-June Georgiana was feeling less welcome on the field: the Duke had grown tired of her presence and the soldiers no longer regarded her as a novelty. She stopped loitering around the guns and reluctantly joined her friends in their card parties and jolly picnics on the hills, and discovered that they too were bored and wished to do more than simply observe the soldiers. It occurred to her that she could organize a female auxiliary corps. She had soon designed a smart uniform, and in July the *Morning Post* informed its readers: 'Her Grace the Duchess of Devonshire appears every day at the head of the beauteous Amazons on Coxheath, who are all dressed *en militaire* . . . and charms every beholder with their beauty and affability.' She continued to parade throughout the summer, inspiring women in other camps to follow suit.

Although Georgiana and her friends did little more than dress up in uniforms and provide good cheer for the men, she had broken with tradition. For the first time aristocratic women organized themselves as a voluntary group, taking up duties to help their men in time of war. Furthermore, Georgiana's idea of dressing up in patriotic uniforms was a propaganda coup for the Whigs, who had suffered for their opposition to the war, and helped to mitigate public hostility towards them and restore the party's popularity.

Georgiana's pleasure at her success was short-lived: one day she discovered that the Duke and Lady Jersey had been taking advantage of her parades through the camp to visit each other's tents. Possibly jealous of the attention Georgiana was receiving and feeling neglected, the Duke made no effort to keep the affair a secret. Lady Jersey regarded all married men – except her husband, who was twice her age – as an irresistible challenge and flaunted her conquest in front of Georgiana, who was too frightened and inexperienced to assert herself.

Georgiana's timidity puzzled her mother – although hurt and mortified it seems that she said nothing to either party. However, the liaison between Lady Jersey and the Duke was short-lived, as Lady Spencer brought an end to the affair by calling on Lady Jersey and outlining the consequences she would face if it continued. The Spencers also gave the Duke to understand that they were disgusted with him.

By the time the King and Queen made their long-awaited official visit to Coxheath on 4 November 1778, Lady Jersey had acquired a new lover. The rain poured down on the day – 'cats and dogs', Georgiana complained – and while the Duke marched his soldiers past the King, Georgiana led the delegation of ladies standing in slippery mud up to their ankles waiting on the Queen. However, the Devonshires' patriotism did not extend to spending the winter in a mud pit; immediately after the royal visit they returned to Devonshire House.

*In the summer of 1778 as Britain prepared itself for a possible French invasion and the Duke performed the duties of Lord Lieutenant of Derbyshire, Georgiana organized a female auxiliary corps. That and her design of this feminized version of the military uniform provided aristocratic women with a patriotic role to play during the war.*

Georgiana's sense of isolation had increased as a result of the Duke's adultery. Despite her unease, she continued to behave towards Lady Jersey as if nothing had happened. Though not all the inhabitants of the camp escaped the consequences of their actions so lightly. Lady Melbourne became pregnant with Lord Egremont's child while Lady Clermont's affair with the local apothecary resulted in a secret abortion. But it was Lady Derby and the Duke of Dorset who, in social terms, paid the highest price.

In December 1778 Lady Derby fled from her husband's house, leaving behind her children and all her belongings. It was a widely broadcast secret that she was hiding with the Duke of Dorset. Her desertion broke one of eighteenth-century society's strongest taboos regarding the sanctity of the family and a wife's obedience to her husband. According to Lady Mary Coke, she had 'offended against the laws of man and God'. In February, two months after the initial excitement, a 'party', consisting mostly of the younger generation of Whigs – Lady Carlisle and Lady Jersey in particular – intended to visit Lady Derby in her exile. Georgiana was caught between her friends, who sought the additional weight of her celebrity, and her parents, who forbade her to have anything more to do with the unfortunate woman. Everyone was waiting to see what Georgiana would do.

The Spencers gave Georgiana a choice: either she dropped Lady Derby or they would never allow her sister Harriet to visit Devonshire House or Chatsworth. Georgiana surrendered, a little relieved to be excused from the unpleasant bickering which surrounded the affair. Then, in April, Lord Derby announced that he would not be divorcing his wife. It was a terrible revenge; by his refusal – it was almost impossible for a wife to divorce her husband except on the grounds of non-consummation – he consigned his wife to social limbo, disgraced, separated and unprotected.

The reputation of the Duke of Dorset did not suffer. He had seduced another man's wife, but while many people looked askance at his behaviour there was no question of excluding him from society. He even remained friends with Lord Derby and continued to be invited to his house.

In July 1779, when the season was over, Georgiana went with her parents to Spa. The Duke did not accompany them, pleading military duty, and spent the summer marching his soldiers at the camp. The English and French aristocrats on holiday at Spa behaved as if the two countries were not at war. Madame de Polignac had been waiting for Georgiana to arrive, and they were such conspicuous companions that their friendship reached the notice of the English press.

Georgiana rejoined the Duke at the camp in October 1779. The combined French and Spanish fleets had been sighted in the Channel; the government expected an invasion force to arrive at any day. She was determined to stay and watch the fight, but the invasion never came and the strain of anticipation was reflected in the drinking and debauchery that went on after dark. Georgiana became fed up with camp life and with the sycophancy she perceived in some of her friends. She returned to Devonshire House without the Duke. Her departure annoyed the Cavendishes, who thought she had no right to go anywhere on her own when she had not yet given them an heir.

Fearing that she would never have a child, Georgiana noted every variation in her menstrual cycle with obsessive diligence. 'The Prince [menstruation] is not yet come,' she wrote to her mother in October, 'but my pains are frequent and I continue the Spa water.' After five and a half years of marriage she was so desperate to conceive that she went to the notorious quack Dr James Graham. Lady Spencer was unimpressed with the doctor's use of electricity, milk baths and friction techniques to encourage fertility in women and cure impotency in men. Society, however, had taken him up and Graham was earning sufficient money to practise out of the Adelphi, where his Temple of Health and Hymen attracted long queues of desperate women. Georgiana saw him for

*The Duchesse de Polignac. The 'Little Po', as she was known, was an intimate of Marie Antoinette and Georgiana. Sweet-tempered and impressionable, she was ruled by her violent lover, the Comte de Vaudreuil, and there were rumours that she and Marie Antoinette were more than just friends.*

a couple of months, and then abruptly stopped. Her wish for a child had been answered, only the child was not hers: the Duke had asked her to accept his daughter Charlotte by his late mistress.

Charlotte Spencer had remained his mistress until at least 1778, but what had happened to her then remains a mystery; it is known only that she died shortly afterwards. Georgiana's thoughts on the situation have not survived – she almost certainly knew of the relationship: articles about it had appeared in *Bon Ton Magazine* and *Town and Country Magazine.* The latter had declared, 'it was the greatest paradox' that the Duke must be the only man in England not in love with the Duchess of Devonshire. After Charlotte's death the Duke sent for their daughter and her nurse, Mrs Gardner. It was not uncommon among aristocratic families for a husband's illegitimate children to be brought up by his wife. Georgiana's cousin Lady Pembroke was generous towards Lord Pembroke's bastard children until he proposed giving them the Herbert name. Georgiana was in raptures at the prospect of adopting the girl. She met her for the first time on 8 May 1780 and told her mother:

> she is a very healthy good humour'd looking child, I think, not very tall; she is amazingly like the Duke, I am sure you would have known her anywhere. She is the best humour'd little thing you ever saw, vastly active and vastly lively . . .

Lady Spencer was baffled by her daughter's excitement. Georgiana was sending the wrong message to the Duke, she thought; she would do better to appear neutral about the child. Georgiana ignored her advice; little Charlotte was all she had of her own to love, and she didn't care where the girl came from. However, her gambling sharply increased just before Charlotte's arrival and continued afterwards at the same level. 'You say you play'd on Sunday night till two,' wrote Lady Spencer in distress. 'What did you do? I hope you are not meant by the beautiful Duchess who has taken to the gaming table and lost £2000. Pray, my dearest G. take care about play . . . and deserve to be what I doubt you are, whether you deserve it or not, the idol of my heart.'

Charlotte had no surname but Georgiana resisted any move which might alert the child to her irregular background. The usual practice was to use the father's Christian name or, if he had several titles, one of his lesser ones, in the place of a surname. After much discussion they agreed on Williams and decided to present Charlotte as a distant, orphaned relation of the Spencers.

Meanwhile both George and Harriet became engaged. The twenty-two-year-old George confessed that he was 'out of his senses' over a certain Lady Lavinia Bingham. Although Lavinia had no money of her own, and did not come from a particularly distinguished family – her father, Lord Lucan, was a mere Irish peer – the Spencers made no objection to the match. At first glance she seemed to be a good choice; it was only later that her more unattractive traits became apparent: she was highly strung, vindictive, hypocritical and a calm liar who maintained a veneer of politeness to her in-laws while freely abusing them in conversation elsewhere. She was also neurotically jealous and loathed Georgiana and Harriet. Georgiana tried not to show her misgivings even though she could sense Lavinia's dislike.

Harriet's engagement took place two months later, in July. She was now an attractive nineteen-year-old, tall like Georgiana, slim, and the image of Lord Spencer with his dark eyebrows and pale skin. She was quieter than her sister, more analytical and less prone to flights of fancy, and she still worshipped Georgiana.

Her choice was the Duke of Devonshire's cousin Frederick, Lord Duncannon, the eldest son of the Earl of Bessborough. She explained to her friends that 'he was very sensible and good tempered and by marrying him she made no new connections, for now her sister's and hers would be the same'. Georgiana was slightly surprised by her sister's choice. She had not thought him the type of man to attract Harriet. He was quiet, not particularly good looking, and not even financially secure – his father was known to have mortgaged all his estates. Harriet admitted to her cousin that his proposal had come as a surprise, writing, 'I wish I could have known him a little better first, but my dear Papa and Mama say that it will make them the happiest of creatures, and what would I not do to see them happy . . .'

Lord and Lady Spencer approved of the marriage because of the Cavendish connection, and probably influenced Harriet more than they realized, but they were also concerned about the couple's financial situation. Harriet's marriage portion of £20,000 went to pay off part of Lord

Bessborough's £30,000 debt. She would be left with a mere £400 a year pin money and £2,000 a year joint income with her husband. Lady Spencer begged Georgiana not to lead her impressionable sister into bad habits, and above all, to keep her away from the Devonshire set.

Georgiana was confident that if she could reform her own life, protecting Harriet would be simple. Since her return from Coxheath she had sought to impress Fox and the other Whig leaders with her political understanding. She followed the debates in parliament and soon became sufficiently well informed to have her own opinions about political issues. She had also perfected the skills required of a political hostess: her dinners at Devonshire House served a useful purpose: waverers could be kept in line and supporters rewarded. She had also learned how to extract information without betraying any secrets in return.

Georgiana absorbed the minutiae of party politics. To an outsider the House of Commons was an inchoate system of temporary factions and alliances named after the men who led them – Shelburnite, Northite and Rockinghamite. There were, in a broad context, two main parties: the party in government and the party out of government. The latter called themselves Whigs, and they contemptuously referred to the former as Tories. The idea of an organized opposition was not acceptable in the eighteenth century – any party which opposed the King was, in theory, committing treason. On the other hand, since 1688 the Commons had prided itself on its independence from the crown. Peers and MPs regarded it as their duty to be both servants to the crown and defenders of the constitution.

The Whigs had to be careful not to appear dangerous or disloyal. Edmund Burke spent much of his time defending the party against such charges by arguing that they were challenging the King in order to safeguard the victories of the Glorious Revolution. The opposition Whigs liked to portray themselves as the true Whigs, martyred for their beliefs by the forces of tyranny.

Georgiana fervently believed this to be the case even if some members of the opposition were rather more cynical. When she wore the adopted Whig colours of blue and buff (taken from the colours of the American army) she did so out of conviction and expected her friends to do the same. She had become one of the party's best-known representatives. Fox was the first to recognize her talent for propaganda and encouraged Georgiana to play a greater role in increasing the party's public presence. When parliament reconvened on 8 February the government was beset by a number of crises. Not only was the war going badly; there was unrest in Ireland and a widespread fear that it might follow the example of America and declare independence. There was also popular discontent at home, fuelled by the Whigs, and hundreds of petitions poured in from around the country demanding democratic reform of the parliamentary system.

After some success in April with Edmund Burke's Economical Reform Bill, which aimed to limit the crown's powers by reducing the number of pensions and sinecures on the Civil List, the Whigs suffered a series of setbacks. Georgiana reported, 'We go on vilely indeed in the House of Commons.' But there was one piece of good news. The eighteen-year-old Prince of Wales, the future George IV, had allied himself with the Whigs. His support, as heir apparent to the throne, absolved them of the charge of disloyalty to the crown, which made it easier for them to attack the King. In supporting the Whigs against his father the Prince was following an established tradition. From George I onwards, father and son had hated each other. Each successive Prince of Wales had thrown in his lot with the opposition. The future George IV feared and resented his parents while they despised him as weak, duplicitous and lazy. Georgiana recorded her first impressions of him in a scrapbook, which she entitled 'Annecdotes Concerning HRH the Prince of Wales'.

*Overleaf, left: George Spencer, Viscount Althorp, 1778. Honest and reliable, Georgiana's younger brother was often called upon to mediate in both his sisters' financial and marital affairs, especially after the death of Lord Spencer in 1783.*

*Overleaf, right: Lady Lavinia Bingham married George Spencer in 1780. She was neurotically jealous of other women, including Georgiana, who loved George 'dearly in the double character of friend and brother'.*

*The Prince of Wales, right. In 1782 Georgiana wrote of him, 'he is inclined to be too fat and looks too much like a woman in men's cloaths.' But they were lifelong friends, and the Whigs counted on her influence with him on many occasions. Vain and petulant, he rebelled against the King with his incontinent lifestyle, publicly taking the actress Mary Robinson, left, whom he affectionately called 'Perdita', as his mistress when he was seventeen.*

> The Prince of Wales is rather tall, and has a figure which, though striking is not perfect. He is inclined to be too fat and looks too much like a woman in men's cloaths, but the gracefulness of his manner and his height certainly make him a pleasing figure . . .

She also called him 'good-natured and rather extravagant'. He was clever, well read, and possessed of exquisite taste in art and decoration, but he was also vain, petulant and attention-seeking. The Prince had been isolated from companions of his own age and tutored by dry old men who saw to it that his life was one long regime of worthy activities. As soon as he could he rebelled against everything he had been taught. On his first trip to Drury Lane in 1779 he saw *The Winter's Tale*, and immediately fell in love with the twenty-one-year-old actress Mary Robinson, a protégée of Georgiana's. She was delighted to conduct a very public affair with him, and the Prince foolishly wrote her explicit letters, in which he called her 'Perdita' – her role in the play – and signed himself 'Florizel'. Like any astute woman on the make, she kept his adolescent declarations – he promised her a fortune as soon as he came of age – and blackmailed him when he grew tired of her.

It was during the Prince's visits to Drury Lane that he first came into contact with the Devonshire House Circle, and in particular with Georgiana and Fox. George III blamed Fox for deliberately and calculatingly debauching his son, but the Prince had already started to drink and gamble before he met Fox, who simply showed him how to do it in a more refined way. The Prince worshipped Fox who, for his part, genuinely liked the boy. On most nights they could be found either at Brooks's or Devonshire House, playing faro until they fell asleep at the table.

The Prince's marked attentions to Georgiana, the fact that he constantly sought her advice on every matter – from his clothes to his relations with his father – fanned rumours that they were having an affair. The Prince was almost certainly in love with Georgiana, but she never reciprocated his feelings. Throughout their lives they always addressed each other as 'my dearest brother' and 'sister', although the Prince was often madly jealous of rivals. The Prince shared with Fox, Lord Cholmondeley and Lord George Cavendish a round robin of the three most famous courtesans of the era: Perdita, Grace Dalrymple and Mrs Armistead. The Prince also pursued Lady Melbourne and Lady Jersey, or perhaps it was the other way round. Less well-informed people speculated that Georgiana was in competition with her friends for the Prince's affection, but a letter from Lady Melbourne suggests collusion rather than rivalry:

> The Duke of Richmond has been here, and told me you and I were two rival queens, and I believe, if there had not been some people in the room, who might have thought it odd, that I should have slapped his face for having such an idea; and he wished me joy of having the Prince to myself. How odious people are, upon my life, I have no patience with them. I believe you and I are very different from all the rest of the world . . .

The Whigs continued their onslaught against the government. On 3 June 1780 the Duke of Richmond, then a radical on the extreme left of the party, moved a resolution that the constitution should be rewritten to allow annual parliaments and universal suffrage. By an unlucky chance, while the Lords were debating the Duke of Richmond's proposals, Lord George Gordon, a mentally unbalanced Protestant fanatic, chose to march on parliament at the head of a large mob. He carried with him a petition from the Protestant Association, a sectarian body which opposed giving legal rights to Catholics.

*The Gordon Riots lasted four days and resulted in 458 people being killed or seriously wounded. Georgiana witnessed much of the violence from Devonshire House. 'I feel mad with spirits at [it] all being over,' she wrote. 'It seems now like a dream.'*

This mob, intoxicated by drink and whipped up by a crazed demagogue, was more dangerous than the over-excited rabble which constituted the usual eruptions of the lower orders. The crowd blocked all the entrances to parliament while Lord George Gordon stormed into the Commons and harangued MPs on the evils of popery. He then rushed out to do the same in the Lords. As MPs tried to leave the House they were punched and kicked by the marchers. By nightfall the protest had turned into a riot that lasted until 8 June when the army arrived and George Gordon gave himself up. Georgiana had stayed on the balcony for four nights, staring at the orange sky as Piccadilly reverberated to the sound of gunfire and explosions. The number of people killed or seriously wounded stood at 458; whole blocks of the city lay in ruins.

The immediate aftermath saw the total discrediting of the reformers and all their movements. The Whigs were blamed for irresponsibly fomenting discontent. Lord North seized the political advantage and called a snap general election on 1 September. Georgiana's assistance was demanded from many quarters: in addition to the canvassing she had to do for the Cavendishes in Derby, the Duke's family pressured her to persuade Lord Spencer to align his interests with theirs.

In addition, Sheridan wanted to become a politician, but his lack of wealth or family connections made it impossible for him to contest a seat on his own cognizance. He pressed Georgiana to help him. She arranged for him to stand in the Spencer-dominated borough of Stafford. He was duly elected and wrote her a grovelling letter of thanks: '. . . It is no flattery to say that the Duchess of Devonshire's name commands an implicit admiration wherever it is mentioned.' A week later, on 25 September, Charles Fox invited Georgiana to accompany him on the hustings when he contested the borough of Westminster. The press was shocked by her boldness, even though she stood on the platform for only a few minutes. Fox whipped up his supporters with speeches about parliamentary reform, the rights of the British people and the consequences of royal tyranny, earning his title 'Man of the People'.

Fox won with a comfortable majority, and his success was unexpectedly duplicated around the country. Despite recent setbacks, the Whigs had managed to reduce Lord North's majority to only twenty-eight, a success that convinced them that it would be only a matter of time before the government collapsed.

*Whitehall, 1775. During the Gordon Riots of June 1780 the mob sacked Newgate Prison and burned down the King's Bench. They exploded the distilleries at Holborn so that the streets were flooded with spirits and the water supply to Lincoln's Inn Fields became alcoholic. The Whig grandees mounted a round-the-clock defence of their houses, as the mob targeted them. Whitehall, too, was strongly defended, though afterwards whole blocks of the city lay in ruins.*

1780–1782

# Introduction to Politics

*The concourse of Nobility, etc., at the Duchess of Devonshire's on Thursday night were so great, that it was eight o'clock yesterday morning before they all took leave. Upwards of 500 sat down to supper, and near 1000 came agreeable to invitation . . . The company consisted of the most fashionable 'characters' . . . The best dressed ladies were her Royal Highness the Duchess of Cumberland, her Grace the Duchess of Devonshire, Lady Duncannon, Lady Althorpe, Lady Waldegrave, and Lady Harrington . . . The gentlemen best dressed were his Royal Highness the Prince of Wales, the Marquis of Graham, and the Hon. Charles Fox.*

LONDON CHRONICLE, 21–23 MARCH 1782

LORD NORTH CLUNG TO OFFICE despite the government's poor showing in the election. Exasperated, the Whigs consoled themselves by fêting the Prince of Wales, who amused them by being rude about his father. He took great delight in annoying his parents; at the ball to mark his official presentation to society on 18 January 1781 he snubbed the ladies of the court by dancing all night with Georgiana. The *Morning Herald* could not help remarking, 'The Court beauties looked with an eye of envy on her Grace of Devonshire, as the only woman honoured with the hand of the heir apparent, during Thursday night's ball at St James's.'

Much against her inclination, Georgiana left London just as the new parliament was getting under way. In February she accompanied the Duke to Hardwick, in the words of a friend, 'pour faire un enfant'. But relations between them had deteriorated rapidly after Harriet's marriage to Lord Duncannon in November. To Georgiana's embarrassment, her sister delighted the Cavendishes by becoming pregnant at once. Despite Harriet's initial reservations her marriage appeared to be free of the tensions which plagued Georgiana's. In February 1781 Lady Spencer wrote to inform Georgiana that Harriet's 'closet is becoming a *vrai bijou,* and she and her husband pass many comfortable hours in it. I trust indeed that all will go very well in that quarter.'

Harriet's good fortune contributed to Georgiana's fear that her own failure to produce a baby was a punishment from God. Sitting alone in cheerless Hardwick every day while the Duke went out hunting was too much for her to bear and she blotted out her days with large doses of opiates. 'I took something today,' she wrote, 'but I shall ride tomorrow.'

The Duke was disgusted when Georgiana still showed no sign of pregnancy after a month at Hardwick. He decided that their stay was a waste of time and they returned to Devonshire House. Still Georgiana rarely appeared in public, and the papers remarked that she had 'become the gravest creature in the world' and complained about her absence from society.

The reason for Georgiana's sudden retirement was not only the disappointment of Hardwick but a crisis concerning Harriet. Less than two months after Lady Spencer had written of the Duncannons' 'comfortable hours' together Lord Duncannon shocked them all by shouting at Harriet in public. Harriet later confessed that she was frightened to be alone with him, since the slightest provocation made him lose his self-control. The Cavendishes regarded Duncannon's abusiveness towards his wife as a disgrace to the entire family. Another incident at a ball in April moved his cousin, the Duke's sister the Duchess of Portland, to write him a warning: '. . . do not flatter yourself that your conduct has escaped observation. It is becoming the subject of ridicule, and your best Friends begin to fear your want of understanding.'

*The public rooms were the main attraction of Devonshire House. They could accommodate 1,200 guests comfortably, whereas in some of the great country houses the crush could lift a person off his feet and carry him from room to room. Some of the finest paintings in England hung on its walls.*

Lord Duncannon apologized; his behaviour, he explained, was caused by worry over Harriet's pregnancy: he feared she would miscarry. The Duchess of Portland's reply showed her contempt. She wrote that it was his conduct 'may have been the cause of this unhappy event'. However, threats and warnings were the only weapons available to the Spencers or the Cavendishes. Eighteenth-century law granted a husband the freedom to treat his wife as he pleased, except in the case of imprisonment and physical torture. Even then, the shame of public scandal deterred upper-class women from seeking legal redress in all but the most extreme circumstances.

Georgiana had ceased to entertain at Devonshire House immediately after the discovery and spent her time caring for Harriet. The Spencers were frightened to leave their daughter alone with Duncannon and kept her away from him as much as they could until she gave birth to a son, the Hon. John William Ponsonby, on 31 August 1781. Not long afterwards Lord Spencer became deaf and suffered a partial paralysis on one side of his body. The double anxiety over Harriet and Lord Spencer drove Georgiana to the gaming tables, and Lady Spencer with her. 'I can never make myself easy about the bad example I have set you and which you have but too faithfully imitated,' Lady Spencer had written bitterly in November 1779. Harriet followed her mother and sister, but with less than a tenth of their income, and without the resources to pay her creditors.

George Selwyn described incredible scenes at Devonshire House to Lord Carlisle. 'The trade or amusement which engrosses everybody who lives in what is called the pleasurable world is [faro],' he wrote. Georgiana had arranged the drawing room to resemble a professional gaming house,

*Overleaf: 'A Gaming Table at Devonshire House' by Thomas Rowlandson, 1791. Georgiana throws the dice while her sister, Harriet, takes money from her purse. Georgiana made numerous vows to curb her gambling habit, particularly after the birth of Little G, but Horace Walpole wrote that she 'will probably stuff her poor babe into her knotting bag, when she wants to play Macao, and forget it'.*

complete with hired croupiers and a commercial faro bank. Lady Spencer was there most nights, throwing her rings on to the table when she had run out of money.

Faro was a complicated game, involving one banker and an unlimited number of players who staked their bets upon the dealer turning over particular combinations of cards. Although it was a game of chance, the odds in favour of the banker were second only to those in roulette. The carelessness with which people threw their money about attracted shady characters to the house. One in particular, a man called Martindale, lured Georgiana into a ruinous agreement. According to Sheridan, 'the Duchess and Martindale had agreed that whatever the two won from each other should be sometimes double, sometimes treble the sum which it was called . . . the Duchess . . . was literally sobbing at her losses – she perhaps having lost £1500, when it was supposed to be £500.'

Lady Mary Coke reported that the Duchess of Devonshire was living a twenty-four-hour day of gambling and amusement. One week, she wrote, Georgiana attended a breakfast at Wimbledon (which continued all day), then an assembly at Lady Hertford's, where she had proposed a visit to Vauxhall Gardens. She took all the Duchesses, sniffed Lady Mary, as well as the most popular men, including Lord Egremont and Thomas Grenville, 'a professed admirer of the Duchess of Devonshire for two years past'. There they stayed until the small hours, keeping the musicians at their posts long after the gardens were officially closed. She did the same thing the next day and the day after that until, returning from another late party at Vauxhall with the Duchess of Rutland, Lady Melbourne, Lord Egremont and Thomas Grenville, she fell asleep in the boat.

The newspapers also reported on Georgiana's activities to the wider world, but she was still their darling. The fawning notices revealed more than just a weakness for society hostesses. A recent upturn in the Whig party's fortunes made papers like the *Morning Herald and Daily Advertiser* eager to be associated with the future regime. The war looked certain to end: General Cornwallis had surrendered at Yorktown. When Lord North heard the news he offered his resignation to the King without delay, but after five years of war George III could not accept the defeat. He ordered the Prime Minister to remain in office and to prepare a counter-attack.

The Whigs felt certain that they would soon be in power. Impatient for North to go, they harassed him in the Commons

*Previous pages: The Vauxhall Gardens was one of the places Georgiana and her friends indulged in late-night parties. In 1777 Lady Sarah Lennox observed her habits: 'The Pretty Duchess of Devonshire . . . dines at seven . . . goes to bed at three, and lies in bed till four: she has hysteric fits in the morning and dances in the evening; she bathes, rides, dances for ten days and lies in bed the next ten.'*

with motions of no confidence. On 20 March, the King at last accepted that the ministry had lost the confidence of the House and could not continue. Lord North resigned but George III refused to accept the Whigs *en masse* and insisted on a joint ministry between Lord Rockingham and the Earl of Shelburne, whose sympathies lay more with the King than with the Whigs. The party accepted this bitter pill, hoping it might eventually be able to push Shelburne out. Having agreed the terms, the Whigs went to Devonshire House to celebrate. Georgiana threw a series of celebratory balls, each one lasting the whole night and part of the following day.

Having so long avoided St James's, the Whigs now trooped into court to pay their respects. The King was too disgusted to hold a proper Drawing Room and sat glumly next to Queen Charlotte, while Georgiana and her friends talked to the Prince of Wales and the Duke of Cumberland. The King grudgingly offered the garter to senior Whigs, and they accepted with a shameless delight which disgusted Nathaniel Wraxall. He watched with embarrassment as 'The Duke of Devonshire . . . advanced up to the Sovereign, with his phlegmatic, cold, awkward air, like a clown.'

Fox was now Foreign Secretary, and under parliamentary rules MPs selected for office had to re-offer themselves to their constituents. Having been impressed by the reaction to Georgiana's appearance on the hustings at Covent Garden in 1780, Fox asked her to repeat her performance, only this time with more fanfare. She accepted without hesitation. The Duke and other grandees decided that Georgiana should lead a women's delegation. Since the crowds had responded so enthusiastically to one woman, they reasoned that five or six would be even more popular.

On 3 April Georgiana performed her first official duty for the party. The *London Chronicle* reported the event in some amazement. In an age of free beer and bloody noses at election time the Whigs' polished handling of public events was disconcerting. Fox stood on a platform beneath three large banners that read, THE MAN OF THE PEOPLE, FREEDOM AND INDEPENDENCE, and INDEPENDENCE and promised he would unite the country in defence of liberty. Georgiana was there with several other women, all wearing the Whig colours of blue and buff. Nothing like it had ever been witnessed before. Milliners' shops began making fans bearing Georgiana's portrait which sold in their hundreds.

A week later, on 8 April, the Whigs made their first appearance in the Commons. At first MPs were disorientated: Lord North and his followers were no longer sitting on the treasury benches; in their place were the Whigs. Their uniform of blue and buff was gone and they wore the formal dress of government, all of them – even Fox – with hair powder, ruffles, lace around their necks, and swords by their sides.

*Opposite: George III hated the Whigs, blaming them for corrupting his son the Prince of Wales. There was also a personal enmity between him and the Cavendishes since he had dismissed the fourth Duke of Devonshire from his post as Lord Chamberlain and had his name scratched from the Privy Council when he ascended the throne in 1760.*

For the first time since her wedding in 1774 Georgiana looked forward to the future. Her optimism was born out of a new-found sense of purpose. In September 1782 she recorded her thoughts about the year.

> If some people would write down the events they had been witness to . . . the meaning of an age would be transmitted to the next with clearness and dependence – to the idle reader it would present an interesting picture of the manners of his country . . . I wish I had done this – I came into the world at 17 and I am now five and twenty – in these eight years I have been in the midst of action . . . I have seen partys rise and fall – friends be united and disunited – the ties of love give way to caprice, to interest, and to vanity . . .

She hoped one day to be 'a faithful historian of the secret history of the times'.

# *Politics*

## 1782–1789

1782–1783

# The Cuckoo Bird

*The Duchess of Devonshire, it is said, means to introduce a head piece which is to be neither hat, cap, nor bonnet, and yet all three, a sort of trinity in unity, under the appellation the 'Devonshire Whim'. Whenever the Duchess of Devonshire visits the capital, a Standard may be expected to be given to the Fashion.*

MORNING HERALD AND DAILY ADVERTISER, 21 OCTOBER 1782

AS SOON AS PARLIAMENT ADJOURNED for the summer Georgiana and the Duke retreated to Bath. They did not return to Devonshire House until the autumn, when the new session was well under way. Accompanying them to London was Lady Elizabeth Foster, described by the papers as the 'Duchess of Devonshire's intimate friend'.

Georgiana met Elizabeth, or Bess, as she affectionately called her, during their first week at Bath. The Duke had rented the Duke of Marlborough's house, one of the finest in town, for the whole summer. The Devonshires were both there to 'take the cure': the Duke for his gout, Georgiana for her 'infertility' – she had suffered two early miscarriages the previous year. The tone of her letters betrays her misery at having to abandon London just when the Whigs had come to power. Twice a day she drank the thermal waters in the King's Bath, the most fashionable of the three pump rooms. The company there was hardly uplifting, comprising the unfortunate casualties of eighteenth-century living: the incurables, the rheumatics, the gout sufferers, and those afflicted with rampant eczema and other unsightly skin diseases. Georgiana sat each morning in a semicircle near the bar with the other childless wives, cup and saucer in either hand, listening to a band of provincial musicians. Bath was, in her opinion, 'amazingly disagreeable, I am only surprised at the Duke bearing it all as well as he does, but he is so good natur'd he bears anything well'.

Two things made life tolerable: watching the new Shakespearean actress Sarah Siddons at the Theatre Royal, and the acquaintance of two sisters living in straitened circumstances in an unfashionable part of town. On 1 June Georgiana informed Lady Spencer, 'Lady Erne and Lady E. Foster are our chief support or else it would be shockingly dull for the D. indeed.' These were the eldest daughters of the Earl of Bristol; Lady Mary Erne was a great friend of Mary Graham, who was probably responsible for the sisters' introduction to Georgiana. Both were separated from their husbands, and lived with their aunt, a Methodist convert, on the tiny income allocated to them by their father.

Georgiana's letters to her mother were full of praise for her new friends. But after a short time there was no more mention of Lady Mary Erne, and Lady Elizabeth Foster – Bess – became the sole topic of her correspondence. She was the same age as Georgiana and already the mother of two sons, yet there was something surprisingly girlish about her. She was slimmer than Georgiana, shorter, more delicate, with thin dark hair framing her tiny face. Her appearance of frailty, coupled with a feminine helplessness and coquettish charm, made most men want to protect and possess her. The historian Edward Gibbon, who had known Bess since she was a little girl, described her manners as the most seductive of any woman he knew.

Bess's family, the Herveys, were not the sort that recommended themselves to Lady Spencer. Eccentric, libertine and untrustworthy, the Herveys were an extraordinary family who had made their fortune in the early eighteenth century as professional courtiers. Bess's father took the well-worn path to a career in the Church, eventually becoming the Bishop of Derry, which brought him

*Previous pages: Georgiana, Duchess of Devonshire, by Maria Cosway, 1782. Aged twenty-five, Georgiana is portrayed as the goddess Diana. Her son, Hart, felt this portrait was the best likeness of her.*

a modest salary. He succeeded to the title of the fourth Earl of Bristol unexpectedly, but his spendthrift habits meant that Bess, her brother and two sisters were brought up in relative poverty.

On succeeding to the title in 1779 the Earl-Bishop inherited Ickworth Park in Suffolk, and with it an income of £20,000 a year. But his good fortune had come too late for his daughters, especially for Bess. She had married in 1776 while still Miss Elizabeth Hervey, a mere bishop's daughter with no dowry and few acquaintances. Her husband, John Thomas Foster, was a member of the Irish parliament. He was careful with money, and uninterested in city life. Later Bess claimed she had married him under parental duress: 'I really did on my knees ask not to marry Mr F. and said his character terrified me, and they both have since said it was their doing my being married to him,' she told Georgiana. Whatever the truth, by 1780 the marriage was in jeopardy.

*Bess's father, the Earl-Bishop. Bess grew up in modest circumstances while her father was Bishop of Derry. On succeeding to the title of fourth Earl of Bristol his income became much more substantial, yet he was still reluctant to help his children financially.*

According to Lady Bristol Bess had formed an 'attachment' with someone other than Mr Foster, for whom Bess felt 'disgust'. However, in public the Herveys blamed the breakdown of the marriage on Mr Foster, who had seduced Bess's maid. Nevertheless, she was willing to attempt a reconciliation, if only for the sake of her two children, and was shocked when Foster demanded a complete separation. He ordered her to surrender their child and their infant as soon as it was weaned, refusing to pay a penny towards her support. The first act was legal in the eighteenth century as the father always had custody of his children, but the second was not under normal circumstances. Unless legally separated or divorced, a husband was liable for his wife's debts and most families ensured that marriage contracts contained provisions for their daughters if there was a separation. Either Bess's family had failed to do so, or Mr Foster had evidence of his wife's adultery and threatened to divorce her if provoked. To compound matters, Bess's father managed to 'forget' her allowance whenever it came due.

Fanny Burney wrote *The Wanderer* to highlight the dreadful vulnerability of such women – respectable but alone and without financial support – to pimps and exploitation. Their status demanded that appearances they could not afford should be maintained while the means to make an independent living were denied them. Bess's newly inherited title made it impossible for her to find work either as a governess or a paid companion. She could easily fall for a man who offered her a better life as his mistress.

*Bess as Lady Elizabeth Foster. Referring to Bess's unhappy marriage and her father's reluctance to support her, Mrs Dillon, a distant relation, wrote, 'Never was a story more proper for a novel than poor Lady Elizabeth Foster's.'*

Bess later confessed 'a wish to be loved and approved . . . with perhaps a manner that pleased': it was an irresistible combination to Georgiana. Bess's desire to serve her new friend was greater than anything Georgiana had ever encountered before. Both the Devonshires were also deeply moved by her misfortunes. However, it never occurred to Georgiana that Bess's untiring enthusiasm for her company might be inspired by her own poverty, which made Bess a *de facto* paid companion.

Bess was good with the Duke, too; indeed he appeared to like her almost as much, and Georgiana congratulated herself on discovering such a perfect friend. Bess realized that both Georgiana and the Duke were lonely – Georgiana obviously so, but the Duke suffered no less in his own way. Since Charlotte Spencer's death he had been without steady female companionship. Georgiana was too caught up in her own life, and too much in awe of him to take the place of Charlotte. Bess could see that they both needed a confidante, a role that she was very happy to play, although it required her to act two quite different parts: with the Duke she was submissive and flirtatious; with Georgiana she was passionate and sensitive. Almost everyone except the Devonshires saw through Bess immediately.

The seventh of June was Georgiana's twenty-fifth birthday and Lady Spencer used the occasion to denounce her daughter's mode of living. 'In your dangerous path of life you have almost unavoidably amassed a great deal of useless trash – gathered weeds instead of flowers . . . You live so constantly in public you cannot live for your own soul.' The harshness of the letter stunned Georgiana, who replied that on her 'nervous days' she cried whenever she thought about it.

Feeling hurt and rejected, Georgiana turned to the sympathetic and understanding Bess for comfort. She could confide in her new friend as she had done with Mary Graham, and without any of the inconvenience – Bess had no husband or home to call her away. The news that Bess had accompanied Georgiana and the Duke to Plympton camp for the annual military review alarmed Lady Spencer. She had no illusions about Bess, but she was astonished that both Georgiana and the Duke had fallen under her spell. She gathered from her daughter's letters that the three were

inseparable. Bess never seemed to leave Georgiana alone, nor was there any facet of Georgiana's life closed off to her. Bess wrote on Georgiana's letters to Lady Spencer, addressing her as if she were an old friend and adding postscripts about her daughter's health and good behaviour. Sometimes she wrote almost the whole body. She was always deferential, but her familiarity with Georgiana grated on Lady Spencer. Her tone revealed a person desperate to make a permanent home for herself.

The harmonious threesome remained at Plympton until the end of September, when Bess developed a bad cough. Georgiana complained she was being very annoying, loudly insisting one minute that she was perfectly all right, and the next admitting to a troublesome cough for the past two years. Georgiana became anxious and full of self-doubt. On 30 September she wrote, 'I did not go out as I was sulky and uneasy and locked myself up all morning.' She admitted she was taking sedatives again which made her groggy and prevented her from receiving friends.

Georgiana blamed her unhappiness on her infertility but there were other worries: her debts for one. On 19 October Lady Spencer told her that she had paid some money on her behalf to a Mr Hicks, who had seemed quite shifty.

> In short, I suspect some mischief or other – that you have bespoke more things than you can possibly pay for and have given him things of value in exchange . . . at all events I beg you will never part with Jewells. I have often told you they are not your own and should be look'd upon as things only entrusted to your care – do not pass over this article without answering.

Lady Spencer spent much of her time thinking up ways to get rid of her rival. She asked Georgiana and the Duke to visit them at Hotwells in Bristol, politely adding that Bess would not be welcome since Lord Spencer was 'too ill to see a stranger with any comfort'. Bess was bitterly disappointed to be called a stranger after all her carefully composed postscripts. 'Poor little Bess', as she styled herself, went into hysterics at the thought of being left alone. Georgiana hurriedly wrote to her mother, 'Lady Eliz. comes with us, Dst Mama, and poor little soul, it is impossible it should be otherwise.' She tried to soften the blow by pointing to Bess's obedient nature: 'she is the quietest little thing and will sit and draw in a corner of the room, or be sent out of the room, or do whatever you please.' She ended the letter with the only sentence that brought comfort to Lady Spencer: 'I hope to see her set out for Nice within the month.'

The two weeks in Bristol were strained and awkward for everyone except Bess. Nearly every morning the Duke and Bess left Georgiana with Lady Spencer to go riding together; they returned before supper and joined the group, playing cards or reading, without looking or glancing at each other again. Their behaviour was suspicious enough for anyone to question their relationship, but Georgiana chose to remain ignorant.

The Duke left after ten days and Bess remained in Bristol with Georgiana and Lady Spencer. When the Duke was not present Bess appeared to think of nothing but Georgiana's comfort. She displayed a combination of servility and bossiness, taking a great delight in fussing round her. She hardly ever used 'I', Lady Spencer noticed; it was always 'we'. Her voice, hair and clothes were all arranged in a faithful, if not disconcerting, imitation of Georgiana's – Lady Spencer was sure that most of her clothes had once belonged to her daughter. Yet Georgiana seemed to encourage Bess's behaviour. They used code words and nicknames for each other: the Duke was called Canis, which was a reference to his fondness for dogs; for reasons unknown, Georgiana was Mrs Rat, and Bess, Racky.

Shortly after their return to London Georgiana announced that she was pregnant again. She was healthier than she had been for many years, but her mental state seemed precarious: she was beset by 'feels' which made her cry constantly and prevented her from sleeping. Georgiana's emotional state disturbed Lady Spencer, who feared it might induce a miscarriage. But she did not imagine that Bess's impending absence might be the cause of her daughter's torment, and her advice to Georgiana was limited to the practical. Firstly she suggested that Georgiana should stay at home; otherwise she would be accused of loving parties 'better than a child'. Secondly she recommended laudanum; 'take a few drops (5 or 6) . . . if you feel any violent [attacks] or agitation . . .' Finally, as usual, disturbed by Georgiana's fear that she was too sinful to take the Sacrament, she urged her to put her trust in God.

Bess was due to leave for France on 25 December. The Devonshires had officially engaged her to be Charlotte Williams's governess at £300 a year and she was to take her pupil abroad to the south of France for the winter. The plan had a neatness to it which pleased everyone. It solved the problem of Charlotte, who had not thrived with Mrs Gardner, offered hope for Bess's health, and provided her with an income. There may have been other reasons for Bess going away. (Surviving letters hint that Bess had become, or contemplated becoming, the mistress of the great seducer, the Duke of Dorset.) She begged Georgiana and the Duke to keep her informed of 'the stories you hear of me . . . that at least I may be justified to you, and that you may know truth from falsehood'. The threat of some scandal would explain why she was sent abroad for so long when the friendship was in its early stages.

Georgiana was distraught at her departure. Lady Spencer hoped, as much as Bess feared, that the separation would mean the end of her reign over the Devonshires. But neither reckoned on the strength of Georgiana's attachment.

## *An Unstable Coalition* 1783

*Her Grace the Duchess of Devonshire has determined not to appear in public till after her lying-in; as she had long been leader of the fashion, we hope the ladies will follow her example, and get into the* straw *as fast as possible.*

MORNING HERALD AND DAILY ADVERTISER, 8 FEBRUARY 1783

ONCE BESS HAD SET SAIL on the packet to France, enriched with money, new clothes and a letter of introduction to the Polignacs, Georgiana was free to resume her former activities. Her long absence from London during 1782 had reduced her to the role of spectator of most of the developments affecting the Whigs. Defying reports by the *Morning Herald* and other newspapers that she would withdraw from public life until the end of her pregnancy, Georgiana now re-established herself as Fox's ally and political confidante. He frequently stopped by Devonshire House to discuss his worries.

The Rockingham–Shelburne Coalition had been in trouble from the beginning. George III would only talk to Lord Shelburne and pointedly ignored all the Whigs' requests for patronage.

*Opposite: Georgiana and Bess. Georgiana is in the foreground with her hand on her friend's shoulder. 'God bless you my angel love,' Georgiana wrote when Bess was abroad, 'I adore and love you beyond description . . .'*

As early as June 1782 some Whigs were already condemning the Coalition as unworkable. Then Lord Rockingham died after being in office for just three months, following almost two decades in opposition. The Duke of Portland took over as the official head of the party, while Fox remained the heir apparent. Rockingham's death further exposed the deep fissures in the cabinet between his supporters and those of Lord Shelburne. On 4 July Fox resigned as Foreign Secretary. Lord John Cavendish, who was Chancellor of the Exchequer, followed – along with most of the Whigs.

The man who benefited most from Fox's resignation was the twenty-three-year-old William Pitt. His political sympathies on economical and parliamentary reform lay with the Whigs, and notwithstanding the fact that their fathers had been bitter enemies all their working lives, Fox hailed him as a rising new star. They were both heavy drinkers and, for the first few months at least, seemed to have much in common. But despite his enthusiasm for political reform, Pitt regarded the Whigs' opposition to the King as factious politics.

By 1782 Pitt had made it clear to all parties that he expected high office to match his talents, so when Fox's resignation created three spaces in the cabinet, Shelburne invited Pitt to become Chancellor of the Exchequer. To Fox's indignation his former protégé stepped into office over the heads of the departing Rockinghamites. From that moment Fox and Pitt were implacable rivals. Fox and Lord North agreed to put their past enmity behind them, and as soon as the Whigs and North's supporters began voting together Shelburne was lost.

On 24 February Shelburne resigned in the face of overwhelming numbers against him. Once again George III resisted the idea of allowing the Whigs back into office. He begged Pitt to form his own government, but the young politician declined, knowing he would have no support. Lord North refused to renege on his deal with Fox and come in on his own. Seeing that no one was prepared to challenge Fox, the King contemplated leaving England. He even drafted his

The Relief of Gibraltar A Cabinet Council
Pub. by Thos. Colley Jan. 1 1783 London
Richmond Fecit


*Right: 'The Relief of Gibraltar: A Cabinet Council', 1783; one of the first cartoons to allude to Georgiana's influence in politics shows her in negotiation with the Duchess of Richmond over a patriotic headdress.*

abdication speech. Finally, though, on 1 April North, Fox and the Duke of Portland tripped up the stairs of St James's to receive the Great Seals of State. North became Prime Minister, Fox was once more Foreign Secretary, and Lord John Cavendish the Chancellor of the Exchequer.

Georgiana kept Bess informed of political developments as they unfolded, although Bess was more concerned with her own affairs – chiefly with the behaviour of Mr Foster. He had made some enquiries about Bess since learning of her friendship with the Devonshires, wanting to know who was giving her money, among other things. His letters gave Georgiana an idea. She advised Bess to hint that if he would allow his younger son to be educated at school in England, the Devonshires would act as godparents and pay for his upkeep.

Georgiana also made plans for Bess's return. She managed to be explicit and yet circumspect at the same time, declaring her love for Bess but adding,

> . . . Tho' for fear of the agitation it would cause us both and of the hurt it would do your dear health, you must not come before I am brought to bed . . . When you do return it will be to Devonshire House, for a month at least, and as your little pride, and perhaps circumstances, may make it as well that you should not absolutely live in the house always with your brother and sister, I will look out immediately for a house for you near us, on condition that you are less in it than here. The summers you shall pass at Chatsworth . . . the autumns hunting with Canis and the winters in London. You shall have your children with you, or at least Augustus . . .

Bess must never leave her, she insisted. One paragraph of hers was blacked out by a later hand. Hidden here, perhaps, are references to Bess's liaison with Dorset or to the sexual dynamics between herself and the Devonshires. It is clear, however, despite the erasures and the imprecise language, that Georgiana could not tolerate an affair between Bess and her husband. She did not say it outright, but her repeated references to the Duke as 'your dear Brother' must have left Bess in no doubt about the kind of relationship she envisaged between them.

Georgiana's feelings for Bess threatened to overcome her devotion to the party. She was horrified when the Duke of Portland suggested that her husband should become Lord Lieutenant of Ireland. The third Duke of Devonshire had governed Ireland for eight years between 1737 and 1745, and, since the huge Cavendish estates over there generated a large part of the family wealth, the choice seemed extremely apposite. On the one hand, she would have her own court at Dublin, her own duties, and the Duke would have to shake off his lethargy and behave like a statesman. On the other hand, she would be deprived of Bess, who would not be able to accompany them because of Mr Foster's injunction that she stay out of Ireland. 'Ah, Bess, I am half dead,' Georgiana wrote when she relayed the news on 5 April. 'I can only tell you I am afraid we are to go to Ireland . . . I declare to God I am half mad.' The dilemma tore her apart: 'My fate is deciding . . . Oh Bess, every sensation I feel but heightens my adoration of you.'

The matter was decided by the Duke, who for similar reasons disliked the idea of moving to Ireland. Georgiana tried to persuade her brother to go in their place. George, however, demurred. He felt too inexperienced to cope with the volatile situation in Ireland. The country was on the verge of revolution, and the Irish parliament in almost open revolt against Dublin Castle. Why, he asked, if the service was essential, was the Duke not prepared to do his patriotic duty? Georgiana replied truthfully that she had tried to change the Duke's mind.

Although she was five months pregnant, Georgiana continued to host political dinners several times a week. When the Duc de Chartres – a cousin of Louis XVI – and several other members of the French court came to London they treated Georgiana as if she were their official hostess. Lady Mary Coke recorded jealously that they 'did not go anywhere but by [her] direction'. The new French ambassador, the Comte d'Adhémar, was already a regular visitor at Devonshire House, having arrived with a letter of introduction from the Duchesse de Polignac. He was not a professional diplomat and owed his position to his friendship with the Polignac clan. D'Adhémar and the Baron de Bésenval were the two great cronies of Little Po's violent lover, the Comte de Vaudreuil, who took advantage of her sweet nature to obtain gifts and favours for his friends. Though Georgiana did not particularly like d'Adhémar's silky manner, she accepted his company because of his connections, and the weekly invitation to the elegant dinners at Devonshire House gave him access to all the social and political gossip he needed for his secret reports to Paris during the peace negotiations.

On 8 May 1783 Georgiana told her mother that the Duc de Chartres was sporting oversized buttons with pornographic pictures on his waistcoat, 'which my sister very nearly died of'. The entertainments she was providing for the French visitors were so original and lavish that even the *London Chronicle*, which normally eschewed reporting such frivolities, printed full descriptions. Georgiana's popularity with the foreigners inspired envy among the *ton*: not only did she enjoy first place in society; her party was also now in power. Bess was also dismayed to hear about Georgiana's success while she was plodding through France with the ungainly Charlotte. However, she wanted to know all Georgiana's movements. 'Dearest ever ever dearest Love,' she wrote in June, 'why have I no letters from you? I cannot express nor describe the anxiety I feel from it, nor how my peace depends on everything that concerns you . . . how necessary you are to my heart.'

Yet the King was determined to remove the Whigs as soon as he found the appropriate means and the Prince of Wales seemed to provide the opportunity. 'The whole world is in an uproar,' wrote Georgiana on 17 June, referring to a row over the Prince's desire to have a proper allowance and his own household now that he was twenty-one. He also demanded an extra payment of £100,000 to clear himself of his debts. The King refused even to consider handing over such a large amount to his delinquent son and the Prince found that few MPs sympathized with his position. Half the cabinet had threatened to resign if Fox gave in to the Prince's demand and yet he could not, having promised the Prince that he would obtain the money for him, go back on his word.

Fox was in despair and predicted the end of the coalition government in a matter of days. But Georgiana took it upon herself to persuade the Prince to drop his demand. Knowing her voice carried its own authority, she wrote him a frank letter, explaining why he would be making a terrible mistake if he caused the Whigs to resign and that 'the thing therefore to be considered is whether it is not in the power of the present Administration to serve you more by staying in than going out'. As Fox was 'bound in honour' to support the Prince, it was up to him to release Fox, 'and you must do it, if you think it right, as if it was of your own accord'.

Georgiana's letter made the Prince realize that the situation was hopeless. He capitulated and accepted the lower sum of £30,000. Thanks to her intervention the Coalition was safe for the moment. Georgiana's action proved her own thesis – that great consequences often develop from 'causes little imagined'. No one in England knew that the fate of the government rested on a woman's influence with a spoilt youth. In five years Georgiana had matured from a girl parading in military uniform into an astute political negotiator.

# 1783–1784 *A Birth and a Death*

*The decorative appendage of female dress and the newest taste, and highest ton, is the golden collar, epigrammatically bemottoed. Her Grace of Devonshire is said to be the fair inventress of this fashion, whose enviable collar bears this sportive inscription: 'Strayed from Devonshire House!'*

MORNING HERALD AND DAILY ADVERTISER, 12 AUGUST 1783

THE PEACE NEGOTIATIONS with the French and American delegates, overseen by Charles Fox, had not yet been concluded when Georgiana retreated from public life for the last weeks of her pregnancy. Her confinement was a great inconvenience for the negotiators, who had relied on her suppers at Devonshire House for informal meetings. 'Mr Fox is careful to avoid every possible opportunity to talk politics with me,' the Comte d'Adhémar reported to his superiors in France. 'The house of the Duchess of Devonshire, where I usually meet him informally, has been closed to us all for three weeks, owing to the lady's confinement. The painful consequences of this event will doubtless make her invisible for even longer . . . and I shall be deprived entirely of this daily means of seeing Mr Fox.'

Georgiana whiled away the time with Harriet, who was also eight months pregnant. In the sanctuary of Devonshire House the two women amused themselves by experimenting with new hats and drawing patterns for dresses. The fashion for false hips and bottoms made of cork to round out the figure, and padded breasts to fill out the bodice had been in vogue since the 1770s. Georgiana added a new element: the false front to disguise pregnancy. She showed her designs to her friends and the false fronts were soon worn even by women who were not pregnant. Georgiana was also responsible for the unprecedented sales of the 'picture hat': wide-brimmed hats, worn with a large sash and adorned with drooping feathers. She had posed in one of her own design for her portrait by Gainsborough.

The only person who was not excited by Georgiana's pregnancy was the Duke. He was convinced that the baby would be a girl. On 6 July Harriet gave birth to Frederick, her second boy. A week later, on the twelfth, Georgiana went into labour herself. The baby was a girl as the Duke had feared. However, Georgiana insisted to Bess that he was as pleased with the child as she was. At least it proved that she was capable of bearing a son.

They decided to call the baby Georgiana Dorothy – Dorothy after her aunt and godmother, the Duchess of Portland. The Prince of Wales and Lord John Cavendish also agreed to be godparents. In accordance with custom, Georgiana lay with Little G, as she called her, for a month. '[Little G] is very much admired,' she wrote to Bess. 'Her cradle, robes, baskets, etc., are, I am afraid, foolishly magnificent.'

Georgiana decided to breastfeed Little G herself, still an unusual step among the aristocracy. The *Morning Post* applauded her, remarking how sad it was 'that females in high life should generally be such strangers to the duty of a mother, as to render one instance to the contrary so singular'. Her refusal to employ a wet nurse was a brave act of defiance. The Cavendishes were annoyed and tried to bully her into changing her mind. On 6 August a harassed Georgiana wrote to her mother, 'what makes [them] abuse suckling is their impatience for my having a boy, and they fancying I shan't soon if I suckled.'

*'The Blessings of Peace', April 1783. Once again Georgiana's work behind the scenes of the political debate is recognized. Here she is depicted as a witch on a broomstick flying over the new cabinet members, who are seen to be giving in to 'peace on any terms'.*

It was difficult to find trustworthy, sober maternity nurses in the eighteenth century and Georgiana's brief experience with one was disastrous. 'She was only rather dirty till last night,' she wrote to Lady Spencer, 'when she was quite drunk.' This alarmed Georgiana but then, she added, 'I learnt that she had been so drunk as to fall down and vomit.' After the incident Georgiana let no one but the nurse, Mrs Smith, help her with Little G. A month after her birth, Little G was christened.

Only one person felt unease over the event, and that was Bess, several hundred miles away and thinking constantly of home. Her letters had hitherto been eloquently pathetic: she was broken by her misfortunes, her health was ruined and her heart crushed like a 'bruised plant [which] cannot regain its vigour, but droops even in the blest sunshine of your affection'. Now, however, she tried to convince Georgiana that her poor Bess was in perfect health and spirits and should be allowed to come home. She repeatedly begged to be allowed to look after Georgiana and her baby. 'You will know how anxiously my heart watched over you in the first moments of your being with child,' she reminded her friend. 'Kiss *our* child for me,' she wrote enviously. 'How happy are those who have a right to be its godmother, but I am to be its little Mama – Canis said so.'

Convinced that they would soon forget her in their joy over Little G, Bess began saving the money she received from the Devonshires' bankers. She had previously accepted Georgiana's gifts

MATERNAL LOVE
The Fashionable Mamma, – or – The Convenience of Modern Drefs
Vide The Pocket Hole, &c.

*Gillray's caricature of 'The Fashionable Mamma' refers to the fact that it was becoming acceptable for aristocratic women to breastfeed their own children rather than hiring a wet nurse. Georgiana breastfed all of her children, which attracted the notice, and praise, of the press.*

*Harriet with her two sons, John William and Frederick, left. The Duke blamed Georgiana for not being able to produce an heir, as her sister had done. However, Georgiana was besotted with Little G, shown with her mother below, despite the general disappointment that she was not a boy.*

*In 1782 the Duke and Georgiana paid for Bess, left, to go abroad to improve her health. The separation was so painful for Georgiana that she was easily convinced to send Bess funds for her travels. In Naples, below, Bess claimed to be one of the favourites at court.*

with a great show of reluctance – 'let it my love, be a debt,' she would insist; now she constantly found excuses to ask for more. It was easy to extract money from the credulous Georgiana.

In August reports reached Devonshire House that she had taken Charlotte to Naples and was sharing a house with two lovers. Georgiana could not bring herself to believe it. 'Pray, pray, my dearest love, forgive what I am going to say,' she wrote Bess. 'I think that the innocence of your conduct and intentions does not make you aware enough of the danger of your situation.' They had also heard that Bess had fallen in love with a certain *chevalier* and was planning to meet him in Turin. 'I must entreat you not to go so soon to Turin,' Georgiana pleaded, 'at least . . . do not go there purposely to meet him.' Why, she asked despairingly, could not Bess behave herself and live with a female companion like any other respectable woman? 'Live with women as much as you can,' she implored, '. . . do try. My angel love, the world is so alive [with stories] about you . . .'

Bess was horrified when she read Georgiana's letter. It had never occurred to her that she might figure in people's letters to their friends and relatives in England. She wrote a long, pleading letter to Georgiana attempting to justify herself, knowing that her future hung in the balance. 'The idea of having made you uneasy counterbalances all. I am wretched till I know you are again tranquil on my account, and assured that I cannot err against your will again,' she wrote humbly, 'let my ruling sentiment be to please you.' She blamed her 'imprudences' on her broken heart due to the loss of her dear children. To her surprise, one letter was enough to reassure her friends and the subject was never referred to again. Fortunately for her, far more pressing matters claimed Georgiana's attention.

Georgiana was in serious trouble over her gambling debts. She had frittered away thousands during the past few years, and secretly borrowed more to hide her losses. Nor could she stop herself playing when she had no money to spare. Furthermore, the Duke's agent, John Heaton, had accused Georgiana of swindling tradesmen, and worse. Chatsworth had been undergoing improvements: Georgiana was refurbishing her private apartments and had also instructed builders to give Devonshire House a much-needed face-lift. But Heaton brought the work to a halt after having heard a rumour that Georgiana was using the services of some craftsmen free of charge in return for passing on a recommendation to the Prince of Wales. Heaton advised the Duke not to pay any of Georgiana's bills until he had investigated the matter. He also informed the Duke, without any proof, that Georgiana was having an affair with the Prince. The world, he said, knew that the Devonshires 'liv'd ill together'.

Georgiana wrote to her mother that while she knew that 'the Duke's confidence in me is such that nobody but myself could hurt me with him', other parts of her conversation with the Duke were less reassuring. Why did he not sack his agent, she asked, since he was so angry at his presumption? The Duke informed Georgina that quarrelling with Heaton 'would quite ruin us'. 'In short,' she wrote to her mother, 'whatever he is, Mr Heaton has so puzzled our affairs that I expect he alone can have the clue. This, however, has determined me to be silent whatever I think . . .'

Shocked to learn that Heaton had so much control over their affairs, Georgiana wondered what would happen if he ever learnt the true nature of her debts. In fact, the Duke was exaggerating Heaton's power because he himself knew so little about the running of his estate. On receiving her daughter's worried letters, Lady Spencer advised: 'Try to show your extravagance was due to ignorance.' She was appalled, like the Duke, that a servant should pass comment on his employer's wife. However, the Duke's brother and uncles did not share Lady Spencer's sense of outrage; they accused Georgiana of deliberately wasting his money. Lord and Lady George Cavendish, who remained hopeful that Georgiana would never produce an heir, resented her depletion of what they regarded as their future estate.

Georgiana was saved from further unpleasant conversations by the arrival of many stalwarts of the Devonshire House Circle, including James Hare and Thomas Grenville. The gaiety at Chatsworth temporarily lifted her spirits. On 21 October she wrote in a happier mood: 'we had a bouncing public day yesterday, and many staid. We have a grand coursing this morning . . . Georgiana is very very fretful, and has for a fortnight past slobbered amazingly.' But more rumours about her reached Chatsworth and infected the atmosphere. Lady George Cavendish told Harriet that everyone knew about her sister and Charles Fox. 'Lady George teazed her cruelly,' Georgiana complained to Bess, 'about the Eyebrow [Fox] and me, and Canis and the Infernal [Lady Jersey], and so blended with some truth that my sister was quite hurt.' The letter mentions that Georgiana had discussed the rumours with the Duke, revealing the extraordinary, albeit one-sided, openness between them. Though he obviously accepted that there was no 'intrigue' between her and Fox, Lady George's comments suggest otherwise.

There is no evidence to prove or disprove the notion that Georgiana and Fox had become lovers. Their correspondence for these years does not survive. Georgiana's demeanour had certainly altered since 1779, when Lady Pembroke assured her son that Georgiana never flirted. Perhaps Bess's skill at playing the flirt had stirred something within her, or perhaps she no longer saw any reason to remain faithful to her adulterous husband. Nothing is certain except that Georgiana shared her contemporaries' horror of breaking the patriarchal bloodline. Towards the end of her life she claimed that he had never been her lover, only her friend. She may have been lying, of course, which would mean that she had shared him with the courtesan Mrs Armistead, who became his mistress in 1783.

In the midst of Georgiana's troubles over rumours and debts, news came from Bath that Lord Spencer was dead. He was only forty-nine. Lady Spencer was devastated. The following day, 1 November, she wrote in her diary, 'I have passed another day half-stunned with affliction and stupefied with laudanum.' She had deliberately concealed Lord Spencer's final illness from Georgiana, fearing to add to her worries. The sudden news of his death made Georgiana ill. She developed a fever and lay sick for almost two weeks. Little Georgiana and the Duke caught her fever, and a month passed before they were able to visit Lady Spencer. When the news reached Italy the English community in Rome was surprised to see Lady Elizabeth Foster go into deep mourning.

Georgiana wanted her friend to return now, but she also took care to remind her that there had to be an equal partnership between the three of them. 'What could be more interesting than our journey last year,' she wrote, 'a man and a woman endowed with every amiable quality and loving one another as Brother and Sister, nursing and taking care of a woman, who was doatingly fond of them, and who bore within her the child that was to fulfil the vows and wishes of all three.'

The Devonshires retreated to Bath so that the Duke, who was suffering from gout, could bathe in the springs. She consoled herself by writing each morning to Bess. Bath was no less painful for the Duke. He also missed his Bess, he wrote:

> This place has been very unpleasant for me compared to what it was a year and a half ago, for then I had the Rat and Bess and good health and fine weather . . . There are many places

in Bath that put me so much in mind of you that when I walk about the town I cannot help expecting upon turning the corner of a street, to see you walking along.

Bess, however, had found other attractions and was no longer in a hurry to return to England. Since making her promise to Georgiana and the Duke to avoid any more flirtations, she had visited Rome with Charlotte and made a conquest of the *bon viveur* Cardinal Bernis. They appeared constantly in each other's company until the Cardinal's public affection for her became a dangerous liability. Bess hurriedly returned to Naples, where she promptly fell in love with a handsome Swedish diplomat, Count Fersen. The Count had recently come from Versailles, where his departure had caused Marie Antoinette to cry in front of her attendants.

Fersen was thought to reciprocate Marie Antoinette's feelings, but it did not prevent him from falling for the 'tragic' and beautiful young Englishwoman in exile. One evening, Bess claimed, he kissed her before she knew what was happening but she reluctantly halted his advances. 'Pray forgive me,' she hurriedly wrote to Georgiana in case she had heard about Fersen from someone else. 'I think better of him than anybody I have seen, but your claims and Canis's on me can never lessen . . . Oh G., are you angry with me?'

Georgiana begged her to return immediately. She had detailed plans for Bess and Charlotte. Bess would no longer be in charge of the girl: her life would be with them at Devonshire House. She conceded that Bess would have to live in her own little house from time to time to avoid gossip, but the three of them would never again be parted. However, the prize no longer seemed so attractive to Bess. Her replies were evasive. Bess let slip that she dreaded her return because it 'will renew all remarks, and observations and conjectures' about her past behaviour. She reminded Georgiana that their 'tender friendship makes me an object of envy, and of course of the malice of others'. But it was neither malice nor envy which prompted Lady Clermont to write to Lady Spencer on 26 February 1783 about 'the lady in Italy' that 'I hear there never was anything so much admired, and that she sees a great deal of company. I wish to God she would run off with somebody.'

The prospect of Bess remaining abroad horrified Georgiana. She was pregnant again, but this time the pregnancy was proving to be difficult and painful. The physical signs were not good, and added to her many anxieties was the fear that she might miscarry. After agonizing for months Georgiana went to see the Duke at the beginning of March about her debts. She wrote to Bess that she had incurred

a very, very large debt. I never had courage to own it, and try'd to win it at play, by which means it became immense and was grown . . . many, many, many thousands. I would not tell Canis . . . whilst I was with child and suckling, because I thought it ungenerous to be protected by my situation . . .

But the Duke was more understanding than she had thought he would be:

What had I to offer for the kind of ruin I brought on him . . . And how do you think he has received the avowal – with the utmost generosity, goodness and kindness. His whole care has been that I may not vex myself . . . My angel Bess, write to me, tell me you don't hate me for this confession, Oh, love, love me ever.

Georgiana lost the baby shortly after her confession. She wanted Lady Spencer to come to her, but her mother could not leave London while the executors were unravelling Lord Spencer's estate, which was in a muddle and worth less than a quarter of what they had expected. It appeared that the Spencers had lost most of their money at the gaming table. Lady Spencer was no longer rich; her income would be a mere £3,000 a year, with the promise of an extra £1,000 from George, once he had paid off the outstanding creditors. She blamed herself for having wasted her son's inheritance and for having corrupted her children by her example. Lady Spencer would never face the world with the same self-confidence again.

Although she was lonely and miserable, Georgiana preferred to remain at Chatsworth rather than go to Devonshire House where she would be surrounded by her friends. 'When as now I feel nervous and shy,' she wrote, 'I had much rather converse with people I know but little of, than with those I know very much better. I feel a dread of going to London.' But events taking place in Westminster meant that she would have no respite.

## 1784 *The Westminster Election*

*If Mr Fox is no longer the* Man of the People, *he must be allowed from the number of females who attend to give him their support, to be at least, the* Man for the Ladies. *The Duchess of Devonshire's attendance at Covent Garden, perhaps, will not secure Mr Fox's election; but it will at least establish her pre-eminence above all other beauties of* that place, *and make her a standing toast in all the ale-houses and gin-shops of Westminster.*

MORNING POST, 8 APRIL 1784

THE COALITION HAD STRUGGLED to remain in power since driving out Lord Shelburne in April 1783. George III's hostility to Fox and his former Prime Minister, Lord North, was so marked that no one thought the Coalition could survive for long. The Prince's unedifying display of greed the previous June had not helped the ministry's popularity. However, their management of the political crisis over the Prince's debts had given Fox confidence.

The cabinet shared some of Fox's optimism when parliament resumed after the summer recess and the ministry announced its programme of reform. The most controversial plan was an overhaul of the East India Company's rights and charters. There were stories of unbridled corruption, exploitation – even violence against the native population. Fox's East India Bill passed through the House of Commons in November with a comfortable majority. However, this easy victory was a smokescreen: there were secret moves afoot to break the Coalition. William Pitt held meetings with the King in early December and together they formed a plot to oust Fox. When the Bill reached the Lords Pitt's cousin, Lord Temple, quietly circulated an open letter from the King that stated clearly that anyone who voted for the Bill would henceforth be the King's enemy. Fox refused to believe the rumours until the sight of the Lords voting down the Bill made him realize that he had been outwitted. George III so loathed the Whigs that when he heard the results at 10 p.m. he immediately sent his officers to Piccadilly to collect the Seals of State from Fox and North.

The next morning, 19 December, William Pitt kissed the King's hand and, at twenty-four, became the youngest Prime Minister in parliamentary history.

Paradoxically, the mood among the Whigs was one of exultation. By issuing an order to the Lords to override the House of Commons the King had at last provided evidence of his anti-constitutional activities. Fox saw the political crisis in personal terms – as a duel between himself, George III and William Pitt. Georgiana had no doubt that Fox would win. As long as the House of Commons supported the Coalition there was nothing either the King or Pitt could do. The Coalition spent the Christmas break preparing for battle. No one thought Pitt could last to the New Year. But they misjudged public opinion. The Whigs were reviled for having forced their way into power in spite of the King's objections – 'storming the closet' as it was known – and Fox's perorations on English liberty looked spurious next to his notorious lifestyle.

The Coalition held regular meetings at Devonshire House; its palatial drawing room was the only place that could comfortably accommodate all its supporters. They were depressing affairs: complaints and criticism drowned out constructive suggestions and fewer and fewer people turned out for each meeting. The combination of the King's support and Pitt's cool determination won over increasing numbers of MPs every week. Pitt watched his majority in the House grow until mid-March and then called a general election.

On 17 March Georgiana went to the opera to hear *La Reine de Golconde*, which included a little piece she had composed herself. That night, however, the theatre was taking place not on the stage but in the stalls. Political rivalry divided the audience and there was much booing and hissing at the arrival of prominent politicians. Georgiana loved this kind of public participation. She went again on the twentieth: 'It was very full, and I had several good political fights.' The Duchess of Rutland jumped to her feet and shouted, 'Damn Fox!' at the boisterous crowd below; Lady Maria Waldegrave retaliated from the opposite box, 'Damn Pitt!'

Rivalry between the parties spread to the streets, aided in many instances by *agents provocateurs*. Pitt rode down the Strand accompanied by a great mob which stopped outside Carlton House and shouted abuse at the Prince. It moved on to St James's, where with difficulty he prevented them from smashing Fox's windows. Later Lord Chatham, Pitt's elder brother, spotted James Hare exhorting a crowd to attack Pitt's carriage. A public debate at Westminster Hall degenerated into a riot and Fox was pelted with 'devils-dung' while his supporters hustled him into a waiting carriage.

The threat of insults or worse did not deter Georgiana from venturing into this turbulent world to aid Fox. She spent a few days canvassing for her brother's constituency and then returned to London for the Westminster election. There were three candidates standing for two places: Fox for the Whigs, and Sir Cecil Wray (a Whig deserter) and Lord Admiral Hood for Pitt. Since Hood was a popular hero from the American war it was really a contest between Fox and Wray. Because of its large franchise of 18,000 voters and its proximity to parliament, Westminster was one of the few constituencies where public opinion really mattered. Pitt would gladly have exchanged a dozen ordinary boroughs to oust Fox from this, the 'people's constituency'. The King simply wanted Fox out. Do whatever is necessary, he ordered Pitt, 'rather than let him be Returned for Westminster'.

As at previous elections, the hustings were erected in Covent Garden beside the polling booths, through which the voters had to shuffle, one at a time, to record their vote in front of the clerk. On the first day of the polls, which remained open for six weeks, the Whigs assembled for a mass canvass. Their helpers had strung up banners and coloured bunting along the main thoroughfares. Fox and a few friends stayed on the platform to harangue the crowd, while the men

and women divided into three teams led by Georgiana, Mrs Crewe and Mrs Damer. Georgiana and Harriet, accompanied by several male escorts, walked through the cobbled streets, handing out specially struck medals to Foxites.

The Whigs frantically urged everyone to join the canvass. By 5 April the Duchess of Portland, Lady Jersey, Lady Carlisle, Mrs Bouverie and the three Ladies Waldegrave were among those parading through Westminster, dressed in blue and buff with foxtails in their hats, soliciting votes from bemused shopkeepers. According to Nathaniel Wraxall, their activities soon got out of hand: 'These ladies, being previously furnished with lists of outlying voters, drove to their respective dwellings. Neither entreaties nor promises were spared . . . and there can be no doubt of common mechanics having been conveyed to the hustings on more than one occasion by the Duchess in her own coach.'

Horace Walpole was ashamed by the way in which some of the voters took advantage of Georgiana: 'the Duchess made no scruple of visiting some of the humblest of electors, dazzling and enchanting them by the fascination of her manner, the power of her beauty and the influence of her high rank.' But others shouted abuse at her and on more than one occasion she was physically threatened.

By the end of the first week Georgiana was exhausted and demoralized. Her voice was hoarse and her feet were sore and blistered from walking on the broken cobbles of Henrietta Street – incidentally home to some famous brothels and therefore a source of much coarse humour in the press. Despite all their efforts Fox was still trailing in the polls. 'I give the Election quite up,' Georgiana wrote to her mother, 'and must lament all that has happened – however, the circumstances I was in will justify me to those it is most essential for me to please and I must pocket the opinions of the rest.' The government was jubilant. 'Their exertions have been incredible,' Pitt's cousin told the Duke of Rutland, 'particularly upon the part of her Grace of Devon, who in the course of her canvass has heard more plain English of the grossest sort than ever fell to the share of any lady of her rank . . . Fox is now clearly defeated.'

Pittite newspapers concentrated their attacks on Georgiana and ignored the other women. 'It is very hard,' she complained, 'they should single me out when all the women of my side do as much.' She denied exchanging kisses for votes: it had been Harriet's idea, not hers. Georgiana was easy to attack because she was already a celebrity. The *Morning Post* was the first to run the story about her kissing voters on 31 March: 'We hear the D—s of D— grants *favours* to those who promise their votes and interest to Mr Fox.' Thereafter it ran vicious stories almost every day. By the twelfth Georgiana could no longer endure it and informed the Duke that she was leaving London to stay with her mother in St Albans.

The surge in newspaper reporting since the 1770s had been accompanied by a greater boldness when it came to ridiculing public figures. This was partly because both the government and opposition were prepared to pay newspaper editors handsomely for attacking their opponents. The government poured money into anti-Fox and anti-Georgiana propaganda. Newspapers such as the *Morning Herald* printed as many nasty stories about her as possible, and print sellers who were close to the government sold thousands of cartoons attacking her campaign. On 3 April print shops were displaying a new and particularly offensive set of cartoons depicting Georgiana in a lewd embrace with a Westminster tradesman.

In a world which prized female modesty Georgiana's drubbing by the press shamed her family. It was not the fact of her canvassing but her method, which was too free and easy. Lady Spencer

*Opposite: The Ladies Waldegrave were among the female Whig supporters who paraded through Westminster soliciting votes; however, none of the women received as much direct criticism as Georgiana. The* Morning Post *wrote that 'Ladies who interest themselves so much in the case of elections, are perhaps too ignorant to know that they meddle with what does not concern them.'*

*Overleaf: A crowd gathers in Covent Garden during the Westminster election. A German tourist watched the mob turn violent after the polls closed: 'In a very few minutes, the whole scaffolding, benches, and chairs, and everything were completely destroyed . . . thus in the midst of exaltation and triumph, they paraded through many of the most populous streets in London.'*

had not objected when her daughters trooped off to Northampton to campaign for George: there they had conducted themselves in a seemly manner. Lady Spencer told Harriet that, 'I know it has been from the best intention you have both been led to take the part you have done, but let this be a lesson to you . . . never to go in any matter beyond the strictest rules of propriety.' Even Mrs Montagu, a champion of women's education as well as a member of the Blue Stocking Circle, thought Georgiana had gone too far: 'The Duchess of Devonshire has been canvassing in a most masculine manner, and has met with much abuse.' But her disapproval of Georgiana did not affect her own activities on behalf of Pitt.

St Albans was a safe haven where Georgiana could forget the recent scenes at Covent Garden. However, shortly after her arrival she received a summons from the party. They wanted her to return immediately. As it turned out, she had left just as votes were shifting in favour of Fox. The Duchess of Portland wrote, 'I am happy to tell you of our success today for Westminster . . . Everybody is so anxious for your return that I do hope you will come to town at the latest tomorrow evening; for if we should lose this at last, they will think it is owing to your absence.'

Lady Spencer could scarcely believe the effrontery of the Cavendishes, or their willingness to sacrifice Georgiana's health and reputation for political ends. She wrote a sharp reply, her bitterness heightened by the knowledge that if her husband were alive they would not treat the Spencer name in so cavalier a fashion. The Duke of Portland humbled himself to make a personal plea. 'Every one is convinced,' he told Georgiana, that 'the very material alteration . . . in Fox's favour' was a result of her work. He also warned that if she were seen to have 'withdrawn' from the election, a loss for the Whigs would be 'the inevitable consequence'.

Lord John Cavendish wrote directly to Lady Spencer on behalf of the Cavendishes to apologize for the treatment of her daughters. But he was also blunt in claiming that 'the censure and abuse has already been incurred; and that if any votes are lost for want of similar application' Georgiana would be blamed. He promised her that they had changed their methods: 'the Ladies go early in the mornings to such persons as they are told are likely to be influenced by them, and talk to them at their coach doors, after which they go to a shop that over looks the polling place and look out of the window and encourage their friends.' He also promised that the party would mount a better defence of Georgiana; henceforth no libel would go unchallenged.

Reluctantly, Lady Spencer allowed her daughter to set off in her coach back to London. Lord John Cavendish's assurances had not convinced either of them. But even though Georgiana hated to be a figure of ridicule, she longed for the theatre and excitement of mass canvassing. In Westminster she ignored orders to remain in her carriage. She not only chatted to voters and argued cheerfully with them, she also took an interest in their businesses and families. Her success lay in her ability to empathize with strangers. She went with her friends from shop to shop making enormous purchases, deliberately overpaying while hinting at the promise of more if the proprietors voted for Fox.

The *Morning Post* complained that Georgiana and Harriet were guilty of more than paying over the odds. It accused them of threatening anti-Fox tradesmen with a Whig

Dighton Del

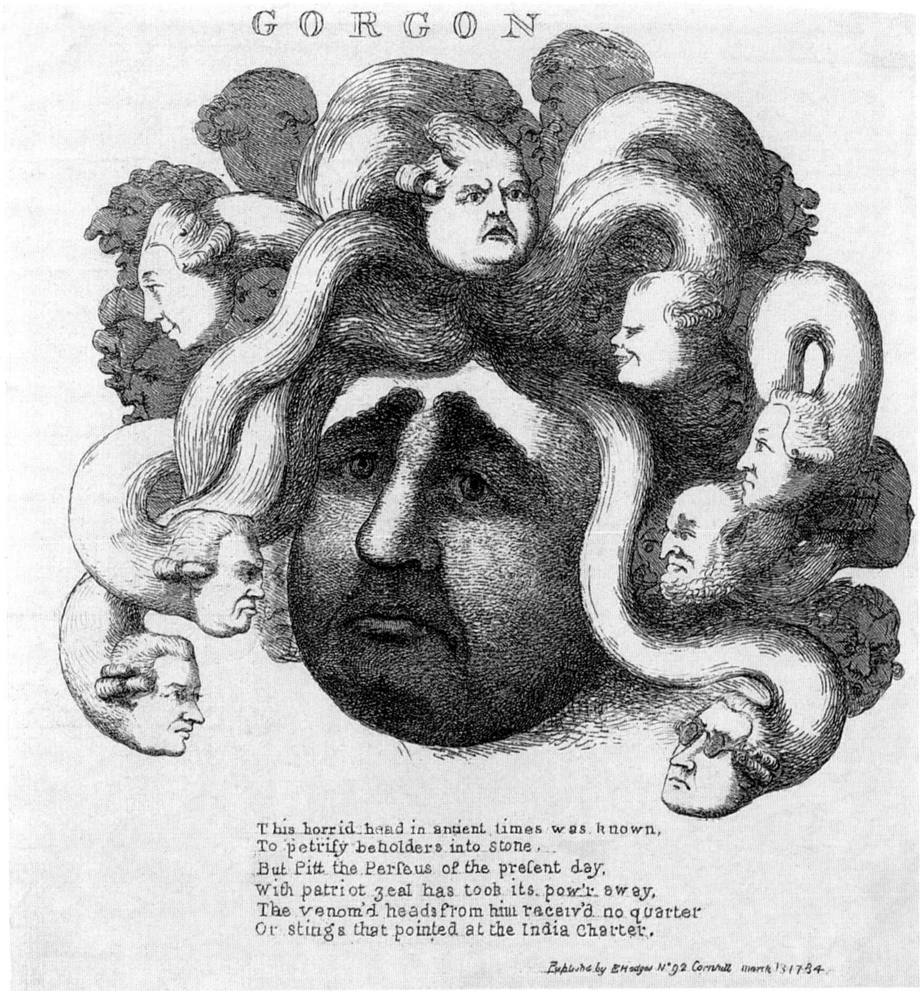

GORGON
This horrid head in antient times was known,
To petrify beholders into stone.
But Pitt the Perseus of the present day,
With patriot zeal has took its pow'r away,
The venom'd heads from him receiv'd no quarter
Or stings that pointed at the India Charter.


*Opposite: Georgiana, by Joshua Reynolds. An unconventional beauty, she was the object of admiration and envy. 'You cannot conceive how vexed I am at the newspaper abuse,' she told her brother, and she begged him not to read the lurid stories the press wrote about her during the election.*

*Left: A cartoon depicting Charles James Fox as a Gorgon. During the Westminster election, the government poured money into anti-Fox and anti-Georgiana propaganda.*

blacklist. Just as Lord John Cavendish had promised, the *Morning Herald and Daily Advertiser* riposted on Georgiana's behalf. For the Whigs, the contest was about the larger issues: Liberty, Patriotism and Duty. In contrast, the pro-government papers concentrated on Georgiana, showing her kissing or bribing electors with favours. The Whig printers tried to raise her above the fray. In the cartoon 'The Apotheosis of the Dutchess' she is lifted up to the clouds by the goddesses 'Truth' and 'Virtue' while 'Scandal' lies grovelling on the ground clutching a copy of the *Morning Post*. The anti-Fox propagandists linked Georgiana's genius for the 'common touch' with being common, hence her nickname of 'Doll Common'. In its daily report on the election the *Morning Post* persistently associated Georgiana with free sex: she was either 'granting favours', caressing her 'favourite member', looking for the 'right handle in politics', or grasping the 'fox's tail'.

The Whigs' defence of Georgiana was anaemic compared to the robust insults made by the government press. The pious images depicting her making sacrifices to the Temple of Liberty failed to neutralize those of her making love to the electors of Westminster. Georgiana was forced to send deputies to buy up the most offensive prints as soon as they appeared in shop windows.

*Cartoons criticizing Georgiana and her friends for canvassing in the streets and undesirable areas. While most of the criticism during the election was aimed at Georgiana and the Whigs, some, such as that above right, attacked George III's apparent disregard for the British people and the constitution.*

THE COVENT GARDEN NIGHT MARE.

A Certain Dutchess kissing
Old SWELTER-IN-GREASE the Butcher for his Vote
O' Times! O' Manners!
The Women Wear Breeches & the Men Petticoats

EVERY MAN HAS HIS HOBBY HORSE

*Many of the cartoons criticized Fox for relying on Georgiana to increase his votes and equated her activities with lewd and unladylike conduct. She is here shown kissing foul-looking butchers for votes and generally mixing with the lowest elements of society. Some print sellers were simply using Georgiana as an excuse for titillation.*

An illustration showing a drunk Georgiana being led in the street. She enjoyed chatting to voters, meeting their families and talking to their wives about homely matters such as nursing and discipline, and also sharing a pint of ale or a tipple of gin; of course, the latter activity caught the greater interest of the press.

Remarkably, the government's efforts failed to turn the voters against Georgiana and her energetic canvass brought in the votes Fox needed. By 22 April he was almost level with Wray; and by the end of April the party's spirits were sufficiently high for them to host a dinner for over 800 electors at the Freemason's Tavern. With only three more weeks to go, supporters in Pitt's camp were understandably sulky. Some suggested that Georgiana should be arraigned before parliament on charges of bribery. Pro-government newspapers increased their output, but the Whig counter-offensive was now working at maximum efficiency and anti-Georgiana posters scarcely survived an hour before being spotted and pasted over.

Through it all, Georgiana and the other women continued to canvass. By the close of polling Hood was first and Fox second, the clear winner over Wray by more than 200 votes. Lady Spencer no longer cared about the outcome and simply wanted Georgiana out of the limelight. This was not what Georgiana wanted to hear just when all her efforts were proving to be justified. The Duke of Portland also insisted that she must stay: the party could show no hint of regret or embarrassment, whatever its private feelings about the Westminster campaign. It had to be a clear-cut moral victory – especially since they had done so badly in the rest of the country. Eighty-nine Whigs, nicknamed 'Fox's Martyrs', had lost their seats.

As soon as the poll closed a triumphant procession of the entire party marched from St Paul's down the Strand, past Carlton House, the Prince of Wales's residence, and along Piccadilly to Devonshire House. Twenty-four horsemen led the way, all dressed in blue and buff with foxtails hanging from their hats. Behind them followed a brass band, and then Fox in a decorated chair, garlanded with laurels and other senatorial insignia. Hundreds of supporters marched behind. The aristocracy followed, dressed in full regalia. The Prince's carriage brought up the rear of the parade accompanied by every member of his household, all in uniform. The Prince of Wales and Georgiana, meanwhile, had slipped through the streets in order to greet the marchers when they reached Devonshire House.

*Mrs Hobart and Georgiana doing battle for their candidates. 'It is very hard,' Georgiana complained of the press, 'they should single me out when all the women of my side do the same.' As this cartoon reveals, women from the other side participated as well.*

*The gardens of Carlton House, the residence of the Prince of Wales. After Fox's victory in the election, the Prince opened up Carlton House for several nights of dinners and balls.*

The Prince of Wales, who had been too drunk for most of the election to be of any help, opened up Carlton House for several nights of dinners and balls. One of the highlights was a sumptuous banquet for 600 guests. The following week on the day of the state opening of parliament the Prince held a *fête-champêtre* in his gardens with music and dancing. The King had to go through St James's Park, past Carlton House, to reach parliament. Embarrassingly for the King, the solemnity of the state occasion was disrupted by the sound of revelry coming from the other side of the brick wall.

Nevertheless, on the first day of parliament the Whig ranks were so depleted they could only muster a miserable 114 votes against the government's majority of almost 300. Pitt's first speech to the House was relaxed and self-assured. He moved his listeners to frequent laughter with descriptions of the Westminster election and Georgiana's canvass, though it was decided that she would not be arraigned for bribery.

Georgiana scarcely registered the fact that she had escaped prosecution; the end of the election had not stopped her hounding in the press or removed her responsibilities. Although the core membership of the party was stable, there were at least a hundred more supporters who had to be prevented from defecting. Georgiana used lavish entertainments and her own popularity to entice waverers back to meetings at Devonshire House, but turtle dinners and gambling nights could not disguise the fact that the Whigs would never be in power while the King reigned. Lord North remained loyal but many of his followers felt there was no point in supporting the defunct Coalition. Georgiana counted each defection as a personal failure.

The Coalition had been a disaster for the Whigs, but it was also the defining moment for their ideology. Henceforth the Foxites would always hark back to 1784: their defeat became enshrined as a near-mythological battle against a despotic King and his lackey William Pitt. For Georgiana 1784 was also a defining year – the personal cost of the Westminster election had been far greater for her than anyone else, but it also established her position. Before the election her participation in party politics had been haphazard and dependent upon circumstance. But it was only after the government had recognized her potency as a campaigner that Georgiana achieved political status in her own right. Her unofficial ties to the Whigs were now official, as the Duke of Portland had made clear when he recalled her to London. Fanny Burney explained Georgiana's position in just a few words: she was the 'head of opposition public'.

At least eleven women had canvassed daily, including Harriet, the Duchess of Portland and the Waldegrave sisters. However, the other women canvassers neither endured the same abuse as Georgiana, nor won the same plaudits; certainly no one libelled Lady Salisbury, who was briefly the Prince of Wales's mistress, with the accusation of nymphomania. Georgiana was marked out for several reasons. First, she brought her own personality to the campaign in an era when the only women who had public personas were actresses and courtesans. Since her marriage she had deliberately courted attention through her patronage of the arts and her flair for fashion. She had appeared as herself and not as a sacrifice to female duty, and this had affronted traditionalists. Georgiana had also challenged eighteenth-century attitudes to class distinction in treating the voters as her equals, which was a serious transgression against propriety.

It was these innovations – her own cult of celebrity and her democratic approach – which differentiated Georgiana then and later as a female pioneer in electoral politics. She was never allowed to canvass openly in London again, nor did other aristocratic women imitate her example. It would be another hundred years before women once more ventured boldly into street politics as Georgiana had not been afraid to do in 1784.

*Lady Salisbury, who with Mrs Hobart canvassed for Pitt during the Westminster election, did not encounter anything like the abuse that was hurled at Georgiana in the popular press.*

1784–1786

# *Opposition*

*The Duchess of Devonshire appeared on Saturday at Drury-Lane Theatre in a* mob cap*; her Grace, ever since her initiation into the business of electioneering, has been much attached to* mobs.

MORNING POST, 3 MAY 1785

'I AM CROSS, MISERABLE AND UNHAPPY. I hate myself,' Georgiana wrote in June 1784, two months after the election victory. She was in debt again. According to estimates in the *Morning Post*, the Westminster election personally cost the Devonshires over £30,000. Georgiana knew that she had spent more than that, although she could only guess at the true figure. She had a pile of credit notes waiting to be paid, but she was terrified of asking the Duke for help. He had hardly spoken to her since her previous confession and their relationship had deteriorated further during the election. He had been mortified by the caricatures portraying him as a cuckold but, more than that, he resented Georgiana's independence and showed his displeasure by allowing her bills to go unpaid. She tried to be philosophical about her own treatment by the press but 'I think it has lowered me', she wrote.

The Duke's silence frightened her. 'As much as I long to see you it is not for me I write,' she wrote to Bess. 'I am certain poor Canis's health and spirits depend upon your soothing friendship.' They were expecting her return, Georgiana had begged her friend to be in England by June at the latest. Bess had not seen England for almost a year and a half and she was beginning to tire of her nomadic life. Since she knew her place at Devonshire House was absolutely assured, there were no more obstacles to her return. Bess informed the Devonshires that they should expect her in August.

Emboldened by the election, pro-government newspapers printed sarcastic asides about Georgiana's inability to pay her debts. However, in July the Prince of Wales involved her in a far worse scandal than mere trouble with creditors. The Prince's latest passion was for Maria Fitzherbert, a respectable and wealthy Catholic widow. Although gratified by his affections she refused to become his mistress. He increased his offer to marriage, and alarmed his friends by throwing himself on the floor and pulling at his hair, sobbing and screaming that she had to be his wife or he would die. It was an impossible wish. Not only would it be unthinkable for him to marry a commoner, twice married, and several years older than himself; two parliamentary acts forbade it. The Act of Settlement stipulated that the monarch had to marry within the Protestant faith, and the 1774 Royal Marriages Act awarded the King sole discretion in choosing the spouses of the royal family. Such a marriage could only end in the Prince's exile. He begged Georgiana, as his best friend, to help him.

Despite her distaste for the affair Georgiana could not resist his pathetic entreaties. However, there was an unspoken antipathy between the two women which made her reluctant to accept the role of go-between. Each sensed a rival in the other. Georgiana compounded her crime in the eyes of Mrs Fitzherbert, who suspected her motives anyway, by taking every opportunity to warn her against such a marriage. Nevertheless, she agreed during one of Georgiana's difficult visits to her house that a trip abroad would be necessary if the Prince persisted in his plan to marry her.

On 8 July Georgiana was summoned at Devonshire House by two of the Prince's cronies, Mr Bouverie and Mr Onslow, who gabbled some story about Prinny having run himself through with

*'A Boating Party of the Prince of Wales at Wimpole'. The Prince of Wales is in the centre gazing ardently at his mistress, Mrs Fitzherbert. The Prince married Mrs Fitzherbert in 1785, against the advice of all of his Whig friends, including Georgiana, who wrote to him that it was 'madness' and that she was 'quite wild with horror of it'.*

a sword. His dying wish, they said, was to see Mrs Fitzherbert but she would not go unless Georgiana accompanied her, and even now was waiting in her carriage just outside the gates.

It was dark when they reached Carlton House. Onslow and Bouverie took them into a room, where they found the Prince dramatically sprawled across a sofa with bloody bandages wrapped around his hairless chest. The sight of Prinny wheezing and crying in what seemed to be his final moments moved Mrs Fitzherbert to agree to become his wife. They sealed the pact with a ring reluctantly supplied by Georgiana. Before the two women parted that night they both signed a deposition stating that 'promises obtained in such a manner are entirely void'. The following morning Mrs Fitzherbert hurriedly packed her bags and departed for France, leaving to Georgiana the task of explaining her absence to the disappointed Prince.

Two weeks later Bess returned from Italy and ignited rumours of an affair with the Duke. Lady Spencer noticed a change in Georgiana's letters soon after Bess joined the Devonshires at Chatsworth. They were far shorter than normal and mostly about generalities – local politics and the races – but there was anxiety beneath their flippant tone. She joked that Bess was like Susannah tempted by the Elders; she had succeeded in making all the men of the house party fall in love with her.

Lavinia and George came to stay in the middle of September, and this at last provided Lady Spencer with reliable witnesses. But George could discover nothing concrete about Bess or her relationship with either the Duke or Georgiana: 'I really believe much more is made of it than need be. [Lady E.] is certainly very pretty and sometimes very engaging in her manners.' However, he found Bess's affectations ludicrous and 'quite sufficient, I think, for anyone to be disgusted' if they weren't already in love with her.

Georgiana also watched Bess closely, although she felt wretched for even suspecting her friend of duplicity. No one noticed that she was anxious although she told Lady Spencer at the end of September that her spirits were low. The Duke increasingly found fault with Georgiana, and when he had nothing particular to point to he criticized her for failing to provide him with a son. Bess, on the other hand, never felt happier or more secure. 'I wish I had a Plympton piece of news [where Georgiana first became pregnant] to communicate to you my dear Madam,' she wrote to Lady Spencer, who was unpleasantly surprised to receive a postscript from her at the end of Georgiana's letter. She added, 'I own I am irresistibly attached to you with all a daughter's respect and affection.'

Bess's flattery only prompted Lady Spencer to urge her once again to go abroad as soon as possible. Coincidentally, there was now a good reason for her departure: even by eighteenth-century standards, which encouraged women to look slight and delicate, Bess was painfully thin. The doctors once again prescribed a warmer climate. She reluctantly agreed to return to France, this time without Charlotte, but with all her expenses met by the Devonshires. Georgiana forgot her doubts about Bess's loyalty and only thought of her imminent loss.

The Devonshires supplied Bess with money and letters of introduction to all their friends in Paris to ensure that there would be no repeat of the previous year's reception. Then, the Duchesse de Polignac, jealous of Bess's relationship with Georgiana, had used her influence with Marie Antoinette to exclude her from Versailles society. Bess implied that the other reason for her ostracism was a rumour: *le tout Paris* talked of a lesbian affair between her and Georgiana. Bess was eloquent in her indignation, although she implied that only Georgiana was under suspicion.

Georgiana's effusive letters guaranteed Bess a rapturous welcome on this occasion. The Duke of Dorset, who had been Ambassador-Extraordinary since 1783, was also in residence; his greeting left no doubt of his interest in renewing their former acquaintance. Bess's letters home contained detailed descriptions of her evenings with the Polignacs, the brilliant parties at Versailles, and suppers at the embassy. No doubt she sought to make Georgiana just a little jealous of the wonderful time she was having without them. However, Bess was silently pleading for Georgiana's forgiveness for a far greater betrayal than the co-opting of her friends: she was three months pregnant with the Duke of Devonshire's child.

Her letter crossed with one of Georgiana's, bring the news that she too was three months pregnant. When Bess counted the weeks she realized angrily that their babies could have been conceived within days or even hours of each other. To console herself she took up with the Duke of Dorset and remained in Paris as his mistress until her pregnancy began to show. She then fled to Italy to be with her brother, Lord Hervey.

Georgiana agreed to give up dancing while she was pregnant but she could not stop gambling, which had grown worse since Bess's departure. In April the Duke at last began to take an interest in her financial plight and wrote out a note of credit for £1,300 to settle her debts. But instead of paying it in to her bankers, she took the note with her to Mrs Sturt's and gambled it away on top of a further £500. At the end of May, when Georgiana was six months pregnant, Lady Mary Coke heard that she had lost over £1,000 at Mrs Hobart's and stayed until 6 a.m. trying to win it back. In July, with only a few weeks left before she came to term, Georgiana was still in the grip of her mania: 'She sits up almost every night at faro,' wrote a friend. 'The Duke has paid five thousand pound for her and She owes three more.' (The Duke was also losing a great deal of money at Brooks's, and between them the two made inroads into their capital. 'I hear the Devonshire Estate is put to nurse,' Mrs Scott wrote sarcastically to Mrs Montagu.)

For Lady Spencer it was not the gambling which frightened her so much as the drugs and all-night binges. 'For God's sake try to compose yourself,' she begged. 'I am terrified lest the perpetual hurry of your spirits, and the medicines you take, to obtain a false tranquillity, should injure you.' However, her letters had no effect. Since meeting Bess, Georgiana had ceased to be so emotionally dependent on her mother. As long as she remained on good terms with the Duke, Georgiana felt reasonably sure of her position, and he had convinced himself that the baby would be a boy.

On 1 September the papers announced that the Devonshires had had a son, prompting a rush of congratulatory messages. But on 2 September they announced a correction: the baby was a girl. Georgiana had given birth to a second daughter – Harriet. Well-wishers dropped by at Devonshire House to find Georgiana happily nursing her new baby. Her lying-in room had been entirely redecorated with white satin. In the centre was a vast bed decked with enormous paper flowers and silver ribbons. Lady Spencer gently padded around so as not to disturb her, having left off wearing silk to avoid making a rustle. Two months later Harriet also gave birth to a girl: Caroline.

The birth of the Duke's other child took place in secret and in squalor; its mother was alone and frightened. In Italy her brother and sister-in-law were quarrelling bitterly and hardly noticed her. It was only in July, when the party reached the little island of Ischia, near Naples, that Bess had the courage to confess the truth to her brother. He was upset but not angry, but he insisted that she should go as far away from people as possible. 'I must go near 100 miles at sea and in an open boat – I must go amongst strangers, perhaps leave my Infant with them. Patience, patience; my punishment is just,' she cried.

The need for secrecy forced Bess to choose the meanest inns along the route. A vivid account of her appalling journey survives in her diary, and is one of the few passages which seems to have escaped the censor's pen. She wrote to Georgiana from Ischia of 'my heart full of sorrows and head of anxiety' but without stating the cause. She wrote separately to the Duke when possible, with more specific complaints which he could only indirectly allude to by way of reply; he dared not write in tones greater than friendship. On the rare occasions that he could trust the courier he wrote awkwardly, unsure how to comfort her: 'I am terribly in want of you here, Mrs Bess, and am every minute reminded of the misfortune of your not being here by things that I see . . .'

On 29 August 1785 the Duke wrote with news of Georgiana's baby girl and added, 'I am very much surpriz'd and impatient at not having heard from you upon a subject I expected to have heard something about by this time.' Bess was in a little town called Vietri on the Gulf of Salerno, having given birth on 16 August in a hostel which also doubled as a brothel – a place well known to her feckless brother. She had arrived two weeks before with Louis, a trusted family servant. He had agreed to pretend that Bess was his pregnant wife, and the mistress of his master Lord Hervey.

The baby was a girl, whom she named Caroline Rosalie. She hurriedly rejoined her brother in Naples, and the baby was lodged with a poor family not far away. She cried at having to leave Caroline with strangers and was in agony over her unused milk, which stained her bodice; she had to cover her breasts with fresh flannels, risking discovery by the servants in doing so. When Caroline was a few weeks old Louis offered to take her to his own family. With Caroline safe, Bess consoled herself with a flirtation with the Russian ambassador: 'Misfortune,' she wrote regretfully in her diary, 'cannot cure me of my vanity.'

Bess remained in Italy for nearly a year, even though the Duke and Georgiana repeatedly urged her to come home. It was not only reluctance to leave Caroline which delayed her return – she did not know how to present Georgiana with the truth. In his usual way, the Duke tried to make light of her fears: 'The Rat does not know the chief cause of your uneasiness . . . but I am certain that if she did, she would not think you had been to blame about it, particularly after I had explain'd to her how the thing happen'd.'

*'The Ambassador's Reception' organized by Marie Antoinette. Bess was stung by the Queen's indifference to her when the Devonshires first sent her abroad. Bess claimed it was down to jealousy and rumour* – le tout Paris *talked of a lesbian affair between her and Georgiana – and blamed Georgiana's 'partiality to me'.*

In the two years since the Westminster election Georgiana had silenced her critics by becoming more popular than ever. Her place within the Whig hierarchy was established. She had grasped the essentials of a successful publicity campaign. This was now the only kind of public political activity open to her, but she used what she had learned to remarkable effect. In December 1784, she sponsored a balloon send-off on behalf of the party.

In 1783 the Montgolfier brothers astounded the court at Versailles by floating a sixty-foot sky-blue balloon 6,000 feet into the air. In their wake, the Neapolitan Vincenzo Lunardi and the Frenchman Jean-Pierre Blanchard arrived in England in 1784. Georgiana gave separate dinners at Devonshire House in honour of the two men. Lunardi repaid the compliment by wearing a silk coat to court in a colour of Georgiana's own invention, called 'Devonshire brown'. But the Frenchman Blanchard allowed her to transform his last British aerial ascent into a Whig political occasion. On 1 December the Prince of Wales and a hundred Whigs and their ladies braved the chill air to join the crowd in Grosvenor Square to watch Georgiana release the ropes of Blanchard's balloon. They all wore blue and buff uniforms, and Georgiana had seen to it that even the stay-ropes were decorated with dual-coloured ribbons. All the surrounding streets were blocked with spectators while the fifty-foot advertisement floated over London.

*Captain Vincenzo Lunardi in a balloon, 1785, opposite. When Lunardi and Jean-Pierre Blanchard brought their hot-air balloons for exhibitions in England, Georgiana jumped at the chance to involve herself and the Whigs. The cartoon, far left, attests to the prurient tendencies of the press – the Prince, sharing the basket with Georgiana, is saying, 'it rises majestically,' while she replies, 'yes, I can feel it.' The actress Mrs Siddons, left, was also the beneficiary of Georgiana's patronage. 'My good reception in London I cannot but partly attribute to . . . the amiable Duchess of Devonshire,' she wrote.*

After her triumph with Blanchard's balloon Georgiana regularly organized popular events to reinforce political and social solidarity among party members. Since arranging Perdita's first appearance on the stage as Juliet in 1776 Georgiana had helped to establish a number of the theatre's most celebrated stars, including Mrs Siddons. Georgiana's patronage of the arts increasingly associated Whiggery with taste, fashion and wit. 'She really is a very good Politician,' a Pittite complained. 'As soon as ever any young man comes from abroad he is immediately invited to Devonshire House and to Chatsworth – and by that means he is to be of the Opposition.'

Sharp of Fleet Street, purveyor of perfumes and toiletries to the gentry, made considerable profits having cornered the market in Georgiana's favourite make of French hair powder. Likewise, Mr Austin, Drawing Master at the Print Rooms, St James's Street, enjoyed a brisk trade in life-size busts and 'curious casts in wax of His Royal Highness the Prince of Wales, her Grace the Duchess of Devonshire . . .' In 1786 there was a minor scandal when one of Georgiana's seamstresses was bribed to reveal her latest design. Several ladies paid for the drawings, each thinking she was the only one. They were all exposed several weeks later when they arrived at a ball wearing the same dress.

Georgiana's popularity meant that she was subjected to scrutiny and with it the propagation of half-truths. There were persistent rumours linking her with the Prince and obnoxious cartoons which depicted them as lovers. It was the Prince's eccentric behaviour which invited conjecture.

During her confinement with baby Harriet he visited her so often that people wondered if the child was his. However, it was not the baby he came to discuss but Mrs Fitzherbert. Seized by emotion, he threw himself about the room, flinging himself on his knees, clasping her hands, and banging his head against a chair. Georgiana repeated, until her head ached, that he ought to talk to Fox.

Mrs Fitzherbert returned home in November 1785, tired of waiting for the Prince to fall out of love with her. As soon as Fox heard of her return he wrote to the Prince, imploring him not to take the 'desperate step' of marriage. An alliance with Mrs Fitzherbert would make it impossible for him to inherit the throne and the party's reputation would be fatally damaged by its connection with the Prince. However, he ignored the pleas of both Fox and Georgiana and the couple were married at Mrs Fitzherbert's house with her uncle and brother as witnesses, leaving immediately for a short honeymoon at a house near Richmond. When they returned the whole of London was buzzing with rumours about their marriage.

The dilemma was particularly acute for Georgiana. The Prince stayed away from Devonshire House but he wrote to the Devonshires, inviting them to visit. Georgiana understood the Prince's anxiety, for where she led the rest of society would follow. The Spencer and Cavendish clans opposed any action which would bestow legitimacy on the union, so she had little choice but to snub them or leave London for the foreseeable future (her mother's preferred option).

Georgiana was saved from further embarrassment by the Prince's debts. They had doubled since 1783 and even his cronies had lost patience with him. The King was not prepared to help without receiving certain concessions in return, including the Prince's renunciation of the Whigs. Instead, Prinny shut up Carlton House, sold his horses and carriages, dismissed the servants, and

*The Royal Pavilion at Brighton. Left, a drawing showing the salon in its first redecorating scheme, 1789, one of many that the Prince embarked upon which changed the residence beyond recognition. The cartoon, opposite, shows the Pavilion in a less glamorous light, with the Prince and Mrs Fitzherbert economizing after he was refused money to clear his debts.*

on 15 July moved to a little rented villa in Brighton. Mrs Fitzherbert followed a short time later, and the two of them lived quietly like an ordinary couple for almost a year. His departure was a great relief to the Devonshires, who decided that Southampton offered a more attractive summer retreat than Brighton that year.

Two weeks later the press got wind of marital trouble in the Spencer family. Although no names were mentioned everyone knew that the latest gossip referred to Harriet and Charles Wyndham, one of the Prince's drinking companions. No one felt sorry for Lord Duncannon. In 1782 the Duchess of Portland had commented sympathetically that Harriet 'leads a melancholy life, at home always, and literally alone'. 'Lady Duncannon has a good heart but a sad head,' opined Mrs Damer, 'quite unfit for all the dangers the circumstances of her life have exposed her to, wanting a protector, instead of which she has fallen to the share of a peevish little mortal . . .' Duncannon subjected her to long periods of neglect punctuated by episodes of anger and abuse. Lady Spencer suspected him of drinking and of gambling at a faster rate than they could afford.

George had found out that Harriet was contemplating something rash and immediately alerted Lady Spencer. The two of them surprised Harriet and carried her off to St Albans before Duncannon discovered anything. Harriet crumpled very quickly and agreed to give Wyndham up. Lady Spencer was not in a forgiving mood: Harriet was never to speak to him again. The Devonshires, who until then had stood by helplessly, intervened at this point. 'Harriet has agreed a change must take place . . . and is anxious to do everything you wish,' Georgiana wrote to George, but she and the Duke thought it would look odd for her to cut him completely.

The Spencers allowed Harriet to return to London, having extracted a promise from the Devonshires to keep her under supervision. George was not entirely unsympathetic, noting to his mother that 'Her sweet husband never comes home till 8, 9, 10, or 11 o'clock in the morning, and that is really poor encouragement for living at home', but still worried that, as far as the family's reputation was concerned, 'her situation still continues a most dangerous one and requires the strictest attention on her own part as well as ours.'

Fortunately for Harriet the return of Bess distracted the Spencer family's attention. 'I really look upon her in every light as the most dangerous devil,' Lavinia told George. The Spencers had come across her while on holiday in Naples, during Christmas 1785. They found a different situation from the brilliant social life Bess described in her letters. 'She is not very well liked by the Italians on account of her want of facility in speaking their language, and her wearing perfume which is here an unpardonable offence,' wrote George to Lady Spencer.

The Duke naturally understood Bess's reluctance to return much better than Georgiana and tried to reassure her by insisting there were few, if any, rumours about the two of them. The longer she stayed away the more Bess resented Georgiana for her good fortune: her children, her rank, her popularity and, above all, her possession of the Duke. Bess's greatest desire was to be a society hostess – like Georgiana. She knew that a respectable woman would not sleep with her best friend's husband or with any man who happened to pay her court. She blamed her promiscuity on the fact that Georgiana had the things she most wanted.

*The third Duke of Dorset, the great seducer. His affair with Lady Derby brought her social ruin. Bess and Georgiana also fell prey to his charms. He served in Paris as Ambassador Extraordinary from 1783. After their affair, he and Georgiana remained friends and he sent her vital information pertaining to her friends in the French royal household during the revolution.*

In June, just before she set out for England, Bess tried to explain herself to Georgiana without admitting to the betrayal: 'All my possible hopes of friendship are connected in you. Without you the World is nothing to me.' Instead of going straight to Calais, however, she made a detour to Aix-en-Provence, where she stayed with the elderly Comte St Jules. There is no record of how they knew each other or of what passed between them, but when she left he agreed to accept paternity of little Caroline, who became Caroline Rosalie St Jules, illegitimate daughter of a French count and an unknown mother. Bess found a surrogate family for her daughter, and set sail for Southampton at the end of July. According to her diary, the Duke travelled to meet her: 'I fear I was glad. I arrive – he had dined out but left a note; he came; Oh, heavens, such moments do indeed efface past sorrows!' There is no mention of Georgiana.

As is so often the case in Bess's diary, her version of events – in which she is always the centre of attention – was more fantasy than truth. The Duke was not alone at Southampton. The Duncannons, Spencers and Devonshires, accompanied by all their children, were holidaying there when Bess landed. Half of London society had joined them. Furthermore the Duke was extremely ill with gout and could only move with difficulty on crutches.

After spending a decent interval with her mother, Bess set off to join the Devonshires at Chatsworth. Bess had not expected to find Lady Spencer at Chatsworth and she had difficulty in hiding her disappointment. There was no repeat of the flirtatious behaviour she had shown with the other guests in 1784. She did not attempt anything in front of Lady Spencer and, when Georgiana's mother was not around, James Hare and Sheridan would tease her if she seemed too attentive to the Duke. Georgiana had other things on her mind: she had received a blackmail letter from Martindale just before Bess's arrival. She had resumed gambling with him during the spring because she owed money to all the other faro dealers and in a short time he had cheated her into a debt of almost £100,000 (the equivalent of £6 million today). Georgiana desperately wanted to confide in Bess and could not understand why she avoided being alone with her.

The Duke of Dorset arrived on 14 September 1786 and took in the situation immediately. He had never been in love with Bess and it didn't bother him to see her flirting with the Duke of Devonshire. On the other hand, he had always admired Georgiana. He wooed and flattered her and before long everyone knew there was an understanding between them. Lady Spencer was so distressed by what she saw.

'I am far from happy here,' Lady Spencer told George, but she felt she had to stay. After Dorset returned to London Georgiana began to suffer mysterious spasms which twisted her entire body. Lady Spencer suspected that some hidden mental anguish was behind them but she could not make her daughter confide in her. Each attack left Georgiana exhausted and she would remain in her room for the rest of the day. With the appearance of great sorrow, Bess assumed her friend's role in her absence, giving orders to the servants and making it clear to everyone that she was in charge. Lady Spencer could not bear to watch her preening and joined Georgiana in isolation. When she revealed Bess's behaviour downstairs Georgiana refused to believe her.

After Lady Spencer left Georgiana promised 'to get some resolution to take place about our affairs . . . you do not know how I do love you – I have often feared trusting to open all my thoughts to you.' A week later, when the house was empty, Georgiana made a partial confession to the Duke about Martindale. Without hesitation, the Duke demanded a separation. Georgiana was devastated; she turned to Bess for support and found her friend unwilling to talk to her. In her diary Bess hardly mentions the incident except to praise the Duke's reaction when Georgiana confessed the debt: 'how nobly, kindly, touchingly did he behave.' Heaton argued that there would have to be drastic cuts in the Cavendish expenditure to pay off the debts: houses would have to be sold, servants dismissed, and on no account was Georgiana to be allowed near London.

George rushed to his sister's defence as soon as he heard of the Duke's plans. The idea that the Duke and Bess might shut Georgiana away in a hunting lodge revolted him. Bravely withstanding Lavinia's annoyance, he invited Georgiana to take the children and live with him at Althorp. The Duke, he added, would be welcome to visit whenever he liked; there was no mention of Bess. But matters were complicated.

If the Duke wanted an heir it would still have to come from Georgiana. For this reason he wanted to have her within easy reach. Georgiana knew that the relationship between the Duke and Bess was such that, if he could not bring her with him when he came to visit, he would never come at all and there would be no chance of a reconciliation: 'which is what of all things your sister dreads,' Lady Spencer told George. (On the other hand, if Georgiana was publicly separated from the Duke Bess would not be able to stay at Devonshire House without scandal, nor would the Devonshire House Circle tolerate her usurpation of Georgiana's role at Chatsworth.) Lady Spencer thought that Georgiana ought to live at Londesborough, the third of the Duke's houses, which was at least fitting for her rank.

Discussions dragged on through November and into December. 'I feel an uncertainty that kills me,' confessed Georgiana. But as time went by the Duke seemed to lose interest and he mentioned the separation less and less. Throughout the ordeal Georgiana felt so ashamed of herself that she hardly noticed her friend's sudden quietness. Bess, who had claimed in June that their hearts were formed for each other, made no offer to follow her wherever she went: if Georgiana were to go in adversity, she would have to go alone. But to Bess's astonishment, Georgiana never reproached her.

On 29 December Georgiana wrote: 'my business goes slow.' Nothing was yet decided but there seemed to be less pressure on her to leave. Lady Bristol had written several times to Bess asking her to visit and she could put it off no longer. The Devonshires left Chatsworth at the same time. On the last day of the year Georgiana's future still looked uncertain but less precarious than before. George allowed himself to feel a little hope: 'A calm has ensued in a certain quarter as I supposed it would when the first violence of the storm had spent itself. How long either will last it is impossible ever to conjecture, but that there will be frequent transmitting from the one to the other is all that one can be certain about.'

## Queen Bess 1787

*On Monday last, the Constitutional Whig Grand Lodge of England held their anniversary at the Intrepid Fox, Wardour St, Soho, in commemoration of the Landing of the Great Deliverer, William the Third . . . among the toasts were 'The Noble House of Cavendish, root and branches – May the blossoms of Liberty never be blighted, nor the Duchess of Devonshire ever be slighted . . .'*

MORNING HERALD, 8 NOVEMBER 1787

THE DUKE REGARDED HIMSELF as an injured man. He required two things of Georgiana: not to gamble away the family estate, and to produce an heir, and she seemed to be incapable of performing either one. He was also furious that she had been deceiving him about her debts for the past two years. By Christmas, however, three months after her confession, the Duke was beginning to have mixed feelings about the proposed separation. He was not so bitter towards Georgiana that he wanted to see her publicly humiliated. Although he preferred Bess's company, he liked having both women around, competing for his attention.

Bess was torn: should she complete her triumph over Georgiana or intercede on her behalf? If she pushed hard enough she could probably force the Duke to separate from Georgiana. But Bess knew that without Georgiana she would not be able to live at Devonshire House or at Chatsworth. Life as the Duke's acknowledged mistress would be dull and constricting. She would become a non-person – ostracized by polite society and despised by Georgiana's friends and family. She hesitated until Georgiana unwittingly made up her mind for her. Instead of blaming Bess or accusing her of disloyalty, Georgiana apologized to her for lying about her debts. All she hoped, Georgiana told her, was that her folly in wasting 'dear Canis's' fortune would not make Bess despise her. The realization that in Georgiana she had a friend who truly loved her was a profound shock and brought out a protectiveness in Bess: she became motherly, even strict, and, though the jealousy remained, there was no further attempt to usurp her place and no more talk of separation.

The Duke took Georgiana to London, where they engaged Sheridan's help to resolve the Martindale problem. No stranger to the art of putting off creditors, Sheridan coached her on what to say. 'The bargain with Martindale entirely depends upon his thinking it my doing unadvis'd,' she told her mother. She had persuaded him to consider only £25,000, but was hoping that he would accept £6,000. They met alone, and to Georgiana'a surprise he believed her display of innocence and confusion and he agreed to settle. (Though she was never completely rid of him; Martindale would continue to demand 'hush money' from her over the years.) Life at Devonshire

A milliner's shop, left, and Buckingham House, St James's Park, below. Georgiana's position as a fashion icon meant that her custom was highly sought after and her style of dress widely copied.

House returned to a semblance of normality. Yet it was a fragile truce: Georgiana was terrified of upsetting the Duke, and he was so suspicious of her now that she admitted, 'I dare not press the Duke nor give him reason to imagine I have a wish or design of my own.'

The Duke insisted on certain conditions before he dropped his plans for separation. Georgiana was not to stay in London any longer than necessary, and her income was to be sharply reduced. In addition, several servants had to be sacked, some of the horses and carriages sold, and all capital projects halted. 'We are distressed, but prudence will set us right,' wrote Georgiana cheerfully. 'I have made a good beginning, having forbid all milliners etc., Dst. M.' She was not concerned by the reduction of her income, thinking that it would be offset by her residing in Bath or in the country, where commodities were cheaper and fashion more sedate.

Georgiana ought to have felt relief but she had told a stupid and terrible lie. The Duke had asked if there were any other debts, and she had admitted to only about a fifth of the total. From now on all her ingenuity would be focused on concealing the truth from the Duke and in keeping creditors at bay. However, the ease with which she charmed Martindale made her realize that the same technique might be used on others. Her friends and acquaintances became a potential source of wealth that she shamelessly mined for loans and gifts. Mary Graham was one of the first to receive her begging letters and gave as much as she could until her husband found out. But there were many others, some near strangers, whose snobbery might be exploited by a Duchess in need.

Yet most of Georgiana's close friends were, like her, gamesters and always broke. She was not the first person in the Devonshire House Circle to beg her jewellers to buy back some of her purchases. Most of the Circle relied on the willingness of one banker, Thomas Coutts, to keep them afloat. A cautious Scot with a weakness for titles, Coutts was determined to drag himself and his wife, a former servant, into the refined society of the *ton.* He courted the Prince of Wales and his Whig friends, seeing in the relationship future lucrative government contracts for the bank and social advancement for his daughters. He expected to be rewarded for his generosity when the King died and Prinny inherited the throne.

In March 1787 Georgiana asked Coutts to become her private banker. He was only too glad to be of assistance to a charming woman who pleaded, 'I am so ignorant of business.' He agreed to oversee her accounts, to provide her with unsecured loans without the Duke's knowledge (a risky and illegal undertaking), and to take on the edifying role, he thought, of her financial adviser. He made a similar offer to the Duke of Devonshire, without revealing his arrangements with Georgiana, and loaned him £7,000 without security and with no time limit. He also took Charles James Fox on to his books.

Coutts assumed that he would be Georgiana's sole banker, and hoped that the personal relationship between them would be as important to her as the financial one. The truth was far more complicated than he realized: Georgiana had inveigled the Parisian banker, Comte Pérregeaux, into a similar relationship to help her manage some £40,000 or £50,000 worth of debts in France. She did not know how much she owed in total, nor did she want to. She gave everyone different figures which represented different debts: gambling debts, purchases, loans from private money lenders, as well as burdens she had assumed on behalf of others. She told Coutts that the Duke knew about all her debts except for £4,500, but the figure was closer to £60,000, and perhaps even more. The first step had to be a complete cessation of all forms of gambling – Coutts urged her to reflect on what 'you risk to gratify this destructive passion' and warned her that 'a gamester goes on in the vain hope of recovering lost sums, till he loses probably all that remains . . .'

*Thomas Coutts, the Scottish banker who managed the debts of Georgiana and many of her friends. He continually warned Georgiana of the perils of her gambling habit: 'A gamester goes on in the vain hope of recovering lost sums, till he loses probably all that remains, and along with it everything which is precious.'*

But temptation was everywhere: the Duke was not prepared to curb his card playing and Lady Spencer, even though she only gambled among friends for small stakes, encouraged Georgiana to play with her. Georgiana brazenly asserted to Coutts and others that she had indeed given up 'playing at faro and insurance at the lottery'. Yet she was secretly doing both not merely for the thrills but also, as Coutts had warned against, in the hope of winning back some of her losses.

Harriet also had her own reasons for seeking relief at the gaming table. It was George who discovered her latest problem by chance. He paid one of his discreet visits on a February morning in 1787, while Duncannon was out, and found Harriet crying with fear. Duncannon had roughly informed her that he had lost a large sum of money at faro. It had to be paid immediately and he wanted Harriet to get it for him.

Duncannon had ordered Harriet not to tell anyone, which naturally made it impossible for her to raise the money from friends or family. He also brought up the subject of her settlement, and he tried to make her sign it over. Harriet was too frightened to refuse, but thinking quickly had added that her brother, as her guardian, would have to give his consent. 'I don't know whether it is or no, but if it is I certainly shall never grant it,' George wrote. He did not know how to help his sister: he could not deny her the money and yet he hated to see it go to her bullying husband. Lady Spencer wanted George to hold out until Duncannon had promised to stop gambling but for Harriet's sake he and Georgiana paid the debt themselves and kept it a secret from the Cavendishes.

Georgiana, meanwhile, had become a victim of her addiction. By 1787 there was almost a complete reversal of power between her and Bess. Now it was Georgiana who desperately clung to Bess, resorting to emotional blackmail when necessary. 'This is the last time perhaps you will ever speak to or love me,' she wrote, for she hadn't confessed all her debts to the Duke. Through a series of schemes she had lost 'an immense sum', but she forbade Bess to tell the Duke, adding that 'you see that doating on Ca how I have used him . . . Say nothing to him until I return – Oh Bess!'

No one had ever needed or trusted Bess as much as Georgiana. But that didn't prevent her from extracting her own reward. Inexorably, she eradicated the boundaries between them and adopted or co-opted friends, interests and parts of Georgiana's character as her own. There is no mention of little Caroline in any of the correspondence but it was probably at this point that Bess disclosed her existence to Georgiana. Georgiana's reaction has not been recorded; however, she had long since renounced her claims to the Duke. But, irritatingly for Bess, the Duke did not renounce his claims to his wife. He refused to live in a monogamous relationship with Bess, or to grant her the precedence she sought over Georgiana.

Georgiana's friends accepted Bess's permanent presence, particularly Harriet who, unlike the rest of the family, knew how much Georgiana relied on her. Bess was too clever to try to alienate Georgiana from her sister. When Georgiana returned to London for the season (that part of the Duke's conditions having been forgotten) Bess never left her side.

Seeing Bess so contented with the Duke, however, made Georgiana long for something similar for herself. The Duke of Dorset could not fulfil her wish. He was in Paris most of the time and they had to be content with writing to each other several times a week. Nor was she deeply in love with him, although she couldn't help succumbing to Dorset's charm even though she knew he was manipulative and vain. He is 'the most dangerous of men', she had written before the affair. 'For with that beauty of his he is so unaffected and has a simplicity and persuasion in his manner that makes one account very easily for the number of women he has had in love with him.' (All of Dorset's correspondence with Georgiana was censored by an unknown hand in the last century.)

*A set of eighteenth-century playing cards, left; fashionable women wearing the trademark ostrich feather headdresses gamble at cards while sinister-looking men take unfair advantage, below. The* Guardian *warned of the dangers for women: 'The Man who plays beyond his income, pawns his Estate; the Woman must find something else to Mortgage when her Pin Money is gone.'*

*Lady Godina's Rout; — or — Peeping-Tom spying out Pope-Joan. Vide Fashionable Modesty.*

*Left: Georgiana at Chatsworth, 1787. She is wearing the muslin gown which Marie Antoinette had adapted from a dress worn by Creole women. The French Queen posed for a portrait in her* chemise à la reine *and caused a scandal.*

*Right: Cartoons satirizing the debauched lifestyle of the members of the royal family, above, and the consequences of gambling debts, below.*

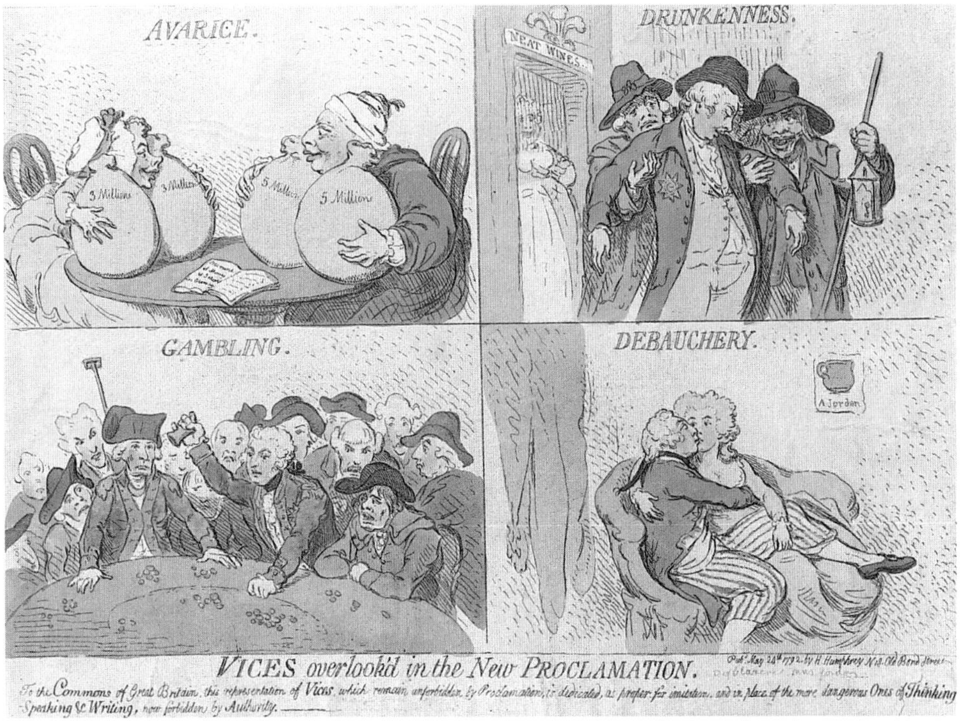

1788 *Ménage à Trois*

*The Gallery of the Graces has no small acquisition in the beautiful portraits of the Duchess of Devonshire, Lady Duncannon, and Lady Elizabeth Foster.*

MORNING POST, 29 MARCH 1788

BESS CHOSE TO REMAIN IN LONDON for the summer while the Devonshires went ahead to Chatsworth. Lady Spencer took advantage of her absence to remain with them until mid-October. The Duke of Dorset was in Paris and for once Lady Spencer found little to criticize during her stay. She reported to George that Georgiana was 'much calmer and better' than last year, and there was no repeat of her 'nervous symptoms'. But it galled her to think that Bess was in London, waiting for her to leave: 'I think she will measure her time by mine,' she wrote. In this she was mistaken; there was another reason for Bess's delay: 'The Duke of Richmond is so in love with Ly Elizabeth Foster,' wrote Lady Augusta Murray spitefully, 'that they say he has made a ridiculous figure of himself, and it is due to his infatuation that Lord Hervey owes his new employment.'

The remorse Bess had once expressed over the Duke of Dorset had not prevented her from making the Duke of Richmond fall in love with her. He was an ideal choice – a sort of insurance policy. He was middle-aged, childless, and lived a separate life from the Duchess, whose health was poor. He also had contacts in the government, and Bess's brother, Lord Hervey, needed some form of employment before his creditors had him arrested. The Duke of Richmond lobbied Pitt on his behalf for the vacant ambassadorship to Florence. There was nothing he wouldn't do for her, and she certainly knew how to make use of him.

Since Bess's recent triumph was known to everyone, guests at Chatsworth were surprised by her subdued demeanour when she arrived at the end of October. When they were alone she confronted the Duke, who 'hardly knew the ill I had hinted to him, and asked me if it was really so. I confirmed it.' She was pregnant again. 'We regret this new anxiety,' Bess wrote in her diary: 'But I felt a kind of pleasure that supported me. How kind he was to me, how soothing and endearing!' Once again she glossed over several important details. The Duke was aware of her friendship with the Duke of Richmond, although naturally she insisted the baby could not possibly be Richmond's. However, the Duke's indifferent attitude towards the child suggests that he never wholly believed her. This time the lovers told Georgiana immediately. Her reaction was typical of what Bess had come to expect: she insisted on accompanying Bess to France in order to assist her when she went into labour. No doubt her desire to be with Bess was compounded by the prospect of seeing Dorset in Paris, but Georgiana's devotion was none the less real. There was no question that she loved her friend and infinitely preferred her company to the Duke's.

However Lady Spencer, having assumed both that Bess was pregnant and that the Duke had ordered his wife to take care of his mistress during her confinement, prevailed upon Georgiana not to go. She accused her of going to Paris with the intention of taking up with the Duke of Dorset. Georgiana reluctantly acquiesced to her mother's order to stay in England. 'I don't know how I shall be able to bear my parting with Bess,' Georgiana wrote on 10 February 1788. The Devonshires accompanied her to Dover. 'Oh it was bitterness to lose her,' admitted Bess in her diary, 'but him – his last embrace – his last look drew my soul after him . . . I see him – he is fixed in my heart – this guilty heart – Oh, why could I not love him without crime? Why cannot I be his without sin?' After eighteen months of a fantasy life she was abruptly reduced to her ordinary state: Lady Elizabeth Foster, grafter, courtesan and destitute wife of an Irish MP. This time, however, she could rely on Georgiana to make up for the Duke's previous indolence over arrangements for the birth. She travelled through France with the faithful Louis and her maidservant Lucille until she reached Rouen on 15 May, supposedly having already come to term.

Instead of the filthy bordello in Vietri there was a 'tolerable' apartment. Nothing happened for almost two weeks. 'What will the Duke think?' moaned Bess; 'that is the last day I was with him, and did not return till I was above two months gone.' Fortunately, she went into labour on the twenty-sixth, just in time for the balance of paternity to remain undecided between the Dukes of Devonshire and Richmond. She gave birth to a boy whom she called Augustus (despite already having a son with the same name) William James Clifford. She had chosen the names with care: William was his father's name and Clifford was one of the Cavendish titles. Her affair with Richmond may have made her anxious to establish the boy's parentage. Clifford, as he was always known, was deposited with another family while Bess collected Caroline from her foster parents. She and the Duke had already decided to send her to Paris to be educated with Charlotte Williams. In her diary Bess confessed to having formed a secret plan to bring Caroline over to England and have her brought up in the nursery with Little Georgiana and Harriet, and she had no doubt she would succeed.

While Bess was in France Georgiana and the Duke got on surprisingly well – better, in fact, than for several years. Georgiana ensured they had little to quarrel over by managing to keep her debts hidden, and she tried to compensate the Duke for his loss by giving him the sort of attention he enjoyed from Bess. Lady Spencer wrote to George about her joy at seeing husband and wife displaying such 'entire confidence . . . easy good humours and [an] unaffected regard and tenderness' for each other. She was disappointed to hear that they were planning to go to France in the summer to meet Bess, but she was mistaken if she hoped either would ever be in love with the other. 'Dr Bess, I know you are safe and therefore not *hurt*,' Georgiana wrote; 'always write to him if you have not time for both.'

Bess pressed them to come to France, but there were obstacles to their leaving. The truth was that they suspected Duncannon of attempting to poison Harriet. It was almost certainly fear rather than malice which guided his actions; he was trying to subjugate his wife rather than kill her. It was not until he put Harriet's life in danger and the doctors had to be called out in an emergency that Duncannon's actions were exposed. He stopped feeding her drugs but the Devonshires took the precaution of putting off their visit to France until the spring.

It was late summer when the Duke of Dorset managed to visit England and by this time Georgiana had decided to end the affair. The shock turned the urbane diplomat into a sad, pleading figure. Concerned that his obvious distress would create a scandal, Lady Melbourne advised Georgiana to allow him hope. But she refused. Only Bess, and probably Harriet, knew what had prompted Georgiana to break off with him. It was the appearance at Devonshire House of a rising young politician called Charles Grey. He was only twenty-three years old, the eldest son of a general from a well-connected Northumberland family. He was a tall, handsome young man with an aristocratic appearance, possessing a high forehead, thick hair, melancholy dark eyes and a long nose. 'He has the patrician thoroughbred look . . . which I dote upon,' remarked Lord Byron, when he first saw him.

Grey delivered his maiden speech in the Commons on 22 February 1787; it immediately won praise. Following her usual practice, Georgiana quickly snatched him up into Whig society, flattering him with invitations to select dinners to meet the party grandees. For many months she tolerated his attentions with the gentle amusement she reserved for her younger admirers – she was seven years older than him and he seemed no match for the sophisticated womanizing ambassador to Paris.

Dorset had the further advantage of having been friends with Georgiana for more than thirteen years. He fitted in easily with the rest of her life; he was safe, light hearted and not without a touch of cynicism. Grey was dangerously impulsive, vain and moody. His violent expressions of love for Georgiana both frightened and fascinated her. The thought of Georgiana juggling lovers no doubt appeased Bess's conscience and she surreptitiously encouraged Grey's suit. By 1788 Georgiana was more entranced by him than she was prepared to admit.

While Bess was away there was a by-election in Westminster. Georgiana had no desire to expose herself to another nationally orchestrated attack on her character and she remained at home while Harriet joined the canvass. Nevertheless she attended the strategy meetings at Devonshire House which allowed her to fight the election vicariously. She also secured a great coup in persuading the Duke of Bedford to donate to the subscription fund much more money than he had originally intended.

*Charles, second Earl Grey. 'He has the patrician thoroughbred look . . . which I dote upon,' remarked Lord Byron. Georgiana began an affair with him in 1787. When the Duke discovered she was pregnant by Grey, he forced her to choose between her lover and her children. 'I have in leaving him for ever, left my heart and soul,' she wrote.*

Fox and Lord John Townshend beat the opposition by a convincing margin and once again the Whigs organized a march of their supporters from Covent Garden to Pall Mall. A procession of 120 carriages, including the state carriages of the Duchesses of Devonshire and Portland, rumbled down the Strand to Charing Cross. Two hundred Whigs on horseback, all dressed in blue and buff, followed. But there were no women present; when Fox and Sheridan addressed the crowd from the balcony of Devonshire House Georgiana remained inside, ignoring calls for her appearance. Lavinia sat with her in the drawing room to make sure she did.

Bess arrived from France shortly afterwards. Despite having written in her diary, 'I will cease to live in error with him,' she resumed her place as the Duke's second wife as soon as she returned. Her permanent residence at Devonshire House kept Georgiana and her mother apart. She continued to make public her opposition to Bess.

Lady Spencer's hostility upset Georgiana, who felt she owed her security at Devonshire House to Bess, certain that were it not for Bess the Duke would have separated from her long ago. It was remarkable how much the balance of power within their relationship had moved in Bess's favour. From being 'a poor little thing', she had become the mainstay of the *ménage à trois*. What had not changed was her obsessive jealousy of Georgiana. Moreover, it was Bess's single-minded pursuit of her which had proved to be the enduring attraction for Georgiana. Her need for attention was so boundless that only someone like Bess would be willing, or able, to satiate it. Georgiana would continue to love Bess for as long as her friend remained preoccupied with her. She was blind to Bess's other faults and simply could not understand why Lady Spencer loathed her.

The visitors staying at Chatsworth this time found the atmosphere harmonious, if a trifle eccentric. Bess's confession about her pregnancy the year before had fixed the *ménage à trois* into certain patterns. It was as if, in order to accommodate the more bizarre aspects of their relationship, the two women had colluded in creating an unreal life based on fantasy and melodrama. When Harriet was there she joined in with them so that everyone was obliged to play along. James Hare wrote a gentle satire on life at Chatsworth called 'A Rational Day in the Country'

*James Hare, a loyal friend and confidant to the Devonshires. He once gently tried to explain his misgivings about Bess to Georgiana: 'I never will be brought to say that she is not affected, tho' I allow it is the most pardonable sort of affectation I ever met with, and is become quite natural.'*

which remarked on their peculiar manners affecting everything from their waking and sleeping hours to their speech and dining habits.

Georgiana still showed no sign of producing an heir, and the Cavendishes referred to her failure almost every day of their visit. She had more reasons than they to want a boy and yet they continued to blame her. Their disapproval made her feel like an outsider, tolerated but not welcomed by her husband's family. 'I do think there is nothing in beauty that equals Chatsworth,' she wrote sadly, 'tho' I like a number of places better. I believe if I had a son I should like it best of all; but there is something in its not being my children's that makes me fancy it is not mine.'

# *The Regency Crisis* 1788–1789

*Most of the Ladies of fashion appeared at the Opera on Saturday in a new head-dress in honour of the Prince of Wales. It consisted of three large white feathers connected by a band, on which was inscribed the motto of the Principality – Ich Dien, and is the most becoming ornament that has graced the female world for many years.*

MORNING POST, 9 FEBRUARY 1789

DR GEORGE BAKER WAS CALLED to see the King on a quiet day in October 1788 and found him drenched in sweat, unable to sit, stand or lie down except in excruciating pain. The doctor noted that his eyes were yellow; an examination of his urine showed it had turned brown, and occasionally flecks of foam appeared on the patient's lips. Even more disturbing were the obvious signs of mental disorder. At times his speech was almost normal, at others rambling and agitated. He was prone to violent rages interspersed with bursts of uncontrolled jabbering. Even the Prince of Wales was so shocked by his father's state that he visited Windsor every day to console his mother and sisters.

Dr Baker informed Pitt on 22 October that the situation was serious and yet so baffling that he could give neither a proper diagnosis nor a prognosis. Newspapers alluded to the rumours, but the lack of real news and the delicacy of the subject made their reports circumspect. The King made a heroic effort to appear in public, which exacerbated his disorientating attacks. Medical ignorance and royal etiquette induced a paralysis at court until, on 5 November, the King jumped from his chair during dinner and attacked the Prince of Wales. He grappled with him in front of his terrified family and attendants and, with the energy of a lunatic, smashed his son's head against a wall. Following an episode the next evening when he chased the doctor into a corner, there was no longer any doubt that the King had lost his mind.

The Regency crisis unfolds like a morality tale in which the foolish are punished and the wise and temperate are rewarded. The reason we know so much about what went on behind the scenes is because Georgiana kept a diary. Her eye-witness account, recorded in a daily journal for her mother – 'my letters will be a regular newspaper,' she had promised – remains the most quoted source material for the period.

Georgiana learned the true nature of the King's illness on 7 November, two days after his assault on the Prince of Wales. Fish Craufurd dispatched a hurried note: 'I can give you no just account of the King's disorder. Nobody can get at the truth but he is certainly very ill and dangerously ill . . . The truth is, I believe, that the King is quite disordered in his mind . . .' She arrived in London on the twentieth to find the party already riven with dissent between those who wanted to wait for Fox, who was holidaying in Italy with Mrs Armistead, and those who were prepared to go ahead without him. There were several men, Sheridan and Grey chief among them, who saw Fox's absence as an opportunity to assert their authority. By law, if the King was incapacitated, the Prince of Wales became Regent. The government would have to resign and the Regent would have the opportunity to choose a new cabinet.

Since the 1784 election scores of Whigs, including the Duke of Richmond, had deserted the party and no longer went to Devonshire House. Georgiana's most frequent visitors were now

Charles Grey, Sheridan and the Duke of Bedford, Lady Melbourne's new lover. Richard Sheridan was envied and mistrusted rather than liked by many members of the party. Fox's friends resented the way he fawned on the Prince of Wales. However, during the Regency crisis Sheridan came to Devonshire House every day, not to see Georgiana but Harriet: they had recently become lovers.

Harriet's affair with Sheridan began shortly after he had broken off with another Whig hostess, Mrs Crewe. Duncannon was ignorant of it but everyone else knew, including Sheridan's wife and his sister Betsy, who never missed an opportunity to malign Harriet. Devonshire House, which provided the setting for so many intrigues, was the easiest place for them to meet, although Sheridan derived little enjoyment from seeing Charles Grey so frequently since they were venomous political rivals.

While Fox was on his way back from Italy Sheridan appointed himself master-negotiator on behalf of the Prince. His meetings with the Prince were shrouded in secrecy, which made him an unpopular leader and damaged the party's morale by encouraging suspicion. Georgiana complained that 'he cannot resist the pleasure of acting alone', and this made him appear to be double-dealing. Yet at the same time the Whigs were terrified of alienating the Prince, and so pandered to Sheridan's egotistical posturing.

*Richard Brinsley Sheridan, playwright and member of the Devonshire House Circle. He achieved a place in parliament thanks to Georgiana's support but was a constant thorn in the side of the Whigs. 'He cannot resist playing a sly game,' Georgiana complained.*

Fox reached England on 24 November, after a breakneck journey covering 1,000 miles in nine days. He had contracted dysentery along the way and was unable to attend any meetings. His supporters wanted him to quash Sheridan's pretensions, but Fox's conversations with the Prince were disappointing: it was clear to him that Sheridan had usurped his place at Carlton House. Fox was too enervated by his illness to have much influence with Sheridan or the Prince.

It is only through Lord John Cavendish that a picture emerges of Georgiana's politicking. In anticipation of the expected change of government cabinet lists were being drawn up. He complained at a meeting at Carlton House that Georgiana was hounding him and that it would 'kill him' to accept the Chancellorship. Georgiana was actively pushing her own choices for certain posts, as well as jockeying with Sheridan to advise the Prince. In contrast to Sheridan's plan – for the Prince to accept whatever conditions the Pitt ministry imposed and then, once in power, to dismantle them – Georgiana thought the Prince ought to insist on being granted the full powers of Regent but to show magnanimity afterwards.

Such a plan would certainly have been the most politic, but the party and the Prince were too distracted by the imminent prospect of power to think sensibly any more. Three weeks of exemplary behaviour towards his family had strained the Prince. A disgusted public read about his nightly parties; he had even been seen lurching up St James's shouting obscenities and jokes about his father. Public opinion began to side with Pitt. Meanwhile, there were several complicated issues to be faced before the Prince took over as head of state. The most important of these was the prospect of the King's recovery. It would be awkward if the King recovered and found that his greatest enemies were enjoying themselves at his expense.

When parliament met on 10 December to discuss the matter Pitt had prepared himself with a list of arguments and precedents dating back to the insanity of Henry VI in 1454. Pitt suggested that parliament should set up a committee to examine the precedents, which would report on its findings within a week. His cool eloquence and the sound reasons he gave for delaying any decision on the Regency made a good impression on the House. Still unwell but anxious to show the House he was still the leader of his party, Fox leapt up to oppose. Pitt, he said, had no right to delay the Regency by one day. Parliament had no right to debate anything regarding the Prince of

A View of the Garden Entrance of St. James's Palace. Published by F. West. 83 Fleet St. London. Vüe de l'entrée au Jardin du Palais Royal de St. Jaques.

*The royal family was not spared the vulgar satire of the press. George III and Queen Charlotte arrive at the garden entrance to St James's Palace, above, while a corpulent Prince of Wales, opposite, lounges in decadent luxury and another member of the royal family, right, indulges in an adulterous liaison.*

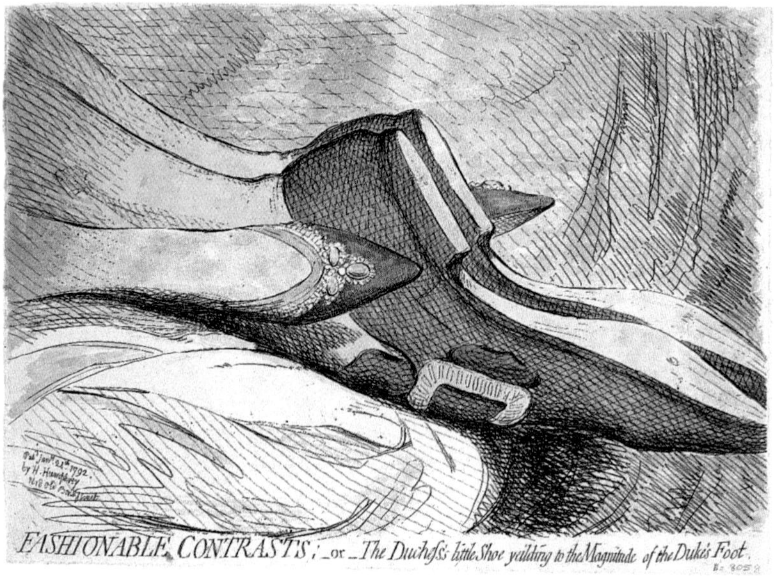


FASHIONABLE CONTRASTS; _or _The Duchess's little Shoe yeilding to the Magnitude of the Duke's Foot.

L. CORNARO
PORT
SYRUP
A VOLUPTUARY under the horrors of Digestion.

Wales, and the government was merely playing for time. In those few minutes Fox had destroyed the party's credibility as the defender of parliamentary rights. By so forcefully championing the Prince of Wales he made the party's battle to limit the powers of the crown appear at best a sham and at worst a sinister plot.

Four days later the Whigs went down to the House to argue for an unrestricted and immediate Regency. The result was a shock: Pitt had won by 268 to 204. 'Fox's declaration of the Prince of Wales's right has been of no small service to us,' wrote Pitt's cousin, William Grenville.

Pitt sent a curt letter to the Prince a few days later outlining the restrictions he would impose on him: the Prince would have no power to create peerages, and he was debarred from conferring any pensions, honours or royal posts. As a final insult, the Queen would be in charge of the Royal Household. Georgiana and her friends were indignant at the harsh conditions. From the beginning of the crisis she had been energetic in employing the tactics which had so successfully demoralized the government in 1784. Georgiana had designed a fetching headpiece, a 'Regency cap', based on the Prince of Wales's crest, made up of three jaunty feathers with his motto '*Ich Dien*' sewn at the base. It caught on to some extent but Pitt was ready for her this time. The Whigs were dismayed to find the government benches uniformly dressed in 'constitutional coats' of blue and red, and they were further discomforted to encounter the majority of people wearing the uniform at public assemblies.

Pitt realized that Georgiana fulfilled a vital function for the Whig party and he was keen to find an equivalent. He was fortunate in having a candidate who had already put herself forward for the post: Jane, Duchess of Gordon. Since separating from her husband, the Duchess of Gordon had entered into a semi-public affair with Henry Dundas, Pitt's best friend and chief political adviser. She was rich, handsome, and a withering opponent in argument. 'The Duchess triumphs in a manly mien; Loud is her accent, and her phrase obscene,' was how she was described by a Scottish wit. Her critics regarded her as a political harpy, 'a horrid violent woman', incapable of acting beyond her two chief ambitions – to be the most powerful political hostess in London, and to secure rich husbands for her five daughters.

For the previous two years she had shamelessly imitated Georgiana, holding regular political dinners for Pitt and Dundas, and organizing specifically Tory assemblies to build up a sense of party as a counter-balance to Devonshire House. Her brashness brought her the rewards she sought: in July 1787 the pro-government *Morning Herald* reported, 'The Duchess of Gordon is now amongst the Ladies most in vogue.' Nathaniel Wraxall thought that she was 'far inferior to her rival', lacking Georgiana's charm or generosity, but that she more than compensated with her utter ruthlessness. Once the Regency debates were in progress she did not hesitate to use her influence on the government's behalf. Wraxall records: 'She even acted as a *Whipper-in* of Ministers . . . she ventured to send for members of Parliament, to question, to remonstrate, and to use every means for confirming their adherence to the government.'

There is no doubt that the Duchess of Gordon was of considerable help to Pitt. In employing her, he was paying tribute to Georgiana's success as the doyenne of the Whig party and acknowledging that certain women, at least, possessed the calibre to be leaders of men. The Lord Chancellor bluntly told Sheridan that his party were fools to waste Georgiana's talents; 'he said she would have been a powerful indeed almost irresistible advocate.' Sheridan replied, according to Georgiana, that they 'had had thoughts of employing me', but it was one more thing on which the leaders could not agree.

In the meantime public opinion supported Pitt. His leadership was praised while the Whigs fought every restriction imposed on the Regency and lost each debate. 'Nothing but treachery going forward – Sheridan heres [sic] Grey has abus'd him, Grey is abus'd by the others,' Georgiana wrote despairingly on 11 January; the enmity between Fox and Sheridan was being acted out by their supporters and destroying any hope of a last-ditch rally against Pitt.

By the end of January the only barrier between the Whigs and ignominy was the King's illness. Fox had given up fighting with Sheridan and the Prince of Wales, and retired to Bath with Mrs Armistead. The Whigs attempted to organize a public address from the borough of Westminster, but with so many bickering and nursing their own grievances, the best the party could manage was to send a petition round various public houses. Fewer Whigs bothered to turn up for meetings at Devonshire House despite strenuous efforts by Georgiana to ensure attendance.

The Regency Bill passed through the House of Commons on 12 February but only a week later, on the nineteenth, official bulletins announced that the King was convalescing. The Lords moved to adjourn the Regency Bill amidst noisy jubilation on the government benches.

The King's recovery released the two sides from any remaining constraints of civility. Sheridan's sister recorded that the Whigs were the object of public derision. Georgiana and her friends braved an assembly given by Lady Buckinghamshire, where they were 'groan'd and hooted' at by the 'Ladies on the Opposite Side'. Georgiana went ahead with a ball she had planned; it fell flat. The Prince made matters worse by provoking several drunken brawls in London clubs; one night the stewards actually threw him out of Ranelagh Gardens.

After a short pause national celebrations began with the formal opening of parliament on 10 March. Fireworks and illuminations marked the event. The Whigs who dared to venture out did so anonymously, squeezing past thousands of flag-waving citizens who cheered and hugged each other in unaffected joy. The carnival-like atmosphere was galling for all the losers but the exclusion from public rejoicing was especially painful for someone like Georgiana; in other circumstances she would have been the organizer.

Georgiana's next public appearance was on 26 March at the Queen's Drawing Room to mark the King's recovery. All the women had received prior notice to wear GOD SAVE THE KING in their caps in a direct riposte to Georgiana's Regency caps. After several heated arguments the Whigs agreed that their side would keep their heads bare. The day was one of the longest Harriet could remember, as 'people did not get away till after eight o'clock though some were there by eleven'. As people filed past her, the Queen 'did not speak to any of the principal Opposition . . . and very cold to the Princes . . . she look'd up at our heads as we past her.'

The exhausted women returned to Devonshire House aching and dishevelled, furious at having exposed themselves to further embarrassment. The Prince arrived a short time later for a quiet supper which he ruined by sobbing and ranting throughout. On 30 March the members of White's held a ball in honour of the King at the Pantheon. Over 2,000 people danced beneath illuminated devices depicting 'GR' and other symbols until the early hours of the morning. The Duchesses of Gordon and Richmond, the patrons for the event, had deliberately appointed only three milliners in London to make the white and gold uniforms to be worn for the occasion in the expectation that the Whig ladies would humble themselves to accept their lead. To their chagrin the Prince and all the Whigs boycotted the ball. Few people noticed the absence of the opposition.

The Prince attended a celebration concert at Windsor three days later, and it was a lesson in mortification. Many of the guests ignored him, his mother glared at him whenever their eyes met

*Jane, Duchess of Gordon, became Pitt's answer to Georgiana as a political hostess. 'The Duchess triumphs in a manly mien; Loud is her accent, and her phrase obscene,' wrote a Scottish wit.*

*Gillray's cartoon, right, criticizes William Pitt and his influence on the Queen during the reign of the mentally ill George III in 1791. In 1783, at the age of twenty-four, William Pitt the Younger, opposite, had become the youngest Prime Minister in parliamentary history. He and Fox were lifelong political rivals.*

An Excrescence; – a Fungus; – alias – a Toadstool upon a Dunghill.

and his sisters were forbidden to speak to him. Pitt's famous winning vote after the Regency debate on 16 December – 268 – was emblazoned above the banqueting table along with his coat of arms entwined with the Lord Chancellor's. 'All this,' complained William Elliot, 'is quite new at Court, and most excessively indecent, as the King is always expected to be of *no party*.'

The Whigs' torture continued for one more day. The service of thanksgiving for the King took place at St Paul's on 23 April, St George's day. The King and Queen, followed by the royal family and the entire household, rode past a clamour of cheers and ringing bells until they reached the cathedral. They were all dressed in the Windsor uniform and, though the King looked thin and frail, there was no mistaking his calm demeanour. Ministers and members of both Houses followed in a slow march behind, which allowed the crowd to give clear indications of preference. *The Times* reported that Fox's carriage was received with 'an universal hiss which continued with very little intermission until he alighted at St Paul's'. Every building was covered in banners and ribbons. As a precautionary measure against the mob, even Devonshire House was decorated with flags and royal insignia. It was Pitt's day. 'He is admired and adored by all who wish well to Great Britain,' wrote one supporter. He was still only twenty-nine.

The Duchess of Gordon was also triumphant. The night of White's ball she hosted a select party which included Pitt, Dundas and Dr Willis; people stopped to applaud them as they walked arm in arm. She had become a significant rival to Georgiana, whose reign over the *ton* for the past fifteen years now looked seriously in doubt. The uniforms, the tribal politics, the use of private female

influence to affect the voting outcome – Georgiana had perfected the technique and the Duchess of Gordon had copied her with successful results.

The Regency crisis established the future path of the two parties: the diminution of the Whigs as a credible opposition and Pitt's unassailable pre-eminence. 'I have often thought,' wrote the Whig peer Lord Palmerston, that 'we have more Wit and Ingenuity on our side than sound judgement in managing Parliamentary matters'. Many Whigs expressed regret at their party's lack of professionalism. 'We despise parliamentary craft too much, and are sadly deficient in it,' complained Lord George Cavendish. Re-reading her journal some years later, Georgiana wrote: 'These fragments, I think, prepare to the disunion and want of method which so soon brought the destruction of opposition about during the years '92 and '93.'

# Exile

## 1789–1799

*Previous pages: In this portrait by Gainsborough, the most famous picture of Georgiana, she wears a wide-brimmed hat of her own design. After the exhibition of the portrait, women all over the country ordered their milliners to make them a copy of the 'Duchess of Devonshire's picture hat'.*

*Little G, above left, and Harryo, above. Georgiana had a remarkably close and loving relationship with her children. 'How different you are from everybody else, how superior to all mothers, even good ones,' Little G wrote to her. Harryo, who had a difficult adolescence, nevertheless later told her mother that she felt 'enthusiasm and adoration, that for anybody else would be ridiculous, but to deny it [to] you would be unnatural'.*

# *The Approaching Storm* 1789–1790

*The Duchess of Devonshire has thought it proper to quit Paris during the present convulsions in that capital. The amiable Duchess was advised to this measure by Madame de Polignac, who told her Grace that she could not depend upon her own safety. The Duchess of Devonshire, it is supposed, has proceeded to Spa.*

MORNING POST, 10 JULY 1789

ALMOST EVERYONE HELD A GRIEVANCE about the way the leadership had dealt with the crisis. Georgiana adopted a conciliatory role and tried to bring the various factions together by holding quiet dinners at Devonshire House. But she, too, retreated from public life and avoided all large gatherings.

By April she was personally bankrupt and in terror of the Duke discovering her debts. She may even have contemplated suicide. 'I really think the best thing is to lay before the Duke the very worst of your situation at once,' Coutts wrote after she implored him for another £6,000. 'If *his* excusing the past, together with *your viewing* the precipice you are standing on the verge of, does not cure you I can only say you have gone beyond the point of recovery.' Fortunately for her, she had means of persuasion: Coutts's daughters were learning French at a convent in Paris and it was within her power to introduce them to the French court. She enlisted the help of the Duke of Dorset and the Little Po and her efforts brought her a brief respite, especially after she had explained to Coutts that money would be forthcoming as soon as she gave birth to a son. Under the terms of the Cavendish estate the Duke would then be able to raise a mortgage, making it possible for her to confess her debts without ruining him.

At the end of May the Duke announced that he had made up his mind to take Georgiana and Bess to Spa. Both women were delighted: Georgiana hoped the waters would help her to conceive, while Bess regarded the trip as an opportunity to see her two children, Caroline and Clifford. Charlotte Williams was to accompany them, and Little G and Harriet, whom they nicknamed Harryo, would stay with Lady Spencer. On 20 June 1789 they set sail for Calais. Georgiana had managed to secure a £500 loan from her brother which was all the cash she had to last her while she was abroad.

The enthusiastic reception Georgiana received from the French temporarily enabled her to forget her worries (Martindale had reappeared to demand some 'quiet' money from her). The Devonshires' visit during such uncertain times was a reassuring sign of normality for the Parisians. French farmers were still suffering the effects of a prolonged drought. Those crops that survived the scorching sun had drowned in the violent storms that followed. In some areas people were facing starvation: there were riots in the marketplace, grain stores and bakeries were being attacked. In April Paris had been brought to a standstill by two days of rioting.

The Devonshires arrived in France three days after the Third Estate had voted to call itself the National Assembly on the grounds that it represented 96 per cent of the country and by rights ought to have the majority share of power. On 19 June the Royal Council met and agreed that the King should call a special session of all the Estates and take a strong line by annulling the proceedings of the National Assembly and imposing his own compromise plan.

Louis XVI did offer a compromise which entailed limiting some of the monarchy's powers, but he remained firm against the other demands: in particular, there would be no union of the three Estates. He declared all the proceedings conducted by the Third Estate since May null and void, and then ordered the deputies to disperse until the next day. Georgiana summed up the futility of the meeting in a letter to her mother: 'the King . . . made a speech to the *tiers* telling them they must desist from their proceedings. After he went, there they staid and voted to annul everything he had done and said.'

On 25 June, three days after the Devonshires had settled at their hotel, there was a revolt among the upper Estates, and the majority of the clergy (the Second Estate) and about fifty nobles (the First Estate) led by the Duc d'Orléans joined the Third Estate. 'The ferment at Paris is beyond conception,' wrote Arthur Young. '10,000 people have been all this day in the Palais-Royal . . . the language that was talked, by all ranks of people, was nothing less than a revolution in the government, and the establishment of a free constitution.'

When the Devonshires were eventually able to drive to Versailles they found the Polignacs and the King and Queen excessively glad to see them. Georgiana found the King looking better than she expected and the Queen looking worse. 'She received us very graciously indeed, tho' very much out of spirit at the times,' she wrote Lady Spencer. On 27 June Louis capitulated and ordered the other two Estates to join the Third. 'The King has wrote to his nobles to join the *tiers*,' Georgiana reported, 'which in fact is giving up his authority entirely . . . The people are wild with joy, and all our friends miserable.' Three days later the Estates merged. That night a riotous crowd surrounded Versailles shouting slogans and dancing to music until daybreak.

Georgiana continued to hold sumptuous dinners for her friends in spite of the deteriorating situation. Yet, it was becoming difficult for her to travel about; 'all is license and confusion.' She was explicit in a letter to her brother of 5 July: 'The troubles of this place are not to be described – the guards refusing to act, the people half mad and the greatest part of the nobles divided in the most surprising manner, so that families are at daggers drawn.' 'I saw La Fayette at the Vicomte de Noailles late,' she wrote. 'They disputed amazingly on Politicks with me. I am *for* the Court on Mme Polignac's account. They are violently against it.' She knew her position was indefensible considering her staunch opposition to the court at home, but Parisian society admired her independent spirit.

The Duke, however, had had enough of Paris and on 8 July Georgiana and Bess, dressed in mourning, made one last visit to Versailles to say goodbye to their friends. Georgiana saw Marie Antoinette alone for a little while, and then the Little Po, who had been a faithful friend to her for fifteen years. Their correspondence had never slackened; for Georgiana's sake she had accepted Bess, helped to bring Caroline St Jules to Paris, and provided countenance to Coutts's daughters. Georgiana said farewell not knowing when she would see her again, or in what circumstances.

The Devonshires were in Brussels, en route to Spa, when a messenger reached them with news of the storming of the Bastille. The report of the governor's lynching and the bloody outrages which accompanied his murder made them fear for their friends. The Polignacs had escaped, fleeing Versailles in the middle of the night. Marie Antoinette had urged them to go, but their departure left her almost completely alone except for her family and a few attendants.

James Hare wrote to Georgiana at Spa on 18 July to give her an eye-witness account of the rioting and to reassure her that Charlotte, whom they had left with a French family, was safe. Georgiana told Lady Spencer that the Duke of Devonshire 'really cry'd from anxiety' at the thought of poor Charlotte surrounded by a 'mad populace arm'd with pistols, swords and bayonets'. However, the Duke's tears were not only (if at all) for Charlotte, but for little Caroline, to whom Georgiana referred very casually in her letters as the 'other pensioner, Mlle de St Jules, a young lady from the provinces'. Very few people knew of her existence apart from the Little Po and James Hare. With several illegitimate children of his own he sincerely sympathized with the Duke and Bess. He not only visited Charlotte and Caroline but also the infant Clifford – he even made sure Coutts's daughters were safe in their convent. By mid-September Charlotte and 'the other pensioner' had joined them at Spa.

The Duke of Devonshire began to talk of their going home, which dismayed Georgiana, who feared her creditors more than the revolutionaries. Coutts had discovered she had been lying to him and refused her plea for another loan. Georgiana now placed all her hopes on conceiving a son. By the end of September she discovered she was pregnant. 'The symptoms are all the same,' she wrote excitedly to Lady Spencer; 'I have no *Wednesday feels*, but some that show that great care must be taken – I have been entirely free from headache this last three weeks which seems to be a sign of being with child . . .' The pregnancy was a last-minute reprieve. Georgiana was so relieved that the first person she informed was Coutts, two days before she wrote to her mother. 'I shall consecrate all my time to quiet of body and mind, that I may not lose the advantage of giving the Duke a son; and before I lie in (if I really am with child), I shall lay everything before him. In the meantime . . . I send an order to Beard to pay you 300. This will, I hope answer all demands . . .'

The Duke was so excited at the prospect of an heir that he immediately cancelled their plans to return to England, fearing that the Channel crossing might cause his wife to miscarry. Bess confided to Lady Melbourne that she dreaded another girl, for her own sake as much as Georgiana's. But the situation in Belgium was hardly safe: revolutionary fever had spread to Brussels and there was rioting in the streets against Joseph II. Unencumbered by ties of friendship, her Whig principles reasserted themselves. This was a great help with regard to receiving mail, since letters addressed via their royal connections mysteriously disappeared while those which came via the patriots did not.

The Spencers and Cavendishes were bewildered by the Duke's decision to remain abroad; Lady Spencer wondered if Bess was pregnant. Their concern increased when the Duke departed for England at the end of December, leaving Bess and Georgiana behind. Neither woman was happy at the prospect – Georgiana had not seen her children for six months and she missed them terribly. Bess dreaded the Duke's absence in such lawless times, but 'I shall stay with her to the last,' she wrote melodramatically.

The Duke had left them not to attend to business matters in England, as they claimed, but because Duncannon had initiated divorce proceedings against Harriet. He had discovered her affair with Sheridan nine months earlier, in March. Although she had promised not to see Sheridan again they continued to meet in secret until Duncannon found out.

The Duke of Devonshire reached England just as the bill for the divorce was about to enter the first stage of proceedings. He found Harriet in a state of nervous collapse, and Duncannon more determined than he had ever seen him before. But once Duncannon realized that his father and all the Cavendishes were taking Harriet's side against him he dropped the suit. The Duke, however, was not prepared to take any chances while Georgiana was still liable to miscarry. He forced Duncannon to agree to accompany Harriet to Brussels and stay with them.

The Duncannons arrived at Brussels a short time after the Duke, not in the least reconciled and their future together as bleak as the winter prospect around them. Harriet's presence gave

*Caroline St Jules, the illegitimate daughter of Bess and Georgiana's husband, the fourth Duke of Devonshire. The Duke's favourite daughter, she received £30,000 from him when she married George Lamb. A few months later, when Harryo married Granville Leveson Gower, the Duke settled only £10,000 on her.*

Georgiana something to think about other than her own problems. For the past few months she had been desperately trying to raise money to satisfy her creditors. She asked the Duke's personal banker Cornelius Denne to advance her £5,000 in secret, which he sent over despite grave reservations. She kept part of it and sent the rest to William Galley at the Lottery Office to lay bets for her. She also extracted money from the Prince of Wales.

She was sickened by herself. Bess was convinced that the Duke had to be told the true state of affairs. At first he thought Bess was talking about a few thousand. Gradually, he realized from her hints that the sum was much greater. But despite everyone urging her to confess before it was too late, Georgiana once again lied when he confronted her. She wrote him a letter in March which was as subtle as it was sad in its contortions to avoid a disclosure. 'Why do you force me, my dear Ca, to an avowal to you which agitates me beyond measure, and which is not necessary now?' she asked, not mentioning that the circumstance which made it unnecessary was the money she had borrowed from the Prince and Denne. She also played on the Duke's fear of her miscarrying. She implored him not to confront her creditors as the true extent of her debts would, she knew, send him into a rage.

The Duke took her statement at face value. However, by the time the baby was due she had borrowed almost £20,000 and was still being persecuted by her creditors. In May she begged a further loan from the Prince, falsely claiming that it would clear all her debts. Harriet, who had no more to spare, tried to help by paying some of the smaller creditors herself. Like everyone else, she dreaded Georgiana becoming agitated and losing the baby. The Duke even agreed to allow the children to be brought out from England because she missed them so much. It was a dangerous and complicated venture which involved the transport of over thirty adults in various capacities as outriders, footmen, nurses, nannies, maids and grooms. As a consequence little Georgiana and Harryo met their half-sister Caroline much earlier than planned.

Caroline's presence among the Cavendish children did invite speculation, and there were other rumours; some people actually claimed Georgiana was not pregnant at all, which made her indignant. It was not only their remaining abroad which caused talk; their choice of a young doctor named Croft seemed obscure. In fact he was the son-in-law of Dr Denman, who had attended Georgiana's previous births. Denman had felt he was too old to make the arduous journey, whereas Croft was robust enough to withstand Continental travel. However, Georgiana was his first notable client and people wondered why the Duke would allow someone so relatively inexperienced near his wife, unless the Devonshires were planning something to ensure that they returned with a son. Lady Spencer joined the party at the beginning of May partly to help quash these rumours.

After the initial turmoil most of their eight-month stay in Brussels was quiet. Georgiana's contacts with the patriots were of great use but the Belgians did not understand her royalist links, and after some of her letters were intercepted the entire party was ordered to leave Brussels. They mobilized as quickly as was possible with four children and a hundred adults to organize. Georgiana was so large she had difficulty walking, her discomfort aggravated by chronic cystitis. Lafayette promised they would not be molested if they returned to France. They did not know where they would stay until by chance the unwieldy caravan bumped into the Duc d'Ahrenberg, who was fleeing in the other direction. He offered them his house at Passy, just outside Paris. They reached the city on 19 May and found it 'perfectly quiet'. Georgiana began to experience pains almost immediately. 'We are thank God got safe into a magnificent house here,' Lady Spencer wrote to George when they reached Passy, 'where I trust it will not be many days before we shall be relieved from the load of anxiety.'

Within a few hours of their arrival Georgiana went into labour. Lady Spencer took charge of the situation. She ordered Bess to ride back to Paris and show herself at the Opéra in order to dispel the speculation about which of the women was actually pregnant. She also wrote to the secretary of the British embassy, Lord Robert Fitzgerald, and to the dowager Duchesse d'Ahrenberg, both persons of impeccable respectability, asking them to come and be independent witnesses to the birth. Bess did as she was asked and appeared in Lord St Helens' box so that everyone might see her slim figure. She arrived back at Passy just before the birth. The message had not got through to the embassy but the Duchesse d'Ahrenberg was there. They waited outside Georgiana's door.

Just before two in the morning on 21 May 1790 Georgiana gave birth to a boy, the Marquess of Hartington. As arranged, the Duchesse d'Ahrenberg entered the room before the family and verified the new-born baby; her cries brought the rest of the family rushing in. 'There never was a more welcome child,' recorded one of the servants. Messengers were immediately dispatched to England. Church bells rang continuously in Derbyshire to relay the news across the county. The Cavendish clan could hardly believe that Georgiana had at last delivered them an heir.

For two weeks after Hartington's birth the joy at his arrival was muted by the fear that Georgiana might die. Duncannon was impatient to return to England but Harriet refused to leave until she could be sure about her sister. It was not until mid-June that Lady Spencer was able to tell George, 'since Thursday there has been a regular and gradual amendment and she is at this moment expressing with a sweet affectionate countenance her gratitude to everybody for their care and tenderness . . .' Within days Georgiana was organizing a round of parties to celebrate. As soon as she felt well enough she enjoyed the attentions of Paris's finest couturiers – a gift from her grateful husband. For the first time in many months she could relax and enjoy herself.

But Georgiana was not insensible to the plight of her friends. Since October the royal family had been virtual prisoners in the Tuileries where they were subjected to the scrutiny of crowds who came daily to stare and insult them. Marie Antoinette still had some freedom of movement and was enjoying a short respite from Paris in the beautiful gardens at Saint-Cloud when Georgiana took her children and Bess to visit her.

They stayed in France until the end of August. Lady Spencer had left in July, taking the children with her. Little G had come down with a strange illness which Dr Croft could not identify and which further convinced them that the children would be better off at home. For Bess it was a supreme irony to know that her arch enemy would be the means of transporting her daughter into Devonshire House; Lady Spencer was too anxious to leave to question Charlotte and Caroline's inclusion in the party.

'I regret the Duchess's departure very much,' wrote Lady Sutherland, echoing the general sentiment among the Parisians. 'As for Lady Elisabeth, she is nice enough but one can do without her, but the Duchess has a thousand good qualities and an excellent heart.' The Devonshires sailed in the first of four packet boats, followed by their servants and luggage crammed on to the three behind. Georgiana rarely let Hartington out of her sight. The trip to the Continent had given her a long-awaited son, and returned Caroline St Jules to Bess. Yet the purpose of the journey remained unfinished: Georgiana still had to confess her debts and Bess's son Clifford was marooned amid the chaos in Paris.

# 1790–1791 *Exposure*

*The liberal, noble spirit of the Lady united to the head of [the Cavendish] family, whose charities are universal and whose benignity of heart is announced by the beaming graces of the most ingenuous, lovely, impassioned countenance ought to have operated as an example . . . Her lively, mercurial temper was also admirably calculated to correct the phlegm of the family, with which she is connected; but fire and water cannot assimilate; and it grieves us to hear, that a separation has actually taken place.*

THE JOCKEY CLUB (PAMPHLET), C. PIGOTT, LONDON 1792

GEORGIANA CAME HOME to find the Whigs split over the merits of the French Revolution. Burke and Sheridan were at the head of rival camps, with Burke claiming it as the triumph of despotic democracy, and Sheridan as a victory for citizen's rights. Some of the younger Whigs believed that radical change would liberate the benign instincts of society and bring about a happy compromise between the aristocracy and the lower classes. The conservative Whigs who followed Burke accepted his argument that it was impossible to control such grand forces of change and that they endangered civil institutions.

Unable to decide which man to support, Fox allowed Burke and Sheridan's dispute to grow until on 6 May 1791 Burke turned an innocuous debate in the Commons on the constitution for Quebec into a platform from which to denounce the new French republican constitution. Fox tried to intervene but Burke turned on his former protégé and announced their irrevocable separation. Both men were pushed to tears by the breakdown of their thirty-year friendship but could not be reconciled.

Years later, Georgiana admitted that she held Fox accountable for his failure of leadership at the critical moment. For one thing, she knew that Burke's devastating criticism of Fox's political beliefs was based on a misunderstanding. Fox believed in the French Revolution as a means of bringing about a constitutional monarchy similar to that inspired by the Glorious Revolution of 1688. He never advocated the deposition of Louis XVI, and he made plain his support for the French monarchy three months later, when the royal family were captured while attempting to flee the country. As soon as he heard the details of the King and Queen's tragic flight to Varennes, of their return to Paris surrounded by a baying mob, and of their imprisonment in separate apartments, he wrote to Lafayette urging him to safeguard their lives.

Georgiana herself would never forget the unruly hatred of the mob, nor her last visit to Marie Antoinette when the taunts of the crowd could be heard outside the gates. Since her return to England Georgiana had allied herself with a select group of Englishmen who were striving to contain the revolution within reasonable bounds. She also wrote to Lafayette and warned him that his reputation was at stake. He replied indignantly that there was not the slightest danger to either the King or Queen. However, the letter campaign did little to help the beleaguered royals, not least because the French resented English interference.

The flight to Varennes briefly reunited Georgiana and the Duke of Dorset. As soon as the news of the failed escape of the French King and Queen reached England he impulsively wrote to her, and they were soon exchanging news with each other almost every day, Dorset passing on official reports from the embassy, Georgiana relaying information from French minister Alexandre de Calonne whom she had befriended at Devonshire House in 1788. In August he sent an express to Bath asking Georgiana to travel to London for meetings at his house but she replied evasively that she could not leave Bath for reasons that she could not reveal to anyone.

The Duke had given Georgiana until Hartington, now nicknamed Hart, was weaned to prepare her accounts. She felt certain that he would want a separation as soon as he learned the truth and she put off the day as long as she could. It was only Bess's vehement insistence that she would take her side which made Georgiana begin the process at all. Now that Bess could have the Duke to herself the two women were closer than they had ever been before. Ironically, Lady Spencer was still scheming to have her rival removed from Devonshire House. She had befriended the children's governess, Selina Trimmer, and used her to spy on and torment Bess. After several months Georgiana noticed that servants were taking their cue from Selina and behaving with marked insolence towards Bess.

Writing to her mother, Georgiana attempted to settle the question of Bess's presence once and for all; she lived with them, she said, because both she and the Duke wanted it that way. 'I am born to a most complicated misery. I had run into errors, that would have made any other man discard me,' she declared, and it was owing to Bess's influence that the marriage had remained intact. 'Her society was delightful to us, and her gentleness and affection sooth'd the bitterness that [my] misfortunes had brought on us.' After this description of her domestic situation Lady Spencer found it difficult to argue. However, she had witnessed Georgiana's unhappiness in the early days, and she would never be able to forget Bess's air of triumph that first summer at Chatsworth.

Hart was weaned in November and Georgiana had no choice but to compile a list of her creditors. Friends as well as family, Sheridan and Hare in particular, begged her not to hide anything. She finally presented a list of over thirty names, some of them surprising, such as 'Scafe, £2,638: brother to a servant', and others which hinted at murky dealings in the City – 'Statta: £3700: an imposition'. The amount came to £61,917 (roughly £3,720,000 today). But, as some had feared, it was a sanitized version of her situation: there was no mention, for example, of the thousands borrowed from the Prince, or of the life annuity of £500 she was paying to William Galley, bookmaker to the *ton*.

In order to show her contrition Georgiana asked her trustees to sign over her settlement to the Duke, which would leave her destitute if they separated. The act, however, failed to appease the Duke or the Cavendishes. Bess warned Georgiana to leave the Duke alone and to trust her to ease him slowly into accepting the sum. Georgiana listened to her advice but the anxiety of waiting for his decision gave her headaches which left her prostrate for days at a time. 'I have not a guess of my future destination,' she confided to her mother.

*Many were surprised when Georgiana's sister, Harriet, agreed to marry Lord Duncannon, later third Earl of Bessborough. Harriet had her own doubts, saying, 'there are some things which frighten me sadly, he is so grave and I am so very giddy.' He proved a violent husband who gambled away their inheritance. Yet he was oddly sympathetic where Georgiana was concerned.*

In February, while the Duke was still deliberating, the Stock Exchange suffered the major collapse of a private share syndicate. According to Lady Mary Coke: 'tis the conversation of the town . . . [Georgiana] has it seems been gambling on the stocks, and to such an extent that her loss is now too considerable to remain any longer a secret.' Harriet was also involved.

The Cavendishes told the Duke he was a fool to support his wife any longer, and at a noisy family meeting to discuss her debts the Duchess of Portland accused her of deliberate malice. 'I got into a passion,' was all Georgiana would say of the confrontation, but she was aghast at the strength of the feeling against her. The Duke's formidable sister pronounced Georgiana's ostracism from the family; henceforth they would cut her in public and avoid her in private.

Her distress was not only financial. Harriet had collapsed with some sort of stroke. She was paralysed down one side of her body and suffering from severe fits. What exactly had happened to her is unclear, and was a closely guarded secret at the time. Mrs Damer thought it was 'some inward disease' connected with a miscarriage. It may have been a botched abortion or, more likely, a suicide attempt. The illness occurred just before the sisters were exposed on the Stock Exchange. While she lay paralysed Harriet caught bronchial pneumonia, which damaged her lungs. The family resigned itself to her imminent death.

The Duke behaved with surprising generosity towards Georgiana and Harriet. Ignoring his family's injunction to abandon his wife and her relatives, he rented a house in Bath large enough to accommodate his and Harriet's children, and moved both families down there. No record survives explaining his precise reasons for taking charge of Harriet and protecting Georgiana. He was not only attached to his sister-in-law but had become more sympathetic to Georgiana; after fifteen years of marriage there were indissoluble ties between them.

Harriet remained at Bath for several months, attended by Dr Warren and nursed by Lady Spencer, Georgiana and Bess through recurring 'spasms' which 'left her very weak'. Dr Warren prescribed a warmer climate as the best remedy. Lisbon seemed an ideal option as the climate was warm and dry and the country was free from political turmoil. The only impediment to the plan was Harriet, who declared she would rather die than go abroad with just her husband for company.

*The Duke and Georgiana spent more time at Bath as the Duke became increasingly encumbered by his gout. A fashionable spa town, it attracted the elite who came to socialize as well as cure themselves in the waters. The entrance to the Pump Room at Bath, above; 'A Modern Belle going to the Rooms at Bath', 1796, opposite.*

Nothing had been decided when the novelist Fanny Burney paid her first and only call on Georgiana in August. She was staying with her friend Mrs Ord while she became accustomed to her retirement from court as Second Keeper of the Queen's Robes. For the past five years she had lived at the beck and call of the Queen and the six princesses who adored and trusted her. Naturally she shared her employers' dislike of the Whigs and believed the rumours which circulated about them at court. She was appalled when Mrs Ord's friendship with Lady Spencer brought her into contact with women of such tarnished character. Her record of her meeting with Georgiana, Harriet and Bess is a unique description of their domestic situation by someone unconnected with their circle.

Burney was just beginning to dismiss Lady Spencer as a prig and a bore when she began talking about Harriet 'with much sorrow, and expatiated upon her resignation to her fate, her prepared state for Death and the excellence of her principles, with an eagerness and feeling that quite overwhelmed me with surprise and embarrassment'. Fanny was shocked by Lady Spencer's reference to Harriet's principles; she knew what everyone in London knew – that Harriet had never been faithful to Duncannon, that she had had an affair with Sheridan, and that Duncannon was only delaying a divorce until his father died.

A Modern Belle going to the Rooms at Bath. Pub^d Jan^y 13^th 1796. by H. Humphrey, New Bond Street

*The novelist Fanny Burney was prepared to dislike Lady Spencer and her family when she met them all in 1791 but found that she liked everyone except Bess who, she wrote, had inherited 'all the wickedness of the Herveys'. About Georgiana she concluded, 'it is impossible to view . . . this celebrated woman without feeling the strongest disposition to admire and like her.'*

The following day while visiting Lady Spencer she had the opportunity to judge Harriet for herself. Burney wanted to despise her but as the afternoon wore on her opinion changed in spite of herself. She admired Harriet's 'simple' dress, her 'unusually lovely Expression' and her efforts at 'expressing constantly something cheerful about her own wretched state, or [being] grateful for the services offered or done her'.

More family members arrived. Selina brought in the little girls, who were in high spirits because it was Harryo's birthday. The 'little French lady', as Fanny described Caroline St Jules, seemed a different creature compared to the 'happy disposition' of the Cavendish girls; she was 'fat and full of mincing little affectations and airs'. When Georgiana and Bess flurried in Lady Spencer made no attempt to hide her dislike of Bess.

By this time Fanny's curiosity was stronger than her moral outrage and she was eager to learn more about this infamous coterie. But Bess seized her, 'to my great provocation', and monopolized her entirely while Georgiana went to talk to Harriet. Their conversation convinced her that 'Lady Elizabeth has the general character of inheriting all the wit, all the subtlety, all les agréments [charm], and all the wickedness of the Herveys.'

This judgement of Bess coloured Fanny's view of Georgiana, whom she regarded as the victim of her friend's designs. 'I did not find so much beauty in her as I expected . . . but I found far more of manner, politeness and gentle quiet.' When she finally managed to escape from Bess and talk to Georgiana she thought she was one of the most pleasing women she had ever met. Fanny recorded, 'it is impossible to view . . . this celebrated woman without feeling the strongest disposition to admire and like her.' Consequently, she considered various sinister reasons that Georgiana might be forced (perhaps by the Duke) to tolerate Bess's presence, which made her 'strongly concerned for [Georgiana] in the situation'.

Her judgement seemed confirmed beyond doubt when she bumped into Georgiana and Lady Spencer walking in town without Bess a few days later. She seemed 'more easy and lively in her spirits, and consequently more lovely in her person . . . It struck me, also, in her favour, that her spirits had before been depressed by the presence of the odious Lady Elizabeth and were now revived by being absent from her.'

'This has been a singular acquaintance for *me*!' wrote Burney when she left Bath, 'that the first visit I should make, after leaving the Queen, should be to meet the head of *opposition public*, the Duchess of Devonshire! . . . I came away impressed with the most mixt sensations of pain and pleasure.' She also detected that something was troubling Georgiana though she could not have known the cause: Georgiana was carrying Charles Grey's baby.

Harriet and Bess had known ever since Georgiana discovered it herself. They had repeatedly warned Georgiana to be careful but she was infatuated with Grey. 'She distracts me,' Bess complained to Lady Melbourne, who had also admonished Georgiana, 'by working herself up to think she is more attach'd to him than I know she can be.'

Georgiana was mesmerized by him. They made no attempt to be discreet, and the public way in which Grey would monopolize her at a party or argue with her if he felt neglected dismayed even the most tolerant members of the Circle. Grey followed Georgiana to Bath while the Duke was away, and was often seen going in and out of the house. His lack of caution made Bess dread the arrival of the papers each day. However, help came from an unexpected, although unpleasant source. Lady Spencer, Bess told Lady Melbourne, 'had received an anonymous letter and her commands are you know absolute and her vigilance extreme . . .' Lady Spencer browbeat Georgiana until she swore to send Grey back to London. She was not even allowed to say goodbye to him. However, Georgiana was already pregnant.

They managed to keep Georgiana's secret safe for as long as the pregnancy did not show. However, by October she was into her sixth month and large. Harriet's health was improving but she still needed to convalesce in a warmer climate and this seemed Georgiana's only hope of escape. Dr Warren had agreed to Harriet's request to recommend Cornwall rather than Lisbon; it was as far as they could go without making the Duke concerned about Georgiana's absence. But before they could put their plan into action the Duke arrived on an unannounced visit: someone in London had told him he ought to see his wife immediately. He confronted Georgiana alone; the sound of shouting and crying terrified Harriet, who lay on a couch in the adjoining room. At one point he called in Bess and berated her for covering up for Georgiana.

After the Duke left the sisters remained in their separate rooms. Harriet could hear Georgiana moving about in hers and she sent in a note of enquiry. The reply confirmed her fears. 'We must go abroad – immediately,' Harriet wrote to Lady Melbourne. 'Nothing else will do, neither prayers nor entreaties will alter him. He says there is no choice between this, or public entire separation at home . . . write to me, come if you can, give us some comfort but do not betray me.'

The morning after the interview Harriet talked to Bess and was relieved to find her common sense and loyalty intact. 'Bess has very generously promised to go with us. I urg'd her to it almost as much on her own account as my sister's, it must have been ruin to her to stay behind.' With Bess's support secured, Harriet turned her thoughts to her mother and husband: 'Lord D. and my mother still both believe we are going to Penzance, and how they will ever be brought to consent I know not.' Lady Spencer had no idea of the scenes at Bath until Georgiana wrote to her saying that Warren had ordered Harriet abroad immediately. She hurried to her daughters, worried that Harriet had suffered a relapse. Her arrival plunged the house into crisis again. 'Vexation and unhappiness surround me. I almost wish myself at the bottom of the sea,' wrote Harriet.

She took some comfort from Duncannon's reaction. He could be magnanimous where Georgiana was concerned and reassured Harriet that he would assist them in whatever plan they chose. In the meantime he went to London to make arrangements for the children. The women endured several more angry visits from the Duke and from Lady Spencer. The lapse of a few days had done nothing to diminish the Duke's rage; Bess did not dare try to intercede, especially as she had recently managed to bring Clifford over from France: he was living with a family in Somerset.

When the Cavendishes heard the news they were unanimous in urging an immediate separation. This was her repayment, they said, after the Duke had stood up for her against his own relatives and accepted her debts against the advice of his agents. Finally the Duke recovered himself sufficiently to make a firm decision: unable to trust himself with Georgiana or Bess he sought out Harriet and burst out, 'If you wish to save your sister and me from the most unpleasant disclosure, break off your going to Penzance and go abroad directly.' That was it, she told Lady Melbourne: after he walked out she realized, 'it is determined as far as the Duke can determine anything . . . His soliciting an open publick separation or not depends upon my entire acquiescence in everything he wishes.'

*Georgiana and Harriet, by Thomas Rowlandson. The sisters frequently appeared as subjects in Rowlandson's drawings, probably because they so often socialized and entertained together.*

By the time Dr Warren arrived the strain on Harriet had brought about a relapse and he had no difficulty in requesting her departure. The Duke ordered Selina and Lady Spencer to take the children to London; the exiles should go immediately to Southampton. The party was to consist of Lady Spencer, the Duncannons and their youngest child, Caroline, Georgiana, Bess and her daughter, Caroline St Jules. However, the news that Lady Spencer was definitely going made Bess reconsider her offer to accompany Georgiana.

Once again Lady Spencer's prejudices had blinded her to the exigencies of Georgiana's situation. If Bess stayed behind her reputation might be ruined but the Duke would have little incentive to recall Georgiana from her exile. In any case, there were far more serious problems to be overcome. None of the party had any money. The Duncannons were massively in debt as usual and Georgiana had only the contents of her baggage. The private incomes of Bess and Lady Spencer were hardly enough to support themselves abroad, let alone seven people. Lady Melbourne gave them what money she could quickly gather without attracting notice, and George paid for Harriet's doctor to travel with them. He had little cash to spare although he sent his agent, Townsend, to accompany the party and conduct all their business transactions for them. In many ways Townsend was better than a line of credit because he was practical and level-headed. However, it was impossible to imagine how they would survive if the Duke remained angry for any length of time.

The Duke had ordered Georgiana to renounce Grey and have the baby adopted as soon as it was born. If she refused he would divorce her and she would never see her three children again. She did not hesitate even though she had no guarantee that the Duke would not change his mind and divorce her anyway. But Grey could not forgive her choice. He was being 'very cruel', Georgiana wrote sadly to Lady Melbourne, who was secretly forwarding their letters. 'I have in leaving him for ever, left my heart and soul; but it is over now . . . he has one consolation that I have given him up to my children only.'

1791–1793

# Exile

*The Duchess of Devonshire, the Dowager Lady Spencer, and Lord and Lady Duncannon pass the summer in Switzerland, and next winter in Nice. The Duke is going to visit them soon. This fully contradicts the vague reports that have been circulated of these noble personages.*

BON TON MAGAZINE, JUNE 1792

GEORGIANA LAY in an airless, shuttered room in a house near Montpellier, waiting to give birth. Although only thirty-four, she feared that her life had run its course. She made a new will, dated 27 January 1792, and took out a life insurance policy for £1,000. Bess and the six-year-old Caroline St Jules were the only people with her; the others had pressed on to Nice on account of Harriet's health. Georgiana composed letters of farewell to each of her children, in case of her death. 'As soon as you are old enough to understand this letter it will be given to you,' she wrote hopefully to her two-year-old son. 'It contains the only present I can make you – my blessing, written in my blood . . . Alas, I am gone before you could know me, but I lov'd you, I nurs'd you nine months at my breast. I love you dearly.'

Georgiana begged the children to learn from the mistakes which had ruined her life, writing to Little Georgiana, 'I die, my dearest child, with the most unfeigned repentance for many errors.' Her final injunction was that they should always be dutiful to their father, loving to their grandmother and 'affectionate to my Dear friend Bess – love and befriend Caroline St Jules'.

The children knew that their mother had been sent away to give birth to an illegitimate child; the proof is in the blacked-out paragraphs which disfigure Georgiana's letters to them during these months. Their Victorian descendants attempted to wipe out every trace of her transgression. But we know from other sources that on 20 February 1791 Georgiana gave birth to a girl. She called her Eliza (a favourite name of Bess's) Courtney (a surname which belonged to the Poyntz family and therefore, unusually, gave no hint of her patrimony). Someone took Eliza from Georgiana's arms almost immediately. The baby was nursed by a foster mother and then, when she was old enough to travel, sent over to England to live with Charles Grey's parents in Falloden in Northumberland.

*Little Eliza Courtney, Georgiana's daughter by Charles Grey. Eliza lived with Grey's parents; Georgiana was never allowed to acknowledge her. When Harriet visited the Greys in 1808 she wrote that 'Eliza is a fine girl, and will, I think, be handsome', but 'it goes to my heart to see her – she is so evidently thrown into the background'.*

Georgiana was never allowed to acknowledge Eliza, although her existence eventually became an open secret. The arrangement ultimately agreed between the Devonshires and the Greys granted Georgiana limited access to the child as her unofficial godmother. She was not allowed to send her private letters or visit her at Falloden, nor does it seem that Eliza ever set foot inside Devonshire House. But Georgiana was granted permission to see her occasionally when the Greys brought her to London. These visits were painful: Georgiana could sense that Eliza lacked the sort of loving attention which her other children enjoyed, so she sent her little presents – poetry, tiny watercolour drawings, and any other scrap of nursery paraphernalia which could be tied up in a ribbon and easily conveyed. But no matter how carefully she composed her letters, she couldn't hide her thwarted maternal feelings.

Though Georgiana came perilously close to betraying herself, she kept her oath and also forbade Little Georgiana and Harryo, who were taken to see Eliza occasionally, ever to reveal their knowledge of the connection. Eliza therefore grew up in complete ignorance about her parentage, thinking that Georgiana was a kind friend and Charles Grey her much older brother. Her treatment in her grandparents' household was marked by indifference. Harriet visited the Greys in 1808 and was miserable at what she saw: 'Eliza is a fine girl, and will, I think, be handsome; but tho' they are kind to her, it goes to my heart to see her – she is so evidently thrown into the background, and has such a look of mortification about her that it is not pleasant, yet *he* [Charles Grey] seems very fond of her.'

Georgiana did not live to see Eliza reach adulthood but she would have been happy with the result. Eliza was the most beautiful of all Georgiana's children which, combined with her sensitive and attractive nature, won her many friends. She married a tolerant and loving husband – Colonel, later General, Robert Ellice – who fell in love with her and rescued her from her life of petty drudgery.

Bess feared that her decision to accompany Georgiana had cost her and her daughter the Duke's protection. Harriet told Lady Melbourne that Bess had been 'excessively [upset] when she first came' and that Harriet had had 'very great doubts whether [Bess] would have [the] resolution to tear herself away'. But Bess was their 'security' in keeping the Duke's promise to bring Georgiana back, and Harriet believed that after the initial shock of leaving 'the natural generosity of her character, and her friendship for my sister will have the leisure to act'.

Georgiana expressed her gratitude by accompanying Bess to Aix-en-Provence to help her to persuade the dying Comte St Jules to adopt Caroline formally, thereby giving her some kind of legitimacy. Nothing survives that would explain Bess's influence with the old man or why he would consider offering his protection to her child. Nevertheless, they succeeded in making him sign a paper just before he died but at considerable cost: the only way Harriet was able to prevent Lady Spencer from fetching them herself was by admitting the truth about Caroline. They joined Lady Spencer on 9 March, having suffered the horrors of the lawlessness and general brigandage along the roads to Nice. The situation in France had worsened since their arrival in Paris in November, and the south was particularly unsafe.

Georgiana had hoped that once the baby was born and safely hidden the Duke's anger would subside and he would let her return. Five months away was already enough for Bess and she had started to hint of her longing for home. Lord Duncannon was also tired of living in hotels; furthermore his eighty-eight-year-old father was ill and wanted to make peace with his son. Even though Harriet was still weak and barely able to move on crutches Duncannon persuaded himself of her fitness to travel. However, in spite of the pain she suffered at the separation from her sons, Harriet declared that 'nothing but absolute brute force shall make me return without [Georgiana]'.

The Duke finally put an end to their speculation in April. His anger had not diminished, and Georgiana was to stay abroad until he fetched her himself. He gave Bess leave to do as she liked. Georgiana was dismayed by his harshness. At least, she implored, let her secretly visit the children. Harriet wrote Lady Melbourne that if the Duke were to let Georgiana visit the children and Harriet to stay abroad 'at least the pretence of returning to me will always save a formal separation as long as I am away'. Only Lady Spencer still hoped for an eventual reconcilement. Firm in this belief, she forbade Georgiana to risk upsetting the Duke by going home now. Georgiana's mask of determined cheerfulness slipped when she broke the news of her prolonged exile to Little Georgiana: '. . . when I am to return is now very uncertain – I hope it will be soon as I do not feel that I have strength to bear so long an absence.' 'When shall I see you all,' she wrote plaintively a month later. 'It will not be long now I trust and I beg of you dst love to make your Papa come and fetch me soon.' Lord Duncannon went home in June and did not return for six months, but Bess stayed with Georgiana.

The children were deeply upset by Georgiana's banishment. 'Mama gone, Mama gone,' Hart wailed over and over. The Duke never saw them; they remained in Devonshire House under Selina's sole care. Lady Melbourne and George and Lavinia were good about visiting them and, surprisingly, Lady Jersey often brought her own children to play. Selina, for all her peculiarities, showed a hitherto unexpressed sensitivity towards Georgiana and did her utmost to help to maintain contact with the children.

The exiles whiled away the time quite pleasantly, socializing with their French and English acquaintances. As Nice was part of the kingdom of Savoy the town was thronging with refugees from France. Georgiana had formed a plan to follow her children's lessons so that she would be able to share in whatever they were learning, and perhaps even help them. She began a course of self-improvement, learning Italian, practising her drawing and music, and studying natural science, which became very important to her in later life.

Quite by chance Georgiana discovered that Mary Graham was also in Nice. The Grahams had been abroad for several years in the vain hope that a Mediterranean climate might improve Mary's health. She was now in the final stage of consumption and beyond help. The two women had a short but emotional reunion. According to her companion Mrs Nugent, one of Mary's last conversations concerned her friendship with Georgiana: no other woman had claimed such an important part in her life. The party had moved on to Switzerland when the news of Mary's death on 26 June reached them. 'I shall never forget her,' Georgiana avowed; '. . . she thought too much of me I am sure; but I have a pride in feeling that she loved me. I wish I deserved her friendship, but the contemplation of what she was adds to one's discontent with oneself . . . how proud I feel in the certainty of her love for me – how humbled in the consciousness of deserving it so little.'

Even though many friends rallied to Georgiana's side, writing letters of support and promising to visit, she felt wretched and unworthy. Up to twenty or thirty letters arrived at each post, of which only a fraction survive. The Duke of Dorset was particularly kind to her: '*aimez moi un peu toujours*' ('always love me a little') was all he asked in return. Although he was ignorant of the true cause of

*While in exile in Lausanne, opposite, Georgiana and her entourage became the guests of Edward Gibbon, left. Gibbon once described Bess as the most seductive woman he ever knew. 'No man could withstand her,' he wrote. 'If she chose to beckon the Lord Chancellor from his Woolsack in full sight of the world, he could not resist obedience.'*

Georgiana's exile, the Prince of Wales also exhibited a rare display of loyalty. Exactly a year after her banishment he wrote to his '*best beloved friend*', that 'no circumstance in life *can ever cause any change in ye the sentiments of yt heart with wh. you have long been acquainted* . . . my ever dearest friend must be fully persuaded yt no *human event* can ever cause any alteration in my sentiments respecting her.'

People knew that a separation between the Duke and Georgiana must have taken place despite official denials, and everyone except the Cavendishes blamed the Duke for the split. The young Whig Thomas Pelham recorded that at a dinner with friends, Dudley North had complained of the Duke's 'selfishness and want of attention, and said . . . that if the Dss had been married to — or to any man who had shown her proper attention and done justice to her merits she would have been one of the most perfect women in England'.

By the time the party had reached Lausanne it had grown into a bulging caravan of English and foreign travellers. They spent the summer on Lake Geneva, at Edward Gibbon's house, enjoying the view over the valley with its silver rivers and dark green forests. The author's sedate lifestyle after retiring from politics was completely overturned by Georgiana's arrival; within days he had thrown his house open to all her guests. The two Carolines, Caroline Ponsonby and Caroline St Jules, found him fascinating and played with him as if he were a doll.

*'William Pitt Addressing the House of Commons on the French Declaration of War, 1793', above; a depiction of the execution of Marie Antoinette on 16 October 1793, opposite. 'I cannot express to you the horror I feel,' Georgiana wrote to Coutts after hearing of her friend's death. 'The impression of the Queen's death is constantly before my eyes.'*

Lord and Lady Palmerston stopped by with some friends for a few weeks, and joined the cooler enclave down by the lake, where the party had rented two houses near Gibbon's. It was through the Palmerstons that Georgiana met the scientist Sir Charles Blagden, with whom she formed a lifelong friendship. With his encouragement she became an amateur chemist and mineralogist of note, later endowing Chatsworth with a collection of stones and minerals of museum quality.

The escalation of war along France's borders in October provided Lady Spencer with the opportunity to take a short break from Bess and her artificial laugh. Switzerland was no longer deemed safe and the party decided that Harriet should go to Italy, where the warmth and relative quiet would continue to mend her health. Georgiana and Bess remained in Lausanne, still hoping the Duke would keep to his word and fetch them. The others began their tortuous journey, avoiding main roads in case they met soldiers, and fearful of going into the mountains which would be too cold for Harriet. Lady Spencer was very frightened: 'Everything in these countries is

in the greatest confusion – the whole road and every Inn full of troops marching to the frontier.' Georgiana had not seen her children for twelve months and the separation was growing ever harder for her to bear. On 30 November 1792 she wrote to Little G that 'This year has been the most painful of my life . . . when I do return to you, never leave you I hope again – it will be too great a happyness for me Dear Dear Georgiana, & it will have been purchased by many days of regret . . .'

The party travelled slowly until it reached Pisa in the new year, where Duncannon rejoined the group. George had found him much improved when he saw him in London, and though Lady Spencer knew enough to be sceptical of any lasting change, she noticed that he was behaving better towards Harriet. Georgiana and Bess caught up with them there, having waited until the last possible moment for the Duke. The French had taken control of the Savoy mountains, leaving open only the dangerous passage over St Bernard which they had to cross through snow and ice, sometimes having to resort to threats and pleading to make the servants continue the trek.

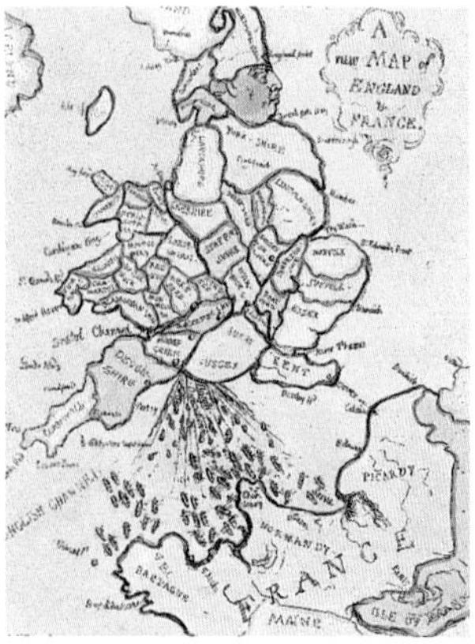


*An anti-French cartoon shows England, in the shape of George III, defecating on France.*

The news of Louis XVI's execution had reached Georgiana before she set off for Italy. Most countries, including Britain, recalled their ambassadors at this point, much to the relief of Lady Sutherland; 'you have no idea of the horror of being at Paris since the 10th,' she had written to Georgiana. Georgiana had known it was only a matter of time before they came for Marie Antoinette, but she was still unprepared for the manner of her death, which took place on 16 October 1793. 'The impression of the Queen's death is constantly before my eyes,' she wrote. The Little Po, still in exile in Switzerland, died shortly after they brought her the news.

London heard about Louis XVI's execution on 23 January 1793. The government immediately expelled the Marquis de Chauvlin, the French ambassador. In retaliation, the French declared war on Britain and urged all British patriots to rise up in favour of the ideals of the revolution. Georgiana's friends in London insisted she should come home. 'I wish most sincerely that you were in England,' wrote Lady Sutherland. 'The Duke of Dorset often talks of you *con amore* as do many other people . . . The best thing I can say of [London] is that the Dss of Gordon is *cut* almost generally.' But the Duke could only bring himself to write short, curt notes to Georgiana about nothing in particular. Devonshire House was reported to be 'dismal and dirty' without her, which at least showed that he was not cheerful at her absence.

Lord Bessborough died on 11 March 1793, aged eighty-nine. As soon as he heard, Lord Duncannon, now the third Earl of Bessborough, set off for London, leaving the exiles in Naples. The city and its environs was a favourite tourist spot for English travellers on the Grand Tour. The King and Queen, and the ubiquitous Hamiltons – Sir William and Lady Hamilton – made the group extremely welcome and they were frequent guests at court. An eminent group of scientists which included Sir Joseph Banks and Sir Charles Blagden had gathered to study such phenomena as the volcanic Mount Vesuvius and they graciously made room for Georgiana at their meetings. These months were some of the happiest and most fulfilled of her life. She climbed up to the top of Mount Vesuvius to watch smoke billowing from the crater, took boat trips around the islands, and investigated the ancient ruins with her new companions.

However, she had no money or jewellery left and Coutts's patience was at an end. He had endured her pleadings and excesses for almost two years, and urged her to return some of the £20,000 she owed him. On several occasions he had even approached the Duke, who refused to talk to him. The new Lord Bessborough reached London just in time to prevent Georgiana's name from appearing on a list of defaulting debtors. He and Harriet were enjoying one of their brief periods of rapprochement; he managed to control his irritation on discovering that she too was on the list.

Georgiana was beginning to give up hope when a letter from the Duke arrived on 18 May. 'Oh my G,' she wrote immediately, 'how can I express my happyness to you . . . the post arrived and your dear dearest Papa's letter telling me to return to you in the middle of the summer . . . in three months at the latest I shall be with you my Dearest children . . .' The party hastily decamped and began the long journey home. They got no further than Rome when Harriet suffered a relapse. According to Lady Palmerston, she had been well at Naples, but the travelling had brought fits of coughing and spitting blood. Harriet was not fit to travel so Lady Spencer elected to stay behind with her in Italy. Harriet was distraught at the idea of being separated from Georgiana.

Georgiana had Bess to comfort her; however, as they neared Ostend both became oppressed by fears of what the future held for them in England. Georgiana in particular felt burdened by worries and regrets. She swore that her life would be different. She would never disobey the Duke

*Lady Emma Hamilton as Ariadne, left. The Hamiltons made Georgiana and her party welcome in Naples, where they were frequent guests at court. While in exile, Georgiana befriended a number of eminent scientists and pursued studies in chemistry and mineralogy. She joined one group in their study of Mount Vesuvius, overleaf, climbing to the top to watch smoke billowing from the crater.*

in anything ever again: 'I return impressed with [a] very deep humility, and the wish of atonement, by doing more for another, and by perfect acquiescence in all *his* intentions and wishes.' She hoped also to benefit from 'increas'd prudence and care'.

They arrived at Ostend just as the French were forcing the Duke of York's army to retreat. Having escaped from besieged Maastricht, risking the bombardment as they crept through its streets, Georgiana and Bess ignored warnings to turn back. There was not a single space on any of the boats leaving the port. Fortunately, in the midst of the general panic Georgiana came across a friend, Lord Wicklow, just as he was heading for his pleasure boat. He agreed to squeeze them on to his little yacht. Some English refugees rushed up and begged to be allowed on but there was nothing they could do, and the boat pulled away from the stragglers who stood forlornly on the quayside as the city burned behind them.

1794–1796

# Return

*Lord Egremont's superb mansion in Piccadilly . . . is sold to Mr Mills, of Yorkshire for the sum as is said, of £16,000. The tenanting of this mansion and of Devonshire House, with the completion of Mr Drummond's and Mr Crauford's [sic], will restore, in the ensuing spring, some of the former splendor of Piccadilly.*

LONDON CHRONICLE, 2–4 JANUARY 1794

THE DUKE WAS WAITING at Dartford with the children to greet Georgiana and Bess. 'I have seen them, I have seen them,' Georgiana wrote to Lady Spencer after the reunion. 'Georgiana is very handsome . . . Harryo is still fat, but with the whitest complexion . . . Hartington is very pretty, but very cruel to me. He will not look at me or speak to me, tho' he kiss'd me a little at night . . . The Duke has the gout but looks pretty well. There was never anything equal to the attention I have met with from him – to the generosity and kindness.' He had surprised her with a smart new carriage. When they reached Devonshire House on 18 September 1793, the entire household was waiting in the courtyard. 'I never knew anything so touching as the reception of the servants,' Georgiana recorded. She admitted she was 'so happy and so anxious'.

Georgiana's two-year separation from the children had affected them badly. She was heartbroken to find that ten-year-old Little G had no self-confidence. Georgiana wrote, 'she never would let me out of her sight could she help it and today she told me I did not know all her faults.' Little G had developed a morbid religious sensibility which made her dwell relentlessly on her sins, real and imagined. Eight-year-old Harryo had become reserved and prickly towards other people. She was also less pretty than her sister, being rather short and plump.

Yet Harryo seemed to have suffered the least, while Hart, now three and a half, had suffered the most. He did not recognize his mother – indeed he screamed whenever Georgiana tried to hold him. He had been so deprived of maternal affection that he associated physical contact with smacks and cold baths. For months he resisted all Georgiana's entreaties to let her touch him. The full reason for his behaviour did not emerge until later: he was almost deaf – an infection had destroyed most of his hearing. The sweet-natured infant of Georgiana's memory had turned into a furious toddler who kicked and bit anyone who came near. The fact that he had caught the infection while under Selina's care added to the tensions between the two women.

The Duke was also marked by the past two years; the pain from his gout, added to a natural tendency to hypochondria, had reduced him to an invalid. Georgiana had made a conscious decision regarding the Duke, and he was pleased to see that he was now her first priority. 'As it is I never go out,' she wrote on 30 September to Lady Spencer, 'but receive 3 or 4 men of the Duke's acquaintance who sit with him and when he is tired come into my room . . . I am impatient to be with the children whom I scarcely leave all day.'

Initially at least, Grey was keen for them to resume their relationship. But Georgiana refused to bend to Grey's demands, even though her love for him had not diminished. Her sacrifice helped to smooth away any lingering bitterness in the Duke, who, for his part, remained angry with Bess for leaving him and taking Caroline St Jules. They resumed their affair but he no longer loved her with the same ardour, nor did he trust her. Although Georgiana would never have allowed Bess to move out of Devonshire House, Bess left nothing to chance, and she sought out the Duke of Richmond, just in case.

When Georgiana finally ventured into society her re-entry was quiet and subdued. The *Morning Post* reported that Lady Melbourne had held a dinner in her honour; after that there was little about Georgiana in the press. Her first presentation at court confirmed the change. This time, she deliberately wore something sober and unremarkable. She knew it would be foolish to pretend she was still the leader of the *ton*.

Georgiana's two-year absence made it easier for her to retire gracefully. She also had little choice – in addition to the rumours about her exile, she was known to be bankrupt, and her banishment had only added to her debts. The Duke was helping to clear some of them, but as usual he could never be brought to sign anything and Georgiana was too frightened to remind him. A return to her old way of life would also expose her to the temptation of gambling. Paradoxically, Georgiana had been free of the urge to gamble during her exile; she had been preoccupied by other interests, especially her scientific studies. Even at Naples, where the opportunity to gamble was everywhere, Georgiana preferred to spend her time at Father Patrini's house, the gathering place for visiting scientists. On her return to London she continued to pursue her new interests. On 23 October Lady Sutherland described Georgiana's routine to Lady Stafford: 'the Duke has got the gout, & the Dss is "at home" every night at 12 o'clock, afterwards she sits with him till 3. She is busy studying *Chemistry*, and goes out little, she is going this morning to a chemical lecture.'

Politics was now a source of much grief to her; the Whigs were hated by the King, despised by the government, and mistrusted by the whole country. Grey, Sheridan and some of the younger Foxites had set up a radical political reform group called 'The Association of the Friends of the People'. Despite his misgivings, Fox was unable to stop them. He was no democrat and advocated political reform as the only means of reducing the power of the crown. Yet Fox's ambivalence towards the Association alienated the conservative wing.

Pitt naturally capitalized on the party's troubles. He began a successful campaign to poach the most talented of the disaffected Whigs. Georgiana spent her first few months trying to heal the rifts in the party by bringing members together at small dinners at Devonshire House. But two obstacles handicapped her efforts to reunite the party: her own guilt at her disgrace, which made her unwilling to be seen too much in public, and the promise extracted by her mother while they were abroad never to meddle in politics again.

For the first time in her life Georgiana disagreed with Fox. He saw no threat in the revolution; she did. He thought England should make peace with France; she didn't. 'I by no means am an advocate for peace for I don't see how it could be made,' she told Lady Spencer on 22 October. The bickering within the party so disillusioned her that in early November she made a dramatic announcement to her mother: 'I promise you from this day, 2 November 1793, I never will say one word of politics in any way whatsoever.' Georgiana did not, of course, keep her promise. She tried to show Grey and Sheridan that their Association was harming the party.

By the summer Fox was leaning more towards the Association than the conservative faction. The Portlands fell out with Georgiana and the Duke over their continued support for Fox. The Duchess of Portland died a short time later of cancer on 3 June, and the following month her husband went over to Pitt, taking more than half the party with him. Among the defectors was George, whom Pitt appointed as First Lord of the Admiralty. Georgiana was devastated by her brother's decision. However, realizing that she would not change his mind, she wrote him a generous letter in which she absolved him of treachery to the party, saying, 'I think your reasons for coming in are the noblest and most upright.'

Devonshire House became a refuge for the eighty or so Foxites who remained – so much so that they were sometimes referred to as the 'Devonshire House party'. Many of Georgiana's closest friends, including Thomas Grenville and the Prince of Wales, stopped coming at all. (The Prince of Wales had fallen out with the Devonshires, having abandoned the Whigs, renounced Mrs Fitzherbert and agreed to marry his cousin Caroline of Brunswick, all in an effort to get the King to pay off his debts.) The Duke of Devonshire was not a supporter of the Association, nor did he agree with Fox's position that Britain should make peace with France; nevertheless his allegiance to the party remained firm.

It was some comfort to Georgiana that the Duke shared her loyalty to the party, and to Fox. But the Whig split of 1794 was a personal disaster for her. There was little or nothing for her to do now that the party had almost ceased to exist. The swift change to her status and reputation dented her self-confidence. Georgiana was also sensitive to the conservative backlash of the 1790s against women who crossed over into 'masculine' areas. Georgiana discovered that opportunities for women to participate in politics were dependent on having a compliant husband, sufficient wealth, and a regiment of male supporters. Georgiana had difficulty in accepting the end of her political career when the Whig party dissolved.

The 1780s had been a decade of extraordinary freedom for women, and not only in the political sphere. During the American War of Independence newspaper reports of women who disguised themselves as men in order to fight were not uncommon, and their patriotism was applauded as much as their actions were derided. In contrast, during the present war women concentrated on making warm clothes for volunteers. Social commentators urged the return to a traditional society in which women knew their place.

Georgiana's new interests prevented her from sinking into inactivity. She exchanged political meetings for scientific lectures and, with the help of Sir Charles Blagden, continued to enlarge her mineral collection. Her progress gave Lady Spencer the opportunity to boast about her: '[she has] a genius for it,' she wrote in September; 'Padre Patrini, one of the first men in that line in Italy, and Sir Ch. Blagden here have both assured me . . . that the degree of knowledge the Dss has acquired and her observations were very extraordinary.' Georgiana became a patron of promising scientists just as in the old days she had been a patron of young actors. One of her notable successes was Dr Thomas Beddoes, whose Pneumatic Institute she helped to establish in 1798, resulting in the discovery of 'laughing gas'.

Harriet, now the Countess of Bessborough, joined Georgiana in her scientific studies. She had returned in September 1794 with her health almost restored, except for a lingering weakness in her legs which necessitated the use of walking sticks. When Georgiana last saw her sister she had been thin and wan; now her face glowed with a light Mediterranean tan and she radiated good spirits. Harriet had fallen in love while in Naples. The man in question was Lord Granville Leveson Gower, a twenty-year-old, who was travelling through Italy before embarking on a career in the diplomatic corps. He was clever, self-centred and extraordinarily attractive. He was politically ambitious, but also hedonistic: he gambled too much, drank too much, and was constantly falling in love. It had never been Harriet's intention to fall in love with him; but he was unabashed by Harriet's initial rebuffs and they were lovers before she departed for home.

Harriet had returned just in time to comfort Georgiana. Grey had become engaged to Mary Ponsonby, a cousin of Lord Bessborough's. The marriage followed quickly afterwards in November. For a while Georgiana was rendered almost speechless with grief. The news arrived

*George, second Earl Spencer, 1799. Georgiana's brother is wearing robes of the Order of the Garter, an honour awarded to him in 1799 in recognition of his services as First Lord of the Admiralty. Despite her promise to abstain from interfering in politics, Georgiana could not resist passing on advice and information to her brother when he was in office.*

*Georgiana's sister Harriet, after she became Lady Bessborough, left. An unhappy marriage with the disagreeable Bessborough led Harriet to have affairs with several men, including Lord Granville Leveson Gower, right, whom she 'lov'd almost to idolatry' for seventeen years and with whom she had two illegitimate children.*

*A cartoon by Gillray of a lecture given at the Royal Institution demonstrating the effects of 'laughing gas' (nitrous oxide). Georgiana helped Dr Thomas Beddoes establish his Pneumatic Institute in 1798, where the gas was later discovered.*

while she was taking the sea air at Teignmouth with Harriet, Bess and the children. Both women did their best to distract her, as did Lady Melbourne, who sent frequent letters from London.

Grey's marriage increased Georgiana's sense of isolation. The disintegration of the party, followed by Fox's retreat to St Anne's Hill, and now Grey's rejection, robbed Georgiana of her all-important role of political confidante. Without these props she had no means of expressing her own suppressed political ambition. Yet she could not imagine a life where she was not in a position to influence a powerful man. In desperation she turned all her attention to George.

Georgiana began to send him unsolicited advice and information. She could not help herself; her need to be involved – to do something important – was sometimes overwhelming, especially when she was unhappy. Writing from Teignmouth in February 1795, she described to him the condition of the fleet in nearby Torbay. She justified the breaching of her promise never to take part in anything political by saying that she was only passing on information: 'Sometimes, people may say to me what they would not venture to you and a hint may be of use.'

Georgiana stayed in the country as much she could for the rest of 1795, occupying herself with her mineral collection and writing to George whenever she had information she thought might be useful. The Duchess of Gordon had taken Georgiana's place as the leading political hostess in society, although the press still made fun of her attempts to set the fashion. Georgiana lived much more quietly than in previous years, which lost her none of her old friends and earned her many more. Lady Stafford wrote that she was pleased to see Georgiana 'living in a pleasanter way this year than usual, with a good society, & less of the nonsence that was formerly'.

Social and political disputes continued to divide the *ton*. The behaviour of the Prince of Wales had once more drawn society into opposing camps. He was flagrantly unfaithful to his new wife, Princess Caroline of Brunswick, whom he married on 8 April 1795, and humiliated her by parading Lady Jersey in public as his consort. He also bullied Caroline in a manner which did him no credit and elevated her in the eyes of the public. Lady Jersey seized every opportunity to insult the young Princess, even contriving to have herself appointed one of Caroline's Ladies of the Bedchamber.

However, by January 1796 there were whispers of a revolt. 'She has reigned with too much despotism to last long,' was Lady Spencer's opinion. 'I would wish you both to remember that she has fairly dropt you, and that there is no necessity when others drop her that you should take her up. In a good cause such a conduct is highly laudable, but surely not in a bad one.' Within less than six months of her prediction Lady Jersey was the most reviled woman in England, while Caroline was loudly applauded whenever she appeared in public.

Lady Jersey's downfall coincided with Georgiana's brief reappearance in public. In June 1796 Fox was re-elected for Westminster and his supporters carried him to Devonshire House. It was the last time the Whigs enjoyed anything that resembled a celebration. The Duke was not present to congratulate Fox on his victory, fearing that it would imply that he supported Fox's advocacy of peace. Instead, at the last minute he asked Georgiana to organize the reception herself. She did as requested but felt embarrassed lest the Lady Mary Cokes of the world should accuse her of putting herself forward without the Duke's consent. She managed the event with considerable style in spite of her reservations. Later she felt ashamed at having enjoyed herself so much and wrote a somewhat incoherent letter to George, insisting that she had not broken her promise to remain out of politics as this was 'an act of friendship to Mr Fox' and she would not have taken part except 'under the particular guidance of the Duke of Devonshire'.

The victory celebration was the last time anyone saw Georgiana for over a year.

*The Prince of Wales's marriage to Caroline of Brunswick was known to be something of a farce as he was already 'married' to Mrs Fitzherbert. He also openly kept mistresses such as the insufferable Lady Jersey. The Prince married Caroline so that the King would agree to pay off his debts.*

The JERSEY Smuggler detected; — or — Good cause for Separation
Divorcement
Marriage vows, are false as Dicers oaths.

The LOVER'S DREAM.
"A Thousand Virtues seem to lackey her. Driving far off each thing of Sin & Guilt."

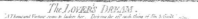

*The BRIDAL-NIGHT.*

Pubd. May 18th 1797. by H.Humphrey. 27 St. James Street.

# 1796 *Interlude*

'DEAR GEORGIANA,' Lady Spencer had written on 2 January 1796, 'your headaches so often proceed from Vexation, and your saying you are low about yourself dwells sadly upon my mind.' For the past few years Georgiana had often complained about an ache in her eyes during and immediately after one of her migraines. In July she went to bed with a headache, but the pain did not abate and after a few days her right eye had swelled to the size of an apricot. Dr Warren examined her and summoned three of the best eye surgeons in the country. The children were dispatched to Chiswick so that they would not hear their mother's screams. Harriet and Lady Spencer joined Bess's vigil by Georgiana's bedside.

Georgiana's illness and the experiments performed on her in the name of medicine were appalling even by eighteenth-century standards. There was no anaesthetic except laudanum, no appreciation of cleanliness or even a basic understanding of the origins of infections. One of the doctors almost strangled her when he tried to force the blood up to her head in the belief that the eye needed to be 'flushed' through. Harriet told her lover, 'After hearing what I did tonight I can bear anything.' On 4 August Lady Spencer described Georgiana's appearance to Selina Trimmer. The inflammation was 'so great that the eye, the eyelids and the adjacent parts were swelled to the size of your hand doubled' and 'every attempt' to lower the inflammation was in vain. An 'ulcer has formed on the top of the cornea and has burst . . .'

They darkened her room after the operations so that she would not know how badly her sight had been damaged. News of the calamity at Devonshire House spread very quickly. Most newspapers reported her illness but with little of the speculation which would have accompanied such news in previous years. Now that Georgiana was no longer the object of envy, people could sympathize sincerely.

Fortunately, Georgiana's health, although not her sight, began to recover quickly. Four weeks after the attack any light or motion still brought on spasms of pain. 'There is little hope of her eye recovering properly, she however is always in hopes and tis best it should be so,' wrote a friend sadly. Georgiana could not see herself properly for the first two months, and that too was a blessing. The children were brought to her in September and warned specifically not to stare or show any fear at her face. She was pathetically glad when they came, and their unrestrained tears enabled her to cry with them without shame.

Lady Spencer was proud of Georgiana's courage. Her harsh experiences during Eliza's birth had taught her a greater fortitude, which she needed, for the infection did not disappear for several months and each time the doctors returned they subjected her to hours of torture.

When Georgiana finally emerged from her sickroom everyone immediately noticed the changes to her personality: there was no laughter or lightness in her, she had also lost too much weight and looked much older than her thirty-nine years. The bottom half of her face was unscarred but her right eye now drooped. She tried to show interest in those around her but the illness had made her introverted. There was no reason why Georgiana could not leave the house, make little visits and receive callers, but she was too shy. Her friends gently tried to help her retrieve some semblance of her old routine, but without success.

While Georgiana retreated into darkness, Bess was enjoying an excess of good fortune. Mr Foster died unexpectedly in November, so her sons Augustus and Frederick could at last come

Price One Shilling
Pub^d March 12 1811 by Tho^s Tegg N^o 111 Cheapside
Rowlandson Del
THE ANATOMIST.


*A cartoon commenting on the brutality of doctors. Medical practices in the eighteenth century were extremely crude; Georgiana was subjected to leeches, electric shock, bleeding, and was almost choked to death in the course of her medical treatments.*

over from Ireland; her widow's jointure would make her financially independent and, most important of all, she was now free to marry again. As if on cue, the Duchess of Richmond died. 'The Dss of Richmond has at last slipt off merely out of attention to Ly E.F.,' Lady Sutherland commented sarcastically. 'It is odd that Mr Foster and she should have calculated so nearly.'

Georgiana generously invited the Foster boys to stay, adding that although she was 'half-blind' she was still anxious to meet them. They arrived on 17 December, the four resident children safely out of the way so that the reunited family could have its first moments in privacy. 'Bess is ill with happiness,' Georgiana told her mother. 'I never saw a more touching sight. They clung to poor Bess, who cried terribly. Mr Foster [Frederick] is plain but a very interesting and sensible young man. Augustus a very fine boy of 16.' Little Georgiana and Harryo, thirteen and eleven respectively, rather resented the intrusion of two shy and gauche Irishmen in their midst. No one would explain why the Fosters did not have their *own* home.

No doubt Georgiana's motives in offering to provide the Fosters with a home were prompted by genuine feeling. But the action also contained a plea to Bess that she should not reject her surrogate, Cavendish, family. Until Bess and the Duke of Richmond became conveniently widowed at the same time Bess's relationship with the Duke of Richmond had posed no threat to the stability of the *ménage à trois*. Georgiana could not accept the possibility of it coming to an end.

Bess promised to do nothing in the short term. She was not sacrificing anything by agreeing to Georgiana's request; the lovers fully intended to observe twelve months' mourning for their respective spouses to avoid accusations of over-haste. Bess was happy in the certainty that when she became the Duchess of Richmond she would at last have the life she craved.

# 1796–1799 *Isolation*

*The daughter of the Duchess of Devonshire, a sweet bud of loveliness, is to be introduced to the circle of fashion in the course of next winter. Devonshire House has of late undergone considerable improvements, and will, ere long, be ready for the reception of its noble owners.*

MORNING HERALD, 28 JUNE 1799

'MY SISTER CONTINUES MENDING,' Harriet wrote in December 1796 to her lover, Leveson Gower. 'But it was thought necessary to perform a most painful operation on her, applying caustics behind her ears and a blister to the back of her neck for four hours. I never saw anything like the agony she suffer'd, & the exertion I made to hold & soothe her brought my old complaint of spasms with great violence.' Georgiana's recovery was hindered by the exceptional cold of the winter. The whole country was suffering: animals froze to death on the hills, people went hungry and the mortality rate among the young and the old rose sharply. The Duke's uncle, Lord John Cavendish, succumbed at the age of sixty-four, dying just two weeks after Georgiana's operation.

The Duke arrived at Chatsworth in an emotional state and went immediately to Georgiana, who comforted him while he cried. The past few months had been deeply unsettling for him. At one point he had feared that he would lose his wife to illness and his mistress to a rival. He was shaken by the experience and yearned for a more stable life. Now that Georgiana was thought to be out of danger he wanted them to live as husband and wife. On 3 February 1797 Georgiana informed her mother that she had received a visit from Dr Croft. 'It has been Croft's opinion lately that I miscarry'd,' she wrote. 'I was not much past therefore tis not possible to judge but it appear'd so.'

A French force of 2,000 men had landed at Fishguard in Wales in February; the troop was easily captured. This had not been the French government's first attempt to invade. William Pitt and his war cabinet tried to maintain the appearance of calm, although in private they were frantic. Spain had switched sides in 1796 and joined France, leaving Britain without a single ally. Napoleon Bonaparte was now Commander-in-Chief and had led the French army to victory against Austria. Georgiana's brother dreaded to think how they would defend the country if Napoleon led his armies to England.

The invasion scare started a run on the banks which Pitt was only able to contain by allowing the Bank of England to suspend cash payments until the situation was restored. The people who suffered most were ordinary debtors who found themselves inundated with calls they could not oblige. Georgiana and Harriet were both caught out by the panic, and Harriet frightened Georgiana by exhibiting the same kind of hysteria that had preceded her collapse in 1791. Since then Georgiana had assumed responsibility for both their debts. 'As indeed I ought,' she explained to a cousin, 'its having been my example and folly that had drawn her in.'

When Coutts brought up the subject with Harriet instead of with Georgiana, she 'was thrown into violent hystericks and past the day very ill indeed'. Georgiana begged him never to do it again: 'All I entreat, Dr Sir, in the future, is that you wd apply to me, but oh, for God's sake never, never to her . . . the calamity of my nearly losing my eye, and, if I recover sight, being in part disfigur'd, has not render'd her state of health more prosperous or her affairs in better plight.'

The burden of carrying Harriet's debts as well as her own forced Georgiana to go to the Duke. In May she wrote over-optimistically that he seemed inclined to help and 'my difficulties [are] settled'. She was not telling the truth since the Duke did not know the full extent of the difficulties. He also put off paying the debts which she had disclosed. Georgiana was loath to press him when he was disturbed by other worries: Ireland appeared to be on the brink of civil war and, like many of the Whig grandees, the Duke still derived considerable income from his Irish estates. Georgiana told Little G that 'if any misfortune should happen in Ireland we should be very much reduc'd in our circumstances'. The events taking place in Ireland revived some of her former energy. She was convinced that a policy of cross-party co-operation over Ireland would be in the island's best interests. The Duke agreed to her request to vote in support of George in the Lords. But her brother took a different view and berated Georgiana for interfering.

It was ironic that Fox resigned from active politics just as Georgiana was beginning to emerge from her own retirement. He would keep his seat although he would no longer attend parliament. He felt that it was useless for the party to oppose Pitt, as the 'Opposition are too unpopular to have anything left to hope for, and the system of party is obsolete'. He retreated to his house in St Anne's Hill. Most of the party resented him for leaving them in the lurch. Sheridan was torn between wishing to show himself a good Foxite and taking advantage of Fox's absence in parliament. Yet he was outraged when he learned that Fox was grooming Grey to be his eventual successor.

Even Georgiana's small dinners for two or three of her friends often ended in acrimonious arguments. Sheridan still went to Devonshire House, accompanied by his new wife Hecca, a pert, talkative girl half his age (his first wife had died while Georgiana was in exile). Georgiana

330

*Previous pages: Chiswick House. Georgiana spent some of her happiest moments at Chiswick House and called it 'My earthly paradise'. She planted lilac, honeysuckle and climbing roses along the walls by her window so that her bedroom there would be filled with scent through the spring and summer.*

understood Fox's despair. He regarded Pitt's suspension of habeas corpus, his restriction of the right to free assembly, and his Treasonable Practices Act, which made it an offence to criticize the constitution, as an attack on the constitution itself. He argued that Pitt was the King's instrument, and that if the influence of the crown had not corrupted the political system, then the bills would not have been passed by parliament. By remaining in the Commons, Fox reasoned, he would be conveying a spurious respectability to a falsely governed institution.

Georgiana vigorously defended Fox against his critics both inside and outside the party. She believed that the majority of the House secretly sympathized with Fox. However, Georgiana's loyalty to Fox clouded her judgement. The House had no sympathy for him and regarded him as a demagogue with suspect views. More members of the opposition defected to the government following Fox's abandonment of politics.

Georgiana continued to write to George, passing on information and offering her insights into Irish affairs. Her commitment, as well as the quality of her comments, finally earned her a grudging respect from him. As pockets of unrest spread to other parts of Ireland she often sent George the private reports of their local agent in the hope that the relatively impartial information might be useful for cabinet discussions. The government's policy of repression struck her as counter-productive, and she argued that legal and civil discrimination against Irish Catholics would only make rebellion inevitable.

'I believe the Government is coming over to the opinion of Duke of D. and indeed all reasonable people, about granting emancipation to the Catholics,' Georgiana told her mother, meaning that George had proved receptive to her arguments. Government policy, however, did not change. Even though some ministers privately thought that the disenfranchisement of Irish Catholics was one of the chief causes of the unrest, the King would never agree to a change in the law, and they could not espouse what was in any case a Whig position.

The Duke was moved by her interest in Ireland even though he disliked anything that distracted her attention away from him. He was in continual pain from his gout and he expected Georgiana to act as his nurse. She was kind towards him and they were more receptive to each other now than at any time past. His habitual reserve with her gradually faded and, after two decades of marriage, they managed to forgive and accept one another. Bess rarely accompanied them to Chatsworth any more. She preferred to remain at Devonshire House, holding soirées of her own which she would describe in chatty letters to Georgiana. In December 1797 Lady Spencer went to stay with Georgiana and the Duke at Hardwick. The scenes she had witnessed made her hope that Bess's marriage would take place soon, as she attributed the happy family atmosphere to Bess's absence.

Georgiana's life had indeed changed. It proceeded at a slower and more gentle rhythm. Before, she had lived in a 'perpetual hurry', always surrounded by people. When the remnants of the Devonshire House Circle visited her now they often found her indulging her considerable creative talents, and with the Duke's acquiescence she amused herself by refurbishing their houses. Chiswick House received the most attention. Georgiana spent some of her happiest moments at Chiswick, calling it 'My earthly paradise'.

Georgiana also invited Charles Grey and his wife to Devonshire House. Incredibly, Mary had no knowledge of the love affair or Eliza. She had no notion why Georgiana should make such an effort to know her but the friendship which developed was genuine on Mary's part. Georgiana's motives were obviously mixed in the beginning, and were almost certainly driven by a desire to be close to Grey. Nevertheless her letters to Mary breathe unfeigned warmth, and in some way, Mary's affection compensated Georgiana for the loss of Grey's. Their first child, Louisa, also became the recipient of Georgiana's particular regard. This was not lost on Grey. In time the relationship between the two women enabled Georgiana and Grey to achieve their own private rapprochement.

Georgiana's period of reflection was cut short in May 1798 by the long-anticipated uprising in Ireland. She blamed the government for 'not consulting enough with the great Irish Lords', meaning the Whigs. Georgiana's Whig principles guided her thoughts; the rebels had to be contained but she was fervently opposed to the use of executions and terror to cow the Catholic population. 'I think the mode of torturing to extract confession so disgraceful and horrid that were it sure of saving Ireland I should deprecate it,' she wrote. She heartily disagreed with the 'indiscriminate manner in which our troops have burnt villages, etc.' and argued that 'We who receive the produce of the labour of the Irish and whose tenants still call the D. of D. their father must feel that this mode of conquest is but a bad [decision] . . .'

Lord Camden, the Lord Lieutenant of Ireland, resigned in June and Lord Cornwallis was dispatched with the greatest urgency to take his place. Georgiana decided that this was the moment for the Duke to make a statement in the House of Lords. The absentee landlords, Georgiana reasoned, were the people most affected by the uprising; it was up to them to reassure their tenants in Ireland and to make it clear to the government that repression was neither desirable nor practical. After much prodding by Georgiana and the other Whig magnates the Duke agreed to speak in support of an inquiry into the state of Ireland. His speech was short, lasting for less than half an hour, perhaps on account of his being 'sadly nervous and frightened', and simply reiterated the Whig view that the government should be conciliatory but firm. Georgiana, however, regarded the occasion as one of the greatest triumphs of her life.

Cornwallis stopped the rebellion without resorting to the destruction and bloodshed that Georgiana and the Duke had feared. The danger was over. For Georgiana, the crisis in Ireland had been a lesson in political independence; instead of taking her cue from Fox, who refused to get involved, she had acted on her own initiative. It was ironic that the demise of the Whig party had, in part, solved her dilemma about showing a masculine interest in politics. Georgiana considered the Irish question to be above politics. She was not guilty of female impropriety, in her view, so long as the beneficiary was the country.

In October, the threat of an imminent French invasion was removed by news of Nelson's dramatic victory at the Battle of the Nile. This was the first major British success in six years. Britain now controlled the Mediterranean while Bonaparte's army remained stranded in Egypt. 'We intend all of us to wear laurels on our heads at the public day,' Georgiana wrote on 8 October. 'I wish to God Buonaparte would do the only thing I think he can do now, surrender himself and his troops to so great and generous a foe [Nelson].'

Georgiana still had bouts of depression, however, and so disliked the idea of people looking at her that she contemplated wearing a mask. 'I am sorry to say that I grow more shy ev'ry day and hate going anywhere except to my own boxes at the play and opera,' she told Lady Spencer. 'I have not seen Ly Sutherland these 3 months, and ev'ry day makes me worse, I think.' However, she was perhaps overly sensitive about her appearance and was by no means ugly: indeed she was not so unattractive as to prevent Sir Philip Francis from falling in love with her.

The sixty-year-old Whig politician paid a visit to Chatsworth in the autumn. Francis was a clever man whose rationality was subservient to a highly emotional temperament. He had sudden and

Georgiana Countess Spencer
Daughter of Stephen Poyntz Esq.

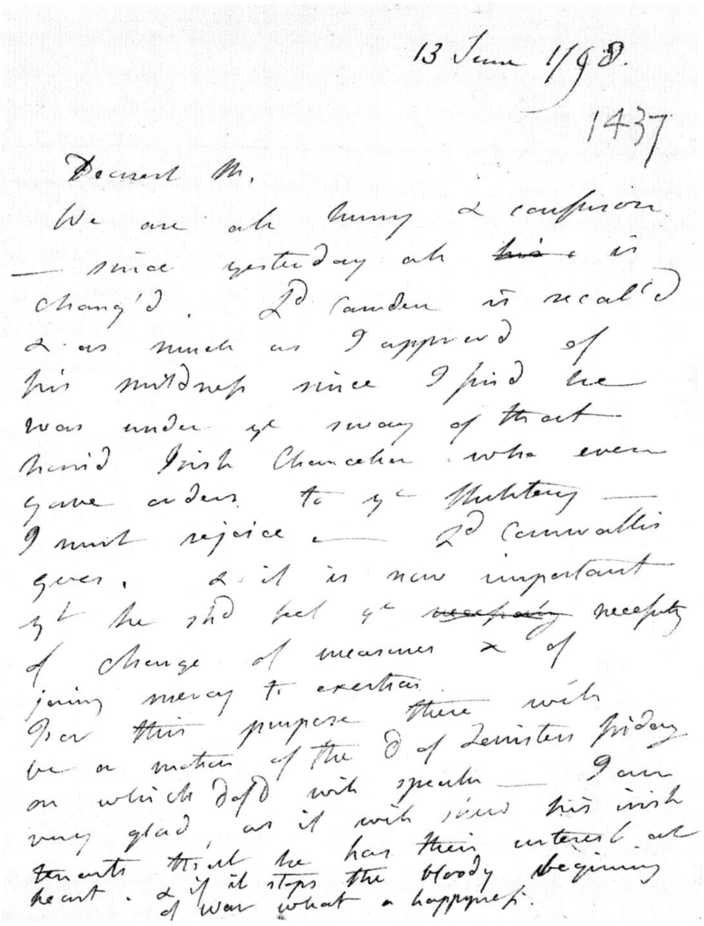
13 June 1798.

1437

Dearest M.

We are all hurry & confusion — since yesterday all ~~his~~ is chang'd. Ld Camden is recall'd & as much as I approved of his mildness since I find he was under ye sway of that horrid Irish Chancellor who even gave orders to ye Military — I must rejoice — Ld Cornwallis goes, & it is now important yt he shd feel ye ~~necessity~~ necessity of change of measures & of joining mercy to exertion. For this purpose there will be a motion of the D of Leinsters friday on which D of D will speak — I am very glad as it will shew his Irish tenants that he has their interest at heart. & if it stops the bloody beginning of war what a happiness.

*A portrait of Lady Spencer, left, shows her in the severe dress she adopted in later years; this letter from Georgiana to her mother, above, is from among the vast correspondence they shared.*

*One of many cartoons accusing Fox of being a Jacobin and a potential traitor to the king.*

strong passions, such as the one which seized him for Georgiana now. Francis wrote to Georgiana that, 'You talk of the shortness of our acquaintance, why, then,' he urged, 'if all this be not mere moonshine, and if we are really and seriously to be friends, we have no time to lose.'

He had not expected to fall in love again at his age but Francis was not ashamed to confess that he had always admired Georgiana from afar: 'The fact, however, is that I have known you many years, and long before the date of our acquaintance. It is true I saw you at a great distance, and as a bird of passage. The planet passed by, and knew nothing of, the poor astronomer who watched her motions and waited for transit. Hereafter, I hope, you will not insist on my seeing you through a telescope . . . I feel like gummed velvet, and wish I could hate you for half an hour, that I might cut you into a thousand little stars, and live under the canopy.'

Georgiana was at first more frightened by her own feelings than by the strength of his. Gradually she felt more secure in expressing her thoughts, and Francis was delighted and flattered that she was prepared to take him into her confidence. An obsessive politician himself, he enjoyed nothing more than a dispute with Georgiana over the future of Whig politics.

There is no record of how or when the correspondence ended; someone destroyed the rest of their letters. Evidence suggests that their relationship cooled after a while, although its effects were beneficial and long-lasting. Her confidence had returned and she began to venture out again in public. Little G was now seventeen, only a few months away from her presentation at court, and society mothers were extremely anxious to invite them both to their parties. Georgiana cautiously accepted a few invitations and was touched by the kindness she encountered. 'I am overpower'd by the court all these great ladies pay me,' she wrote, half pleased and half in jest.

*Sir Philip Francis fell in love with Georgiana in 1798 when he was sixty and Georgiana, at forty-one, had suffered through her long exile and painful treatments on her eye. 'I feel like gummed velvet,' he wrote to her, 'and wish I could hate you for half an hour, that I might cut you into a thousand little stars, and live under the canopy.'*

Georgiana's relationship with all three children had improved considerably during the past two years. Hart had started at Harrow, and the experience of living with other boys was making him less temperamental and more outgoing. Harryo was, in Georgiana's opinion, turning into 'a very clever nice girl, but I do not guess what she will be as to person, however I should not despair – I remember how many people us'd to run down my poor G – and now the same people are puffing her too much.' Georgiana was closest to Little G. '[You are] my dear and chosen little friend,' she told her, 'for such you would have been to me had I not had the happyness of being your mother.' Despite their contrasting temperaments – Little G was still quiet and shy – they understood each other and shared many interests, particularly a love of books. Georgiana treasured Little G's company so greatly that she could never bear to say a harsh word towards her.

But there was one subject which divided Georgiana from her children, and that was Bess. None of the Cavendish children liked her even though they accepted Caroline St Jules and Clifford. Their view of Bess was coloured by Lady Spencer's and Selina's antipathy, but their dislike needed no extra encouragement. They thought her silly and affected and, in the way of children, they could sense Bess's ambivalence towards their mother. 'My mind was early opened to Lady Elizabeth's character,' Harryo wrote many years later, 'unparalleled I do believe for want of principle and delicacy, and more perverted than deceitful, for I really believe she hardly herself knows the difference between right and wrong now. Circumstances have altered her conduct and situation at different times but she has invariably been what even [as] a child I understood and despised.' Both Harriet's and Georgiana's children enjoyed tormenting Bess, although Caroline St Jules never joined them.

Georgiana could not properly explain Bess's place in the household without going into embarrassing details. But she tried to show her children that she loved Bess and trusted her

*Portrait of Elizabeth, Lady Webster, later Lady Holland, 1795. Lady Holland hoped to usurp Georgiana's place and make Holland House the centre of the Whig universe but she had neither Georgiana's popularity nor her experience.*

implicitly. The fact that the Duke of Richmond had still not proposed to Bess made Georgiana sad for her, knowing that she had staked her future on the marriage. Georgiana, Harriet and Bess had been waiting since 1797 for him to formalize the relationship, and at various times, when an announcement seemed imminent, said their goodbyes and exchanged their fond reminiscences.

The Duke of Richmond's hesitation became an embarrassment to Bess. Not only did it highlight the objections of his family, it reminded people of Bess's history. There was much conjecture at the delay: Lady Holland, whose elopement with Lord Holland gave her no right to comment on Bess's morals, thought it a wonderful joke. 'He is always talking and writing as if he intended to marry her, and yet the marriage is not more advanced than it was two years ago,' she wrote in her diary on 26 March 1799. When Bess brought up the subject of their marriage the Duke's answers were reassuring and yet equivocal, leaving her with little alternative but to wait until he made up his mind.

Bess's frustration with her own life was increased by her jealousy of Georgiana. There was as yet, however, no real cause for her to worry. The Duke of Richmond still showed every sign of proposing, and Georgiana still suffered from many handicaps, not least her debts. Periodically she would have a crisis – a call for repayment or trouble from an angry creditor – and she would beg her weary friends and family for further assistance. In April 1799, after another of her dramatic appeals for money, Lady Spencer wrote that 'She assures me there is no more owing (but alas I know not how to rely upon her).' Georgiana had sworn she had confessed all her debts to the

Duke after her return from exile; although everyone wanted to believe her they suspected she was concealing the truth. 'She is and always will be imprudent in the highest degree,' Lady Spencer was forced to admit, 'but I trust in God she is not intentionally dishonest.'

However, Georgiana often enjoyed long periods of calm. She grew less reluctant to receive visitors and resumed the practice of holding select dinners for the Whigs who still attended parliament. Charles Grey once again stopped by every evening to discuss the day's events in the Commons. When Sheridan began work on a tragedy called *Pizarro*, adapted from the highly successful play by Kotzebue, *Die Spanier in Peru*, he invited Georgiana to contribute a song. It opened on 24 May, ran for an unprecedented thirty-one nights and sold more than 30,000 copies.

She followed up her collaboration with Sheridan by preparing one of her poems for publication. She had started 'The Passage of the Mountain of St Gothard', which describes her homeward crossing from Italy into Switzerland, when she was still in exile. Although she wrote 'The Passage' in the form of a travel poem ('I wander where Tesino madly flows,/from cliff to cliff in foaming eddies tossed') it contained a veiled apology to her children for leaving them. 'Italy, farewell!' Georgiana wrote in the first stanza. 'To thee a parent, sister I consign . . . Whilst every step conducts me nearer home.'

Once Georgiana was satisfied with 'The Passage' she distributed a number of copies to her friends and family, telling them she would add her own illustrations later. Somehow a printer got hold of one of the copies and a pirate edition appeared in the *Morning Chronicle*, full of mistakes and misprints which horrified and embarrassed Georgiana. However, the poem was an immediate success, far outselling a prose work of hers entitled 'Memorandums of the Face of the Country in Switzerland'. (In 1802 the Abbé Delille translated 'The Passage' into French; Italian and German translations followed, all of which earned Georgiana considerable plaudits, but no money.)

Meanwhile Georgiana and Little G had become inseparable. Georgiana wanted Little G's coming out to be a success and she forced herself to chaperone her daughter to every party. The Devonshires held a magnificent ball and supper at Devonshire House to mark her first season. The household clattered with activity in the days before the ball. No one turned down Georgiana's invitation. Some came out of curiosity, others out of loyalty, and a few out of nostalgia; all were surprised by the ease with which she had recaptured the atmosphere of Devonshire House parties. According to the *Morning Herald* the ball was a triumph.

Georgiana's re-entry into society coincided with the Prince of Wales's return to respectability after his notorious affair with Lady Jersey. Freed from Lady Jersey's influence, the Prince was anxious to be re-admitted into the Devonshire House Circle. His friendship with Georgiana resumed at the level of its former intimacy, as if there had never been a breach. The *Morning Herald* announced their reconciliation in September 1799, with a report of their joint trip to the theatre: 'On the entrance of his Royal Highness, *God Save the King*, was loudly called for and sang, amidst the reiterated plaudits of the whole audience, who seemed to feel an ecstatic pride in the presence of their Prince.'

Those who knew Georgiana well noticed how she had gained in self-assurance since her illness: she was more confident not only about her appearance but also about her intellectual capabilities. She stopped apologizing for her enthusiasm for politics and made no attempt to disguise her interest in Napoleon's progress. The troubles in Ireland, and the war against France in general, had persuaded her that she could explore the possibilities of a political life outside the party. As it was, the Whigs were split and Georgiana had no role to play.

# Georgiana Redux

## 1800–1806

# *Georgiana Redux* 1800–1801

*Busy preparations are on foot for a course of splendid galas, next month, in the higher circles of fashion: the Duchesses of Devon, Rutland, and Gordon are to take the lead.*

MORNING HERALD, 23 APRIL 1800

GEORGIANA'S FIRST FEW DAYS of the new century were troubled. She was again hunted by creditors and all she had managed to raise was £50 from George. The Duke of Bedford rescued her, offering a loan of £6,000: 'I think it is not more than you may, in the opinion of the most scrupulous, accept from a friend,' he wrote. Knowing her well, however, he insisted on a strict timetable for repayment and even drew up a 'memorandum of the transaction between us that there may be no possible mistake'. The memorandum was, of course, useless as a legal document and if he believed that its existence would guarantee the safety of his money then he did not know Georgiana well at all.

Georgiana was not alone in her difficulties. For Harriet and Lord Bessborough the situation was already hopeless. They had never managed to curtail their expenses and the combination of his and Harriet's previous gambling debts had bankrupted them. They had turned to the Duke in November 1799, and the family, principally the Duke, Lord Frederick Cavendish and Lord Fitzwilliam, agreed to contribute £10,000 each into a trust which would be administered on the Bessboroughs' behalf. However, this plan foundered when Harriet's husband objected at being given no say in the trust.

The Duke became so exasperated with his cousin that he threatened to give him nothing. Bessborough eventually agreed to an arrangement which gave him a life interest in his estate in Roehampton. After his death it would belong to Coutts. The ever-generous Duke of Bedford submitted to being appointed one of the trustees. The new arrangement freed Georgiana from the additional burden of Harriet's debts; 'my heart is full of gratitude for the ameliorated prospect before me,' she told Lady Spencer on 22 January, adding an unnecessary falsehood: 'By May I shall be clear of any debt.'

Georgiana began writing seriously again after the Duke of Bedford's timely intervention. In April she ruefully confessed to George 'that I am guilty of having wrote the epilogue to "de Montfort" to be spoken by Mrs Siddons tomorrow'. She started work on a religious drama and a few months later collaborated with Harriet on a tragedy.

However, Georgiana was mainly preoccupied with Little G's preparation for her presentation at court on 22 May. Lady Spencer had provided her daughter with the best masters in London and her training had been impeccable. Georgiana was determined to do the same for Little G. The rituals of a court presentation were extremely demanding: grace and a dignified ease were paramount – the poor execution of a curtsy could ruin a girl's first season. Unfortunately Little G had not inherited her mother's poise or co-ordination. Georgiana was worried by her tendency to keep her head down and she seemed unable to effect the same curtsy twice.

By every account Little G's court dress was a dramatic success: white crêpe trimmed with blonde (a form of silk lace), cords and tassels. She wore the Cavendish diamonds and, importantly in Georgiana's opinion, no rouge. Devonshire House was in a twitter of excitement on the morning of the twenty-second. The footmen were dressed in special liveries, and Harryo and Caroline

*Previous pages: A portrait of a mature Georgiana by Angelica Kauffmann.*

*Opposite: Francis Russell, fifth Duke of Bedford. Unlike many of Georgiana's friends who lent her money, the Duke of Bedford was shocked when she failed to repay him and ended their friendship. He courted Little G, but did not propose, and compounded the sin by later courting the daughter of the Duchess of Gordon.*

watched from the stairs as bouquets arrived hourly from well-wishers. All the family were there, except Lady Spencer. Bess's presence, and the fear that the weight of memories would make her cry, caused her to stay away.

The Poyntzes, Cavendishes and Spencers, including the Duchess of Marlborough and the Marchioness of Blandford, accompanied the Devonshires to court in a grand statement of family pride and loyalty. The *London Chronicle* reported that it was the most crowded Drawing Room since the Regency crisis. Lady Jerningham described the scene to her daughter: 'we went to the Drawing Room at three o'clock, and remained standing till six, in the most violent crowd I ever yet saw: the three Rooms filled with hoops, swords, and each step . . . bringing danger of suffocation.' Georgiana reported the day as a success 'beyond my warmest hopes'. Little G remembered to keep her head up, and the Queen was extremely civil, which was remarkable considering that only three years earlier she had banned all opposition ladies from appearing at court.

A few days later Georgiana gave the first of a series of balls following Little G's presentation and was pleased to note how many compliments her daughter received for her unpretentious manner and elegant dancing. Georgiana unobtrusively assessed her dancing partners for signs of interest. Two stood out by the end of the first evening: the Duke of Bedford and Lord Morpeth. At thirty-five Bedford was certainly not too old for Little G, although he had several illegitimate children and currently enjoyed two mistresses – Lady Melbourne and a Mrs Palmer. The Duke's liaisons aside, his wealth, Whig credentials and generosity recommended him to Georgiana. Morpeth she was not so sure about even though he too was a personal friend. He was only twenty-seven, which was in his favour, but this was offset by his manner, which Georgiana sometimes found a little pompous. 'I believe he has many great qualities and would make a woman happy,' she decided; 'he is rather too *cold* for [Little G].' He had been linked with several women, including Lady Jersey.

While Georgiana waited for one of the men to reveal his intentions, she took Little G around London. She wrote contentedly to Lady Spencer, 'She is so much admired – it is said they are glad that at last a civil Duchess's daughter is come out.' The *ton* hailed each of her parties as triumphs and they received fulsome plaudits in the newspapers. Georgiana was determined not to allow politics to interfere with Little G's coming out and no one was excluded from the guest list. In June she gave a supper ball for 1,000 people for which she garlanded all the rooms in the house with real and paper roses.

The season was over by July and Georgiana gave her final, and most lavish entertainment – a breakfast at Chiswick. Lady Jerningham attended and recorded that there were 'Several Bands of Musick' as well as a 'Temple which was . . . prettily decorated with flowers'. There were also 'about 20 covers'. After the eating and drinking was finished, 'the young ladies danced on the Green. Lady Georgiana Cavendish (a tall, Gawkey, fair Girl, with her head poked out and her mouth open) dances however very well . . .'

In July Georgiana and her family removed to Bognor Regis for the summer. Georgiana was exhausted but extremely satisfied with her work. There were only a few irritants to mar her enjoyment. Mrs Fitzherbert's reappearance was one of them. The Prince had humbly asked her forgiveness and on 16 June she gave a public breakfast to mark her return to society as his 'wife'. The *ton* had no choice but to include her whenever the Prince was invited.

It was a relief to Georgiana to be by the sea, out of reach of society. Her letters for these weeks have disappeared, probably because Harriet was nine months pregnant with Leveson Gower's child and waiting to come to term. It is extraordinary that they managed to keep the pregnancy a secret. This time there was no anonymous letter to Lord Bessborough, no exposure or disgrace. Harriet simply remained out of the way for a time. The baby was a girl, and Harriette Stewart, as she was named, was farmed out to foster parents. Like Georgiana with Eliza, Harriet tried to keep in contact with her by acting as the girl's godmother.

The family went to Chatsworth in the autumn so that Little G would be able to mix with her possible suitors in a more relaxed setting. Little G gave no indication that she had a preference for anyone and Georgiana, remembering how her own parents had influenced Harriet and herself without meaning to, did not want to press her. Morpeth showed his hand in November but the courtship proved to be awkward since Little G was so shy.

Just before Christmas Morpeth finally had the courage to propose and was accepted. Georgiana still had reservations over his total disregard for religion and his penchant for gambling. But Little G seemed genuinely happy and Morpeth was not a bad match. Lady Spencer also approved: 'Indeed,' she told George, 'I see much to hope and think well of this marriage.' The Duke of Devonshire showed his pleasure with a generous settlement of £30,000 on Little G, and arranged for her to have £1,500 a year pin money. Morpeth had only a small allowance. Georgiana, who had learned a good deal about the psychology of money over the years, advised the Duke not to be too generous in the beginning because it would circumscribe his actions later when, for example, Morpeth entered parliament and required more help.

Charles and Mary Grey were among the first people to be informed by Georgiana. The Prince of Wales was particularly effusive when he heard the news, calling Georgiana 'my dear sister', and referring to the widespread joy in 'the numerous circles in which you are so beloved'.

Everyone else was sincere or, as in Bess's case, sincerely trying to be sincere. 'I have ever lov'd you so much as if you were mine,' she declared. What she said was no doubt true but it was not the whole truth. Her own Caroline, handicapped by her illegitimacy, could never hope to make such an illustrious marriage. She would never be presented at court, never have her 'year' like Georgiana's daughters. Bess was also miserable waiting for the Duke of Richmond to propose and was beginning to wonder if she were wasting the residue of her youth on a worthless venture.

Bess soon received news that Lady Bristol had died. She and her mother had been growing apart for some time and Bess had not even known she was ill, but she took to her bed and produced alarming physical symptoms of grief. Two weeks later Bess tried to force Richmond into action by announcing that she had decided to quit England on account of her mother's death. Richmond gave no sign that he even recognized the hint.

Bess was, therefore, in some desperation when she offered to stay behind and nurse the Duke of Devonshire while Georgiana took Little G down to London to buy her trousseau. The marriage was set for 21 March. Bess's 'altruism' set people talking at once. It was a clear threat to Richmond that if he did not propose soon he would find himself replaced by the Duke.

Georgiana had become more open, more approachable. Devonshire House was filled with callers again, as in former times, although Georgiana could not always receive them: her health had never properly recovered since the infection in 1796. The sight in her remaining eye was poor and she was becoming frail, continually subject to coughs, colds, migraines and intestinal troubles. Dr Erasmus Darwin, the grandfather of Charles, recommended the dubious practice of submitting Georgiana to powerful electric shocks, using primitive electrodes placed above the temples as a way of 'galvanizing' her eye.

*Kedleston Hall, design for a painted Breakfast Room by Robert Adam, 1768, left; design of the Great Drawing Room at Montagu House, 1782, below; the Great Staircase at Carlton House, the home of the Prince of Wales, right. What the members of the* ton *didn't spend on gambling they put into updating the interiors of their houses. The Georgians were passionate about interior decoration. Robert Adam's use of neoclassical detailing was particularly popular.*

TREASURY
G R Orders for keeping all improper Persons out of the Public Offices
Success in the East
Justice of Emancipating Catholics
Gillray, del. 1801
INTEGRITY retiring from Office! ___
Men, in conscious Virtue bold!
Who dare their Honest purpose hold.
Nor heed the Mob's tumultuous cries:
And the vile rage of Jacobins ___ despise.

*A Gillray cartoon depicting the unanimous resignation of William Pitt's cabinet on 18 February 1801. A dignified Pitt is followed by Dundas and Grenville at right, while the unruly opposition under Sheridan are at left.*

Sometimes the pain in her eye forced her to dictate letters. But she did not allow her disability to interfere with her voluminous correspondence. There had been important developments since the crushing of the Irish rebellion and Napoleon's defeat in Egypt. On 9 November Napoleon seized power from the Directory in a *coup d'état.* Most people, both inside and outside France, hoped his arrival signalled the end of the revolution and the return of calmer times.

Napoleon certainly encouraged the thought: in December he made a personal offer of peace to each of France's enemies. However, he had broken every treaty he had ever made, so on 3 February 1800 William Pitt announced to the House of Commons that the government was determined to pursue the war. The House voted on the issue and Pitt won decisively. The debate brought Fox out of his retirement. He made one of his most impassioned speeches, pointing to the intransigence of a government that was not even prepared to consider peace. Fox's view met with approval outside parliament. People were tired of the war, and expressing a desire for peace was no longer considered treacherous talk. The Whig Club meetings reached double figures again.

As Britain had rejected his offer of peace Napoleon went on the offensive. Within a few months he had reconquered Italy, pressured the Russians into becoming his allies and obliterated the Austrian army at Hohenlinden. Spain and the Baltic powers, Denmark and Sweden, also ranged themselves against Britain. The threat that a rebellious Ireland posed to British security convinced Pitt that the two countries had to become united under a single government. Pitt also wanted emancipation for Irish Catholics, seeing it as the only guarantee against civil war. The Devonshires supported Catholic emancipation but could not see the point of a Union because of the destabilizing effect it would have on the existing hierarchy. Pitt won. The Union officially took place on 1 January 1801, and 100 Irish MPs were added to the House of Commons, bringing the total number to 658.

Five weeks later, on 5 February 1801, to the astonishment of the nation, Pitt stepped down from office, ostensibly over the King's refusal to grant Catholic emancipation. He felt it would be national suicide to leave in Ireland a permanent underclass of disenfranchised and disaffected Catholics. The King, on the other hand, considered any weakening of the Test and Corporation Acts which enshrined the Anglican state as a betrayal of his Coronation Oath. He could not in good conscience allow Catholics to be admitted into parliament or to enjoy any other political rights without 'overturning the fabric of the Glorious Revolution'. After seventeen years of uninterrupted and unchallenged rule no one dreamt that Pitt could just walk away.

There were, of course, several contributing factors to Pitt's resignation. He was exhausted, crippled with gout, demoralized by the lack of progress in the war, fed up with the infighting of his cabinet and tired of having to placate George III over Britain's military setbacks. But Pitt's decision was ultimately prompted when the King publicly vowed that 'I shall look at every Man as my personal Enemy, who proposes that Question [of emancipation] to me.'

# *Peace* 1801–1802

*The Duchess of Devonshire was last week much indisposed, but her friends were yesterday gratified by her re-appearance in public. In the evening her Grace attended a musical party, under her patronage, at the King's Head, for the Benefit of Mademoiselle Morelle, a celebrated performer on the harp . . . The evening went off with great éclat and was succeeded by a Ball, which continued to a late hour.*

LONDON CHRONICLE, 5–7 OCTOBER 1802

THE PRINCE OF WALES WAS PACING up and down the courtyard when Georgiana's carriage arrived at Devonshire House. She had been travelling for several days and had not heard the news of Pitt's resignation. Pitt was out but he had urged his colleagues to remain at the pleasure of the new Prime Minister, Henry Addington, the former Speaker of the House of Commons. Half the cabinet, including George, had ignored his request, but the rest remained in their places.

People could hardly believe the choice of Addington. He was a quiet, respectable nobody; perfect as the Speaker, incredible as Prime Minister. Georgiana had met him a few times at Bognor Regis and found him pleasant enough. 'I like both him and Mrs Addington very much . . . he is simple and good-natured,' she had written. His father was one of the King's physicians, and in the rarefied world of aristocratic politics no one could really accept a *doctor's* son as the King's First Minister.

From her first day back in London Georgiana began keeping a political diary; news was coming in by the hour. She was the recipient of confidences from all sides. Lord Morpeth kept her informed about Pitt's circle of friends, George about the ex-members of the cabinet, Fox and Grey about the Whigs, and the Prince of Wales about his own plans. What hope could there be for Addington's administration, she wondered, 'with all the talents of opposition on one side against it and the talents of this administration at least neutral'?

Her first concern was that the opposition should not further damage its tattered reputation by behaving rashly. Her second was for her brother's reputation, but his subsequent actions made both his sisters extremely proud. 'He crowns the most brilliant administration by the most honourable retreat,' was Georgiana's characterization of his prompt resignation. 'The country respect him and carry him to the shires . . .' Georgiana had the added satisfaction of seeing George lose his lofty, ministerial reserve as he followed her friends to Devonshire House.

There had been treachery in Pitt's cabinet: the Duke of Portland, Lord Westmorland, Lord Liverpool, and even his brother Lord Chatham had opposed Catholic emancipation. The King had sent for Addington as soon as he learnt of Pitt's intentions, although Addington was Pitt's friend and at their first meeting had actually tried to dissuade him from resigning.

Georgiana accurately perceived that Pitt's sudden resignation had fragmented party politics into a constellation of factions. It was no longer Whigs versus government but Addington versus all his enemies. The new government was in essence a coalition between former Pittites who opposed Catholic emancipation, and friends of Addington.

Everyone was waiting for Pitt's next move when the King suffered a return of his old malady on 21 February. Dr Willis was recalled to Windsor, and the Prince once more faced the possibility of a Regency. However, the King recovered after only three weeks. The Prince deliberated over whom he would choose as Prime Minister if he became Regent but had reservations about all the main contenders and was probably relieved when the restoration of the King's sanity closed the matter.

George III's recovery heralded a return to normality, of a sort, in parliament. Fox resumed his seat in the Commons, but it was not his return which received the most attention. The House held its breath the first time Pitt took his seat on the back benches. A familiar routine returned to Devonshire House as more Whigs followed Fox's example and began to attend debates. Georgiana was once more hosting political dinners for the party, and the Prince resumed his practice of consulting her on every issue, much to Mrs Fitzherbert's annoyance.

There is also circumstantial evidence that Georgiana and Grey were, if not lovers again, closer than ordinary friends. He came to Devonshire House most days while Mary Grey remained tucked away in the country with the children. He also gave her a locket containing their hair and a lock of Eliza's with the words IL M'EST FIDEL inscribed on it, and other people noticed some sort of unspoken understanding between them. But it was far from being the passionate, reckless affair it once had been. Grey couldn't quite tear himself away from Georgiana, but nor was he truly in love with her. 'Black [Grey] is now very good-natured to me,' Georgiana told Lady Melbourne, to whom she always had to play down the affair. 'But I do not see him often [alone] and I do not believe

*This cartoon portrays the government formed under Henry Addington after Pitt's resignation as unfit for the task of leadership. Georgiana condescendingly described Addington as 'simple and good-natured'.*

anybody knows I do see him.' One reason she saw less of him was because he had also taken up with Hecca, Sheridan's unpopular second wife. Mary Grey also became aware of Grey's relationship with Mrs Sheridan; in the manner of Lady Jersey, Hecca had made sure of that.

There was now a new generation of clever women and ambitious young men, and even though the old guard was still in command it would not be long before youth pushed aside old age and infirmity. Some of the younger Foxites complained with some truth that Fox was out of touch with political realities. They were encouraged by Sheridan, who wanted to capitalize on Addington's pro-peace stance to make a pact in exchange for seats in the cabinet. Fox, on the other hand, was at best neutral towards Addington – or the 'Doctor', as he was nicknamed. Notwithstanding the Prime Minister's anti-war aims, his opposition to parliamentary reform and Catholic emancipation disgusted Fox and prompted endless discussions at Devonshire House.

Addington had enough intelligence to realize that he needed to strengthen his ministry with talent from the opposition benches. Tentative offers were made to Grey and a few others such as the Duke of Bedford and Lord Moira. None of the Whigs accepted the bait.Georgiana's own views were definite on the matter. She was willing to erase eighteen years of hostility towards Pitt in order to achieve an ideal: a coalition government which combined the best talent of all sides.

She had abandoned Fox's 'influence of the crown' ideology as irrelevant to the politics of the day. She did not rate Addington's skills as a politician and saw it as the duty of the Whigs to end the

*'Proclamation of Peace at the Royal Exchange', 1802. After almost a decade of war, Britain signed the Treaty of Amiens with France on 25 March 1802. 'Peace! Peace!' Georgiana wrote to her mother.*

war; this, she believed, could only be achieved in coalition with Pitt. Regarding her own place in politics, patriotism, she repeated, gave her the right to interfere.

By October 1801 Addington had worked out a peace proposal for the French. He knew that the supporters of Pitt's administration could hardly be expected to vote against their own policies so once again he turned to the Whigs. Grey later justified his brief negotiations with Addington on the grounds that peace was more important than opposing the Doctor. But Sheridan tried to twist the episode to discredit him and a bitter and divisive quarrel erupted between the two men and their supporters.

Addington plodded on without the Whigs' help, and although they laughed at his inability to string a logical sentence together, his government remained on course. Perhaps his very dullness lay behind his success. Nevertheless Addington achieved in less than a year what had eluded Pitt for almost a decade – peace. On 25 March 1802 France and Britain concluded the Treaty of Amiens and war was officially over.

## 1802–1803 Power Struggles

*A decent regard to* female dress, *is we trust, about to be restored. In consequence of a notification on the cards of invitation, the Marchioness of Townshend's late rout was composed of persons in* full dress. *The Duchess of Devonshire has given the same precautionary hint, and the decorous example, will, it is hoped, run the* whole *line of female fashion!*

MORNING HERALD, 4 APRIL 1803

NOT EVERYONE SHARED Georgiana's enthusiastic response to the treaty ('Peace! Peace!' she wrote to her mother). Lord Grenville's party sulked because it disliked the terms, and the Whigs were gloomy because it appeared to confirm Addington's position. Bess also had little reason to celebrate; five months earlier, in October 1801, the Duke of Richmond had finally admitted that he had no intention of marrying her. After the initial shock Bess felt rage and disappointment. She knew that his decision had been partly influenced by the objections of his family. 'He must be conscious of how wrong his conduct has been to me,' Bess wrote to Lady Melbourne. 'Tho' had he not luckily for me, broke thro' my romance by showing me he had to a certain degree not only resisted but subdued his attachment to me, I might have long gone on as I did these four years.'

*Charles, third Duke of Richmond. His decision not to marry Bess – after a four-year affair during which both of their spouses had conveniently died – was at least partly influenced by his family, particularly his niece Lady Charlotte Lennox. 'Lady C L is an odious being and I should like to be certain of never seeing her again,' Bess wrote.*

Georgiana knew how her pride suffered, and tried to include Bess in as many of her activities as possible. When Morpeth's father, Lord Carlisle, invited the Devonshires to visit Little G and Morpeth at Castle Howard Georgiana made sure that Bess was one of the party. Georgiana was content in her life, not least in her happy relations with Little G and Morpeth; 'they do seem to prefer coming to me to anything,' she told her mother proudly. Consequently, she missed Little G's company when the couple left London to live with the Carlisles, as custom demanded they should until Morpeth's father died. Georgiana also derived considerable satisfaction from her writing. But she no longer sought to be in the public eye. Now, especially, she was loath to do anything that might embarrass her children.

*Lord Morpeth, above, had been linked with several women, including Lady Jersey, before he proposed to Little G in December 1800. 'I believe he has many great qualities,' Georgiana said of him, '[but] he is rather too* cold *for [Little G].' Little G and Morpeth went to live with his family at Castle Howard, left, after their marriage.*

Georgiana entertained regularly now and her parties always received favourable attention in the press. She also continued to be on good terms with the Duke even though their respective ailments often made them crotchety with each other. Lady Spencer felt that the Duke's tendency to morbid hypochondria placed an extra strain on Georgiana.

It was inevitable that something would interfere with Georgiana's happiness. By the end of 1801 the Duke of Bedford's money had run out and she had no means of paying him the interest on the loan. When she first hinted to him that she might default on her payments he was shocked. Georgiana had assured him that the £6,000 would clear all her debts. When he realized that no payments would be forthcoming, he was furious, thinking she had used him. Unlike so many of Georgiana's friends who shrugged their shoulders and knew better the next time she asked for money, he resolved never to speak to her again. Bedford's disavowal of their friendship, after his unwavering loyalty during her years in exile, was the first time Georgiana had ever suffered a direct rebuff for her deceitfulness. The experience finally made her realize that she could no longer live by lying and prevaricating.

Georgiana turned to religion for strength. She had always maintained her faith in God, although for most of her life religion had been a source of guilt rather than comfort to her. She went to hear her friend Dr Randolph, the Duke of York's chaplain and a regular preacher at Bath, and felt inspired by his sermons. On Christmas Day 1801 she wrote to him about her resolution to 'form some plan thro' my relations and to gain their confidence, by sacrifices in expence, etc., and then to write to all those with whom I have form'd engagements, state my case to them and see if they will be satisfied with gradual payment . . .'

She had already started to work with Coutts on the daunting process of listing and classifying her debts. It was a sad task; each one had a little story or an excuse attached. Georgiana entrusted a letter to Coutts's care, which in the event of her death he was to present to the Duke, exculpating the banker from any wrongdoing and urging her husband to take 'my character and my children's welfare into consideration'.

Georgiana wanted to tell the Duke of Bedford about her repentance, but he wouldn't see her. Shortly after writing to Dr Randolph she heard news that could not have been more unwelcome – Bedford was courting the Duchess of Gordon's youngest daughter Lady Georgiana. Reconciliation between Bedford and herself, she was certain now, would be impossible. Three weeks later the Duke of Bedford was dead, having collapsed while playing tennis.

Georgiana was distraught. 'The family mourn and D of D allows me to mourn as deeply as I chuse,' she told her mother on 8 March. 'I go in a few days with the Morpeths to Chiswick as I cannot bear the sight and commiseration of people who think they have a right to see me.' But her secret was safe; Bedford had ordered the destruction of all his papers and no one knew about the loan. Georgiana had some satisfaction in watching the Duchess of Gordon make a fool of herself by insisting that Bedford and her daughter had been officially engaged, in flat contradiction of Bedford's brother, now the sixth Duke, who claimed that his brother had never expressed any intention of marrying Lady Georgiana.

Georgiana was determined not to fail in her resolution to change. She curbed her personal expenditure and dedicated herself to organizing charity galas and fund-raisers. Something of Georgiana's former celebrity had returned and she was mobbed whenever she appeared in public. Lady Spencer was not very sympathetic: 'as to the crowds that follow you,' she wrote, 'it is a small inconvenience to anybody used to crowds as you have been.'

*The offices of Coutts and Co. at 59 Strand, London, above; 'Bills of Exchange' by Thomas Rowlandson, 1800, right. Charles James Fox was among Georgiana's gambling friends who was happy to receive a letter from Coutts offering to loan him money in order to 'extricate you from hands that are less liberal than, I* Hope, *mine are'.*

However, Georgiana was plagued by more than crowds. Everyone in the family began to receive spiteful anonymous letters, even her daughters. Harriet wrote to Leveson Gower, 'I found my Sister in a great fuss at one she had also receiv'd, very abusive of us all – Bess, K [the Duke of Devonshire], our whole Society, not omitting your Brother's wife and Lord Carlisle, but chiefly again attacking me . . .' Harriet suspected that the author was the same person behind the nasty paragraphs which appeared about them in the *Morning Post*: Sheridan. He had altered since his marriage to Hecca. Instead of being a drinker he was now a drunk, his love of melodrama had turned into a propensity for hysteria, and his humour had slipped into sarcasm and cynicism. Harriet was revolted by Sheridan now, but she had become an obsession for him. He stalked her movements and terrified her with his violent monologues. In August 1802 Sheridan barged his way into her hall. When she sent her maid to say she was out, he answered, 'I shall walk up and down before the door till she comes in.'

Georgiana longed to make a fresh start. 'I must make my future life,' she wrote to Coutts, '(if I can snatch it from blame) an eminent example of good. And how is this to be done?' No one seemed to be prepared to forget. Bess was not much help to Georgiana. All she could think about was her humiliation at the hands of the Duke of Richmond. She could not bear to live as Georgiana's dependent friend again so she chose instead to go to France. After the peace thousands of British tourists were flocking to Paris. Bess left in October 1802 with Caroline St Jules and Frederick Foster to join the sightseers. She had an excuse for being there, and for her wretchedness, since they travelled with her niece Eliza Ellice, who was dying of tuberculosis. Georgiana had wanted the whole family to accompany her but the Duke would not travel because of his gout.

Bess was not alone for long: Harriet and Lord Bessborough followed with their son Duncannon, who had recently alarmed them all by falling in love with Harryo, only to jilt her for Lady Jersey's daughter Elizabeth. Harriet declared it would kill her to have Lady Jersey as her son's mother-in-law, and the family hurriedly decamped to Paris. Morpeth and Little G, who was pregnant, also went to visit. Half of Whig society, including Fox and Mrs Armistead, the Hollands, James Hare and Robert Adair, followed. Just before his departure Charles Fox had informed his friends that he and Mrs Armistead had been secretly married for seven years. Georgiana wrote congratulating him; but 'all his friends are very angry with him', Harriet recorded. For herself, she saw nothing wrong in him formalizing a liaison of sixteen years. 'The odd thing is that people who were shock'd at the immorality of his having a mistress are still more so at that mistress having been his wife for so long.'

Georgiana was miserable at being left behind to nurse the Duke. She promised her French friends that she would come over as soon as possible, knowing the Duke would find an excuse not to go. The English visitors found Paris much changed; no money had been spent on maintaining the fabric of the city for the past ten years because of the political instability there, and the centre was run-down and dirty. Bess complained that deference among the lower orders was non-existent, although she encountered little actual hostility. She made a half-hearted attempt to socialize with the new and *ancien* nobility. She was also aware of how much Georgiana's children disliked her, and dreaded the Morpeths' arrival. Georgiana argued with Little G about Bess and succeeded in making her promise to be kind.

The letters exchanged between Georgiana and Bess show the deep bond that existed between the two women. When they wrote to each other it was in the language of parted lovers: '*My dear Bess,*' Georgiana wrote plaintively in December. '*Do you hear the voice of my heart crying to you? Do you*

*A portrait of the former courtesan Elizabeth Armistead, as Mrs Charles James Fox. Though she and Fox had had a public liaison for sixteen years, friends were shocked when in 1802 Fox announced that they had been married for seven of those. 'It don't signify, my dearest, dearest Liz,' were his last words to her.*

*feel what it is for me to be separated from you?*' In turn, when Bess was low she imagined Georgiana no longer needing her: 'don't forget,' she pleaded. 'I don't mean that, but don't accustom yourself to do without poor little me.' The reports of Georgiana's activities as the doyenne of the Whig party made her feel unwanted and insignificant. Devonshire House was regaining its former stature, and with the peace looking unsteady there was speculation that Addington's government would have to go.

Only three issues, Fox claimed, interested him now: parliamentary reform 'in some shape or other – Abolition of all Religious Tests as to Civil Matters, and Abolition of the Slave Trade'. He wrote to Georgiana, saying, 'I am more and more for complete retirement.' She did not believe him and as soon as he arrived in London arranged for him to meet her brother for an informal talk. She was certain that if they did not make the mistakes of the nineties, the old opposition and new opposition might coalesce. Georgiana spent the next few months consolidating her contacts in each of the factions by holding political dinners almost every night. Georgiana was also winning converts to the Foxite side, which had grown to almost 100 MPs since the 1802 election. Lord Morpeth, for example, renounced his former Pittite affiliation. The political landscape was changing quickly even though Fox and Pitt were absent from the scene; Pitt was nursing his gout and Fox would not leave St Anne's Hill. Georgiana kept him regularly informed of developments and in spite of himself his interest was piqued by her letters.

Left: *Bess, 1802, sporting the fashion for cropped hair dubbed* à la Titus. *The style was affected by few women, other than Bess, over the age of forty.*

*This page: The Post Office, by Thomas Rowlandson, above. Letters written by Georgiana and her friends were doubly censored, first by the author, in fear that they might fall into the wrong hands, and later by Victorian ancestors who actually blacked out incriminating passages, as this letter from Georgiana to Bess shows, right.*

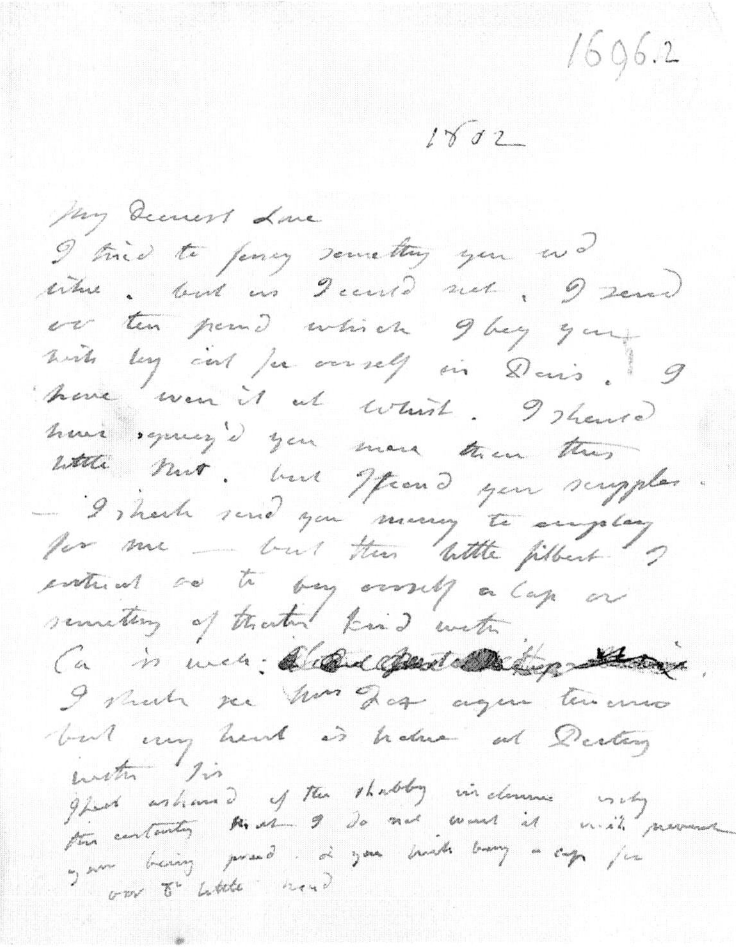

1696.2

1802

My Dearest Love
I tried to fancy something you wd like. but as I could not. I send you ten pound which I beg you with beg it for yourself in Paris. I have won it at Whist. I should have squeez'd you more than this little Nut. but I fear'd your scruples — I shall send you money to employ for me — but this little filbert I entreat you to buy yourself a Cap or something of that kind with
Ca is well: [redacted].
I shall see Mrs Fox again tomorrow but my heart is broken at Dorking with Sis
I feel ashamed of the shabby inclosure only the certainty that I do not want it with prevent your being proud. I you will buy a cap for your dr little head

Since Fox was not interested in participating, Georgiana could do little with the links she was forging between George and the Grenvilles, Fitzwilliam, Canning and the Prince of Wales. As winter gave way to spring Fox was beginning to reconsider his quiescence. The Grenvilles were so keen to get rid of Addington that Lord Grenville mentioned the unmentionable to Pitt, and suggested that the road to victory lay in 'uniting all the leading men in Parliament without exception'.

Bess returned to England just before Britain declared war on France on 18 May 1803. Eliza Ellice, her niece, had died and it was not prudent for English visitors to remain abroad. Several thousand of them, including James Hare, were trapped and declared prisoners of war when war broke out. Bess's depression lifted when she saw how the domestic situation at Devonshire House had changed during her absence. The Duke and Georgiana had entered a bad patch and were both desperate for her company. The Duke wrote to her several times emphasizing how anxious he was for her to come and assuring her of his 'fixed and unalterable' friendship. Bess accepted his offer of her old position without hesitation.

Bess's arrival in London coincided with Harryo's and Caroline Ponsonby's presentation. She made no attempt to have Caroline St Jules presented as a French émigrée, although some people thought she might, but watched enviously as Georgiana's daughter rode off in a train of carriages. Whatever had been given to her in life, she felt, had been offset by what lay out of her reach. She also noticed that Georgiana's welcome was a little distracted; politics was consuming all her time. The way forward was clear to her: the Whigs should join forces with the other opposition parties.

1803–1804

# The Doyenne of the Whig Party

*His Grace the Duke of Bedford has erected in the Garden at Woburn, a Temple consecrated to Friendship, and decorated with busts and poetical tributes to his most valued intimates. The bust of Mr Fox is honoured with some beautiful lines, from the elegant pen of the Duchess of Devonshire.*

MORNING HERALD, 2 JULY 1804

AMONG THE TOURISTS RETURNING from France was the new Duchess of Bedford, the former Lady Georgiana Gordon. The sixth Duke had naturally gone out of his way during his visit to Paris to be courteous to his late brother's putative fiancée and, almost in spite of himself – certainly in spite of his Whig friends – found himself proposing before he departed.

Georgiana tried very hard not to be bitter about the marriage and instead concentrated on preparing Harryo for her season. She did not feel as comfortable with Harryo as she had with Little G: Harryo was too quick to judge and not afraid to speak her mind, which disconcerted her mother. Harryo's obvious contempt for Bess also strained relations between them. The terms under which Bess had returned to Devonshire House had not escaped Harryo's notice, and it made her resent the woman more than ever. As for her father – she despised him for preferring the ridiculous Bess to her mother. While the family was staying in Bath she complained to Little G: 'Our mode of life is not diversified. We are still in this Hotel, Papa thinking it, I believe, Paradise regained. Lady Eliz. and Sidney [the dog] both unwell, both whining and both finally as agreeable as you know I always think them. Mama, in an hotel, as everywhere else, kinder more indulgent and more unlike the Lady or the Dog, than I can express.'

Harryo was not looking forward to her coming out. She was aware that she had not inherited her mother's looks or figure, and her lack of interest in fashion was partly a defence against unfavourable comparisons. But she was not shy like Little G and her witty conversation made a strong impression on visitors to Devonshire House. Georgiana sensed her daughter's dread of being teased because she was plump, and went to considerable lengths to ensure that she was never allowed to feel left out. However, Harryo did not attract any suitors.

As soon as the season was over Georgiana turned her attention to politics again. The outbreak of war had reshuffled political alliances to some extent, but not enough to make a difference to Addington's hold on power. Georgiana would devote the next two and a half years of her life to one cause – that of seeing Fox in office, in a government made up of all the most talented men in parliament, which would bring peace to Europe.

As a general rule, the Victorian descendants who took it upon themselves to preserve their grandparents' papers employed a rigorous policy of sexual segregation: women's letters were destroyed, men's letters were preserved. In many archives Georgiana's letters are mentioned but have not themselves survived. However, the following account, pieced together from fragments, restores her to the tableau of political history.

The Whigs had no interest in supporting the government once the war was in progress. Addington's pro-peace position had been the only link between them. The Prince of Wales was hysterical about the dangers facing the country if France invaded. The Prince wanted to do something, to fight like his brothers, but his father would not allow him to hold a military position. He began to toy with the idea of saving the country by organizing a coalition against Addington. He discussed his plans with Georgiana, who promptly offered her services as a go-between.

She sounded out Fox on the Prince's behalf, but he was cautious about becoming involved with the Prince. Fox was prepared to contemplate co-operation with his former opponents but only if their aim was to bring peace to Europe rather than seek to defeat France, and if they could agree on Catholic emancipation. But Fox was frankly pessimistic. Georgiana was not deterred by his lack of enthusiasm. She and the Prince agreed that their next move should be to collar individual members of Grenville's party and convert them to the idea of a coalition. The obvious candidate for Georgiana's initial approach was George and she wrote to him on 8 July 1803 of the possibility of creating 'a union of Talent and respectability'.

As a result of Georgiana's efforts the idea of some sort of co-operation gained currency. Fox considered the Prince to be malleable, Sheridan 'treacherous' and Carlton House as a whole 'unsteady', but he was prepared to wait and watch. Sheridan did not improve his position with the Prince by ranting in public that Georgiana had polluted his mind with the 'Grenville infection' and tricked him into abandoning faithful friends like himself. Neither Fox nor Pitt had any intention of working with the other. But Georgiana was convinced that if the two men could meet they might reach an understanding. She wrote Fox a confidential letter pointing out that it could only be to his advantage if Pitt joined them, since 'his sentiments and opinions coincide with yours and . . . he is sincere in working for Peace'.

Georgiana fell ill shortly after writing the letter. Her health had become a serious handicap. The problem this time was a stone in her kidneys. 'She had a very bad night,' wrote Lady Spencer

to George on 15 September. 'Sir Walter and the Duke sat up with her almost the whole night.' Harriet was also at her side and cried as she watched her sister's sufferings: 'No Medicine, not the strongest, nothing that can be given her, has as yet taken effect. Six and thirty hours have already elapsed in the dreadful pain. I sat up with her last night. She was put into a warm bath and bled, which reliev'd her at the time so much that she slept from four till near seven leaning on my Arm and quite still.' It was almost a month before the *Morning Herald* reported that Georgiana was receiving 'daily visits of the Nobility, who warmly congratulate her Grace on her perfect recovery'.

Although the attack had left her weak it also increased her determination to promote her plan. Fox groaned when he received a summons from her to come to a meeting at Devonshire House. However, the meeting was successful in galvanizing the Whigs; the general consensus afterwards was in favour of limited co-operation if the occasion was appropriate.

For most of the session Georgiana remained at Bath with the Duke, Bess and Harryo, drinking the waters and trying to wean herself off laudanum. The heavy doses prescribed by Dr Farquhar had left her with an addiction to the drug. Having fallen into the trap of 'false tranquillity', as Lady Spencer termed it, several times before, Georgiana was determined not to succumb again. Fox sent her a continuous stream of reports of political developments, and she was not idle: the Prince's 'unsteadyness' required continual vigilance, and she was prepared to risk her friendship with him to counteract Sheridan's influence. She was one of the few people from whom the Prince was prepared to accept advice and even, occasionally, opposition.

*Thomas Grenville, 1841, by Camille Manzini. The Whig politician, a member of the Devonshire House Circle, pictured here late in life, met Georgiana soon after her marriage to the Duke and reputedly never married because of his unrequited love for her.*

Georgiana's intervention helped to maintain the general momentum towards a coalition. All that was needed was an excuse – a reason for the Grenvilles and Foxites to work together – and this finally appeared in the shape of a debate on army recruitment policies which Fox supported despite opposition from Sheridan's wing of the Foxites. The way was clear for the two sides to make a formal agreement.

On 26 January 1804 Thomas Grenville invited Fox to go riding. Grenville spoke earnestly of his brothers' 'wish to co-operate with me (and friends of course) in a systematic opposition for the purpose of destroying the Doctor's Administration'. His only proviso, to which Fox agreed (assuming that it would never come about), was that Pitt should also be invited to join the coalition against Addington. The inclusion of Pitt was exactly what Georgiana had hoped for since the combination of Pitt, Fox, the Prince and Lord Grenville would prove to be invincible. Pitt knew this, but he could not see himself sharing power with his old enemy. Nor did he want to join forces with his cousin Lord Grenville again; indeed, they were now barely on speaking terms.

London filled up after the Christmas recess, but Georgiana remained at Bath with the Duke, the two of them lying like invalids on chaise-longues in the overheated drawing room, nursing themselves with delicate self-absorption. Georgiana was now forty-six and the damp weather had brought on an attack of rheumatism. She was bored even though there was plenty to occupy her time: despite her remorse and her genuine attempts to re-structure her debts the unpaid bills continued to pile up in her closet in Devonshire House. She was once more begging her friends for money, the Prince in particular. Writing from Bath she asked him, 'if you should happen to be at all rich, a very small *cadeau* would make me comfortable . . .'

She cheered up considerably when the new Duke of Bedford invited her to write a poem about Charles Fox. The Duke was having busts made of all his friends which he intended to arrange in a pantheon to Whiggery at Woburn and he thought it appropriate for Georgiana to provide the inscription for Fox. She took it as one of the highest honours ever bestowed on her and consulted

L'Assemblée Nationale; — or — Grand Cooperative Meeting at St. Ann's Hill. — Respectfully Dedicated to the admirers of a "Broad-Bottom'd Administration"

the playwright Richard Fitzpatrick, who had offered to help. After reading the poem he wrote back, 'I admire it extremely and think that, (like everything I have seen of your writing) it bears the marks of true poetical genius . . .' True genius or not ('And whilst extending dedication for/Ambition spread, the baneful flames of war/fearless of blame, and eloquent to save, Twas he, twas Fox,' etc.), the inscription bears witness to Georgiana's and Fox's remarkable friendship, as well as to the adoration he inspired among the Whigs.

Now that Harryo was out of the nursery, Selina would have to find another family, yet no one except Bess wanted her to go, and in the end, Selina remained loosely attached to Devonshire House, somewhat removed from the day-to-day running of the house but close enough for Bess to feel her presence.

Georgiana remained at Bath until February when the Prince wrote to her with the news that his father had once again become deranged. This was the second time in three years. The Devonshires dismissed their doctors and hurried to London to prevent Sheridan or anyone else from monopolizing the Prince at this crucial moment. Two weeks later the doctors were reporting an improvement in the King's condition and the Prince put away his plans for a Regency government. Georgiana had been so caught up with affairs in London that she failed to take note of the bad reports coming from Bath about Hare, who died on 10 March 1804. He had never recovered from his ordeal as a prisoner of war in France, and a long walk with Lady Spencer on a chilly and damp afternoon had turned a head-cold into pneumonia. Georgiana was shocked. His death had torn a hole through the middle of the Devonshire House Circle and both she and the Duke wished to be alone. Bess shared their grief; Hare had known all their secrets, helped them in many of their scrapes, and had never betrayed his knowledge.

When Georgiana re-emerged from her mourning she found that Sheridan and his friends were still trying to secure the Prince's support for Addington. Apart from Sheridan there seemed to be two further obstacles to all the opposition parties working together. The first was the antipathy between Fox and Pitt, and the second was the Prince's aversion to having any dealings with Pitt. Although many people played a part in bringing these antagonistic men together, Georgiana's contribution was particularly effective – perhaps even decisive – in each case.

George Canning watched the Fox–Grenville–Carlton House alliance work well together and decided that Pitt was making a mistake in staying aloof from the opposition coalition. Once again he turned, via Granville Leveson Gower, to Georgiana, and asked her to persuade Fox to see Pitt. Even though Fox still thought Pitt was a 'mean', 'low-minded dog', he now accepted that the coalition could not succeed without him. But the Prince was less practical and still objected to his inclusion.

The next time the Prince visited Devonshire House he agreed with Georgiana that, 'no one party alone was strong enough to do any good, but that a union of all the great talents in the country was what he look'd to as the only measure that could be of any use.' 'I am ready to meet him half way,' he told her, 'but surely some little advance on his part is due to me.' Leveson Gower was duly given the message to take to Pitt. The outcome of these delicate manoeuvres was that a broad understanding between the parties (Sheridan excluded) was reached and Addington's government was doomed. By the middle of April Pitt, Fox and Grenville were co-ordinating strategy. On 19 April the government was defeated by one vote in a debate about India. It staggered on for several more days until Addington finally gave up and resigned on 30 April 1804.

Georgiana had already begun to feel sceptical about Pitt's intention to include Fox in the new government. She had heard rumours that he was holding private meetings with his own friends. Her fears soon proved to be justified: the King had no intention of allowing Fox into the cabinet and told Pitt it was a 'personal insult' to suggest his name. Fox was magnanimous when he heard the news; at a crowded meeting at Carlton House he urged his side to work without him. But the meeting closed with a unanimous decision to remain aloof from the new government: without Fox there could be no alliance with Pitt. This was splendid news for the Whigs. It meant that Pitt would be as isolated as Addington had been, and that his government would be vulnerable to attack.

Georgiana performed her usual trick of arranging delightful entertainments at Chiswick to boost party morale. In June Gillray commented on the Whigs' new-found solidarity in a cartoon of the coalition entitled, 'L'Assemblée Nationale; or – Grand Co-operative Meeting at St Ann's Hill', which showed Mr and Mrs Fox hosting a party. Pictured in the middle was Georgiana, holding a fan with the words THE DEVONSHIRE DELIGHT OR THE NEW COALITION REEL written across it. Although the cartoon was inimical towards the party in general, it affirmed, if there was ever a doubt, Georgiana's pre-eminence among the Whigs.

*Gillray's cartoon 'L'Assemblée Nationale; – or – Grand Co-operative Meeting at St Ann's [sic] Hill', 1804, shows a reception given by Mr and Mrs Fox (Mrs Armistead) for various factions of the opposition. The three Grenville brothers – Lord Buckingham, Lord Grenville and Thomas Grenville – are in the foreground bowing to Fox. Georgiana, Harriet and George, second Earl Spencer, are standing behind the seated Mrs Fox. Mrs Fitzherbert sits on the sofa receiving the fawning attentions of Lord Carlisle.*

1804–1806

# 'The Ministry of All the Talents'

*A woman more exalted in every accomplishment of rapturous beauty, of elevated genius, and of angelic temper, has not adorned the present age . . .*

MORNING CHRONICLE, 31 MARCH 1806

THE DEVONSHIRES WENT TO THE SEASIDE for their health and busied themselves with family matters while the opposition waited for Pitt to call parliament into session. Georgiana was worried about Harryo, who was argumentative and miserable because of Duncannon. He still could not make up his mind between Harryo and Lady Elizabeth Villiers, Lady Jersey's daughter, and was pursuing both girls. Even more galling to Georgiana and Harriet was the fact that Lady Jersey had succeeded in making the impressionable Duncannon infatuated with her; if she ordered him to marry Lady Elizabeth there was no doubt that he would. 'I feel anxious about Harriet and Duncannon,' Georgiana wrote to Little G. 'It must not go on – something must be decided and that is one reason why I wish her to go to you as I think you will judge better than I can.'

Georgiana was frightened when she saw Harryo's common sense overruled by her passions. Her behaviour made it difficult for Georgiana to be candid with her or talk to her as a friend. Harryo's adolescence was a complete contrast to that of Little G, who had never subjected her mother to sullen silences or nurtured slow-burning resentment. Little G was pregnant with her third child in September 1804, when she wrote to Georgiana: 'One cannot know till one has separated from you how different you are from everybody else, how superior to all mothers, even good ones.'

However, Georgiana's persistence succeeded in wearing down some of her daughter's defences. At the age of eighteen Harryo finally discovered the element of friendship which had been missing in her relationship with Georgiana. While she stayed with Little G at Castle Howard she wrote to thank her mother for her advice about Duncannon and added, with a touching earnestness, that her feelings towards her had changed: 'I never knew thoroughly what I felt for you till I left you . . . I am sure you alone could inspire what I feel for you, it is enthusiasm and adoration, that for anybody else would be ridiculous, but that to deny it [to] you would be unnatural.'

Georgiana had accepted Harryo's reserve as punishment for the years her children spent as orphans but Hart's partial deafness and isolation hurt her the most. Harrow had helped to draw him out, but he still disliked physical contact and sisterly teasing provoked hysterics. Bess was the only one whom he seemed to trust, which might have made Georgiana jealous had she not been relieved to see Hart talking to someone. She arranged for him to stay with Bess at the seaside while Harryo was at Castle Howard. 'I am full of anxiety on this subject and the fortnight he is away shall be very anxious,' she confided to her mother. But 'I have great dependence on Ly E's care and she has influence with him . . .'

With both her children away, Georgiana was able to devote her energies to the crisis developing around the Prince. Since the King's illness the power of Carlton House had increased: it was no longer merely the allegiance of a few men but a recognizable party in parliament. No one connected with Pitt doubted that as soon as the King died or lapsed into insanity the Prince would have his revenge on his father's men. Almost immediately after taking office Pitt began negotiating

*'The Reconciliation' refers to the attempt by Pitt and his followers to broker a truce between King George III and his son, the Prince of Wales. Georgiana and her friends panicked at the possibility that Prinny would betray his friends in order to make peace with his father, but they needn't have worried.*

with the Prince's friends to see what would gain his support for the government. Lord Moira and George Tierney thought he should arrange a reconciliation between father and son.

The interview was set for 12 November 1804 and as the day approached the Prince showed all the signs of a man set to betray his friends. There were crowded discussions at Brooks's and Devonshire House about how best to prevent the wayward Prince from deserting the coalition. Together, Georgiana and Fox primed the Prince on what he should say to the King and then waited anxiously for his return.

The meeting was a disaster for Pitt. Father and son attempted to be polite but as the King spoke almost non-stop and barely listened to the Prince's replies it was hardly a reconciliation. The Prince returned to London in a much steadier frame of mind, and Georgiana was able to inform George that 'he has put a stop *in fact* to all proceedings . . . He conveyed to Mr Pitt thro' Ld Moira that he could not enter into any negotiation that did not include all his friends.' Pitt was astonished and dismayed when he discovered that his plan had failed at the last moment.

Fox was jubilant; as a result of Georgiana's and his intervention the Prince had remained firm. He told Grey: 'Opposition *seems* now restored (at least) to what it was before the Duke of Portland's desertion . . .' He ended his letter by saying, 'you will be glad to hear that the Duke of Devonshire is doing something handsome and kind about the Duchess's debts.' The combination of her creditors' harassment and her friends' pleading had forced Georgiana to own up to her husband. 'Be freed, dearest, I conjure you,' Bess wrote; 'it is better things should be as [bad] as they are, than you go on temporising as you have done, promising I am afraid and not able to perform and therefore exasperating people . . .' Bess's pleas were echoed by Robert Adair and Fox, who feared that even if she did confess to the Duke she would lie about the sum.

Georgiana knew her friends were right. She was exhausted and no longer had the energy to fight off her creditors. She would be mortified, she confided to the Prince, if her children ever learned the truth about her, and described the 'constant anxiety and humiliation of knowing one has been to blame for want of caution and getting into bad hands, and yet feeling the impossibility of escaping'. However, Georgiana was fortunate that Bess and Harriet were there to give support just as they had after the great confrontation thirteen years earlier.

The Duke had been expecting a sum of £5,000 or £6,000, not the £50,000 Georgiana eventually presented to him. Bess stepped in immediately to act as a buffer between the two of them, but her fears proved exaggerated. The Duke did not shout or threaten a separation from Georgiana. 'There never was anything so angelic as the Duke of Devonshire's conduct,' wrote Bess in her syrupy way to her son Augustus Foster. 'The many conversations I had with him on the subject . . . increased my admiration and attachment to him. I feel secure now that she will avoid things of this kind for the future and though the sum is great, yet it will end well I am convinced.'

The decision, when it finally came, was more than generous. It took into account Georgiana's requirements as well as her foolishness with money. Her income was doubled to £2,000 a year, but the extra thousand was consigned to Mssrs Farrar and Altman, who were to be in charge of the liquidation of her debts. Her creditors would be paid by degrees and by the time Hart came of age the restrictions in the fourth Duke's will against raising a mortgage on the Cavendish estates would have expired, thereby allowing for the residue of Georgiana's debts to be paid off in one lump sum. The Duke even saw to it that her extra expenses such as her opera box and charitable subscriptions would be taken care of by Mssrs F and A. 'I shall never have a plague of money,' Georgiana wrote joyfully to Little G. 'I have kept from you the agitation which this has occaision'd. And am very happy and grateful to the blessed author of my happyness.'

Matters were never simple where Georgiana's finances were concerned, however, and even though she had made as full a confession as was possible for her, there were many debts which she had forgotten or hoped had gone away. Once the news leaked out that the Duke of Devonshire was going to settle the Duchess's debts, literally hundreds of creditors came forward with further claims. Some of them were genuine but others were frauds and Georgiana herself had trouble distinguishing between the two. For the rest of the year, more claims continued to trickle in, depriving Georgiana of the relief she had earned through her courage. Shortly after her confession Georgiana suffered excruciating pain from another kidney stone. The entire household remained awake for several nights until it passed.

Georgiana tried not to dwell on her debts and returned to politics as soon as she had recovered. Fox asked her to work alongside him and she became one of his chief whips. The Whigs were weak in the Lords; Georgiana organized a recruitment drive just before the opening of parliament urging supporters to register (no peer may vote in the Lords unless he declares his intention at the start of each year). Georgiana and Fox were determined to let nothing fall to chance. When it came to hunting down wayward votes Georgiana was tireless, ill or not, and was prepared, in the case of the slave trade debate in March, to pick up some of the lazier members and convey them to the House in her own carriage.

Although Pitt had managed to persuade Addington (who accepted a peerage as Viscount Sidmouth) and his followers to join the government, his support could not counterbalance the coalition. On 10 February 1805 a report was published containing allegations of malfeasance against the current First Lord of the Admiralty Henry Dundas (recently ennobled to Viscount Melville), Pitt's oldest and best friend, his chief support in the cabinet. On 9 April in a crowded Commons, MPs voted to impeach Melville by a majority of one vote. Two months later Sidmouth resigned, bringing the government to its knees.

The opposition continued to harry the government. In May Georgiana held a joint ball with Lavinia in honour of the coalition. Despite their long rivalry Lavinia behaved graciously for the first and only time in their acquaintance, and invited Georgiana to 'do the honours'. Georgiana reported that 'it was the most solidly magnificent ball I ever saw at least of late years'. It was also Georgiana's final and most public triumph.

While political struggles abated, Georgiana was surrounded by her family and friends and happily engaged in the light-hearted pursuit of amateur theatricals with Lady Melbourne and the Lambs. To her relief Harryo was no longer fretting over her cousin Duncannon, although this was because he had since dropped both her and Lady Elizabeth Villiers. Georgiana was also pleased to notice a marked improvement in sixteen-year-old Hart, who had started to respond to her overtures of friendship. The change had come about following Caroline Ponsonby's sudden engagement to William Lamb, the future Viscount Melbourne. Hart was distraught by the news; he secretly loved Caroline and had planned to marry her when he came of age. As she had done with Harryo, Georgiana managed to break through Hart's reserve and comfort him. They embarked upon a correspondence which later held some of his most precious memories of her. In what would prove to be her last letter of advice to him, Georgiana wrote, 'I live in you again. I adore your sisters, but I see in you still more perhaps than even in them what my youth was. God grant that you may have all its fervours and cheerfulness without partaking of many of the follies which mark'd the giddyness of my introduction into the world.'

The combatants were in their places by mid-January. Pitt had been buoyed by the success of the Battle of Trafalgar on 21 October which, though it had resulted in the death of Nelson, had also destroyed Napoleon's fleet and with it his ambition to launch an invasion of England. But Napoleon's defeat of the Austrian army at the Battle of Austerlitz destroyed the Third Coalition agreed between Russia, Prussia, Austria, Sweden and Britain earlier that year. Pitt's diplomacy was in ruins; the political future of the government looked bleak. A few days later Pitt collapsed at his home. He died on 23 January 1806 at the age of forty-six, having sat in the Commons for twenty-five years to the day.

The Pittite hegemony was over. Fox expressed his disbelief at the news 'as if there was something missing in the world – a chasm, a blank that cannot be supplied'. Georgiana echoed his sentiments to Hart. She had devoted over twenty years of her life to fighting one man who had 'fill'd an immense space in the universe'. Scarcely a day had passed without Pitt's name being mentioned. He had shaped their lives to such an extent that for a brief period the Whigs were at a loss.

*Left: Caroline Ponsonby, as Lady Caroline Lamb. When she announced her engagement to William Lamb, Georgiana's son, Hart, was distraught. Her mother, Georgiana's sister Harriet, was not happy either: 'My poor Caroline's fate is probably deciding for ever,' she wrote.*

*Right: Georgiana, Lady Melbourne and Mrs Dawson Damer, by Daniel Gardner, as the 'Witches Round the Cauldron' from* Macbeth.

*A cartoon satirizing the forced bonhomie between George III and the Whig administration.*

The King searched for alternatives to the Fox–Grenville Coalition but no one was willing to take the job. Bracing himself for the worst, he sent for Lord Grenville and invited him to form his own ministry. The government was quickly dubbed 'The Ministry of all the Talents' since Fox and Grenville invited Addington (now Sidmouth) to join them. The new government was the broadest and most inclusive of the entire reign of George III. However, after the initial euphoria there was a vicious scramble for places. It was an unfortunate and unseemly beginning. However, it was eventually settled that Lord Grenville was to be Prime Minister, Fox Foreign Secretary, George Spencer Home Secretary, Charles Grey First Lord of the Admiralty, and Sheridan Treasurer to the Navy, a generous position considering his past antipathy to the Coalition.

Georgiana wisely remained in the background until the government was formed, but once the ministers had kissed hands she re-emerged to head the celebrations. 'Last night we had a splendid assembly of the new ministry,' she informed Hart. 'The Prince sat up late with us till Mr Fox (who looks quite smart in powder) went to sleep by me or nearly so.' In the spirit of reconciliation and co-operation she held a supper for the outgoing ministers and their wives, telling Hart: 'The Dss of Gordon came and was very gracious, it was very forgiving of me to ask her.' Night after night London society passed through the doors of Devonshire House to pay their respects to the newly anointed leaders. Some were respectful, others sullen, and a few made such obvious attempts to curry favour (such as the Duchess of Gordon), that they made themselves ludicrous. 'The Dss of Gordon has made it up with me I perceive,' Georgiana joked to Hart, 'for she has asked us to a ball on the 6th. I hear she calls me, "the head of the administration".' Twenty years earlier Georgiana had been called the 'head of the opposition public' by Fanny Burney; this new title filled her with far greater satisfaction: 'we the administration,' she crowed. She joked with Little G, 'We are all statesmen and stateswomen and grown very dull and important.'

A few weeks later Georgiana fell ill with what appeared to be jaundice. At first the doctors thought it was another kidney stone and she seemed to rally for a few days. But on 22 March she rapidly deteriorated. Harriet moved into Devonshire House and sat up all night with her while she suffered a prolonged shivering fit. On 25 March Bess wrote in her diary: 'a better day' but she complained that 'crowds come to enquire'. On the twenty-sixth Georgiana suffered a fit which lasted eight and a half hours. The doctors shaved her head and put blister-plasters on her skin which did nothing to alleviate her illness and only increased the pain. The doctors did not know it but she had an abscess on her liver; there was nothing they could have done for her except make her comfortable, and in this they miserably failed.

By the twenty-seventh everyone in Devonshire House knew that Georgiana was dying. The family, friends and servants waited for the end to come. The crowd outside the gates grew in size. The Duke wrote to Selina on 29 March: 'If the worst should happen I hope you will be so good as to stay at Devonshire House for the present, for I shall not be in a state of mind to attend to anybody, or to receive or give any comfort whatever.'

Georgiana died at 3.30 a.m. on 30 March 1806. The Duke, Bess, Harriet, Lady Spencer and Little G were with her until 'nearly the end' and were reported to be 'quite delirious'. 'The Duke has been most deeply affected,' wrote a friend to Leveson Gower, who was on a diplomatic mission to St Petersburg. 'And has shown more feeling than anyone thought possible – indeed every individual in the family are in a dreadful state of affliction – Oh God what a loss they all have to lament – all who knew her lament her . . .' Thousands of Londoners streamed into Piccadilly to pay their respects. Friends came to Devonshire House to share their grief with the family. Fox sat on a sofa, tears rolling down his cheeks. The Prince was stunned: 'the best natured and best bred woman in England is gone,' he said. Both Harriet and Bess wrote eloquently and at length of their grief, but nothing remains of Lady Spencer's or the children's thoughts. Nothing, except for a tiny scrap of paper. It contained a message from Little G:

> Oh my beloved, my adored departed mother, are you indeed forever parted from me – Shall I see no more that angelic countenance or that blessed voice – You whom I loved with such tenderness, you who were the . . . best of mothers, Adieu – I wanted to strew violets over her dying bed as she strewed sweets over my life but they would not let me.

# *Epilogue*

*For no less than 33 years have we seen [the Duchess of Devonshire] regarded as the glass and model of fashion, and amidst the homage which was paid to her, she moved with a simplicity that proved her to be unconscious of the charm which bound the world to her attraction.*

MORNING CHRONICLE, 31 MARCH 1806

'THE RECOLLECTION ALONE REMAINS, and regrets, never ceasing regrets,' Bess wrote to her son Augustus six weeks after Georgiana's death. 'Regrets only to be equalled by the angelic, the unequalled qualities of the friend of my heart, my dear, my loved, my adored friend . . . she was the only female friend I ever had . . .'

Bess was alone and unprotected without Georgiana. The day after her death, she wrote in her diary, 'we are a family of sufferers.' But she was not part of the family and even though she referred to 'we' and 'our loss', she was frightened that Georgiana's children and Lady Spencer would insist on her leaving Devonshire House. Georgiana's body lay in state for five days beneath the gaze of an unending file of mourners. On 5 April the coffin was removed from the Great Hall. 'I am no longer calm,' Bess wrote in her diary, 'no longer soothed. I cannot describe my own feelings.'

The Duke remained in his room, except for one night when, Bess claims, 'he was hysterical. I stayed late, very late with him. I then went feebly to my room – when I got there I saw in his anxiety he had followed me.' The family abandoned Devonshire House after the departure of Georgiana's coffin; the children and the Duke went to Chiswick House, Bess to Roehampton with Harriet. Georgiana's children were undecided as to how treat her.

Georgiana had anticipated that her death would jeopardize Bess's situation at Devonshire House, not to mention that of Clifford and Caroline St Jules. To safeguard her friend, she had made Bess the sole guardian of her papers. Georgiana had left behind thousands of letters: it would take weeks, if not months, to sort through them, and Bess had absolute discretion to do as she pleased with every one. The importance of Georgiana's gift did not escape her, nor did it leave the family in any doubt as to Georgiana's wishes concerning Bess. For perhaps the only time in their acquaintance, Bess made a special attempt to be sensitive to Lady Spencer and refrained from making the most of this last victory. On 8 May she sent Lady Spencer a lock of Georgiana's hair curled inside a piece of paper which read: 'Dear Madam, The enclosed paper is the only thing that I *can* take the liberty of asking you to accept.' Lady Spencer's reply has not survived.

There is no doubt that Bess arranged Georgiana's papers to suit herself, selectively destroying or preserving letters to leave a record that was detrimental to Georgiana's reputation and beneficial to hers. She was simply incapable of behaving in any other manner. But her grief was real. In July she wrote to Augustus, who was in America: she felt numb, she said, although Dr Farquhar had told her 'it was always so' after terrible shock. Georgiana was 'the constant charm of my life. She doubled every joy, lessened every grief. Her society had an attraction I never met with in any other being. Her love for me was really "passing the love of woman".' But now that Georgiana had gone there were no further impediments to Bess taking her place.

Events overtook the children's desire for Bess to leave Devonshire House. First Clifford came home on leave from the navy, then Hart fell ill and Bess offered to nurse him. The Duke naturally

*'Whig Statesmen and their Friends', 1810, by William Lane. From left to right: William, fifth Duke of Devonshire; Henry, third Baron Holland; William, second Earl Fitzwilliam; bust of Charles James Fox; John, first Baron Crewe; Frederick, third Earl Bessborough; John, second Earl of Upper Ossory; Dudley Long North; General Richard Fitzpatrick; George, first Marquess Cholmondeley; George, second Marquess Townshend; Lord Robert Spencer; St Andrew, thirteenth Baron St John.*

*Little G as the Countess of Carlisle holding a miniature of her mother. 'I wanted to strew violets over her dying bed as she strewed sweets over my life,' she wrote soon after Georgiana's death, 'but they would not let me.'*

found that he could not do without Bess to look after him. Then Charles Fox developed dropsy in August and his condition became so serious that the Duke offered him Chiswick House as a quiet refuge from London. Bess made all the arrangements concerning the servants, and took it upon herself to issue bulletins to the public about his health. 'She is a disgusting beast,' raged Lavinia, who was furious at the way Bess had succeeded in taking centre stage. Bess was also among those present when Fox died on 13 September 1806. She attended Fox's funeral and sat with Georgiana's children while the Duke performed his duty as one of the eight pall-bearers. Four months later the King dismissed the coalition after it attempted to grant Irish Catholics the right to hold officer rank in the army. The Whigs did not form another government until Grey became Prime Minister in 1830.

Bess remained at Devonshire House after Fox's death; her manner subtly changed, as if Georgiana had bequeathed to her not only all her papers but her position too. In November Harryo informed Little G that Bess was shameless in her 'laying down the law when Lord M. and you are away'. Worst of all, she had to watch Bess usurping her mother's place: by rights Harryo should have sat at the head of the table. 'Lady E. F. is very disagreeable in doing the honours instead of me,' she told Little G; 'which for every reason in the world is painful to me.' Harryo feared a confrontation with Bess; Caroline, Harriet's daughter, however, had no compunction in goading her when the opportunity arose.

A year later Little G felt obliged to write to Hart, asking him not to avoid his father because of Bess's presence. 'I feel all her conduct and hate it as you do, but I wish you to behave towards and concerning her as Harryo does, never giving her a handle against you or a just cause of complaint to my father.' Two years after this Little G wrote to Hart to inform him of 'the most painful event': Bess and the Duke were to be married.

The only person who took Bess's side was Harriet. But even she hoped that Bess would not try to marry the Duke and usurp Georgiana's place as the Duchess of Devonshire. 'Tho' we have no right to expect it,' she admitted. Georgiana's death had destroyed something vital in Harriet: 'no one knows, G,' she told Leveson Gower, 'not even you – how I suffer.'

In the autumn of 1809, Bess and the Duke announced their engagement. Harriet tried hard to forgive her, telling Leveson Gower:

> I really love Bess, and think she has many more good and generous qualities than are allowed her, but I think she has the worst judgement of any body I ever met with; and I begin to think she has more *Calcul*, and more power of concentrating her wishes and intentions, than I ever before believ'd . . . Yes, Dear G., I shall stand alone against my whole family and *her* [Georgiana's] children as favouring an event which God knows pains me more than any I believe, and taking part against them and against the Memory of what I lov'd best on earth . . .

The Duke informed the children and Lady Spencer of the marriage a few days after the event. 'I wish you, my Dear Lady Spencer, not to answer this letter,' he wrote on 17 October 1809, 'as it must be disagreeable to you to do it, and I shall know by other means whether you approve or disapprove of my conduct.' Hart wrote a cold acknowledgement to his father which made no mention of Bess, and a heated letter of complaint to his cousin Lady Caroline Lamb: 'Hardly till I see it can I believe that the woman could have the assurance to take that name always so sacred to us, and hence

*Harryo and Granville Leveson Gower with their children. After her marriage to Leveson Gower Harryo adopted both children from her husband's previous liaison with her aunt Harriet. Though she remained jealous of Harriet, she doted on the children, who were, in effect, her own cousins.*

forward to be so polluted.' Harryo did not know how she would bear living at Devonshire House with Bess as her stepmother. Fortunately, a suitor stepped forward to ask for her hand. Harryo had been in love with him for some time, but the connection was nevertheless surprising – the suitor was Granville Leveson Gower, Harriet's lover and father of her two illegitimate children. He was thirty-six and anxious to have a legitimate family of his own. Harriet had accepted that she could not hold him and had given him her blessing to woo Harryo. Her love for him, however, had not diminished and his marriage to her niece caused her intense anguish. 'I must put down what I dare tell nobody,' she wrote in 1812. 'I have heard or spoke that language [of love] and for 17 years of it lov'd almost to idolatry the only man from whom I could have wish'd to hear it, the man who has probably lov'd me least of all those who have profess'd to do so . . .'

The Duke made it clear which daughter he preferred. In 1809, when Caroline St Jules married George Lamb, the Duke gave them £30,000. A few months later, when Harryo married Leveson Gower, he gave them only £10,000. Bess made no complaint about the Duke's unfairness. Although Bess had finally taken Georgiana's title, she never possessed her popularity or her influence, and the Cavendishes and Spencers were never more than civil to her. Shortly after her marriage she wrote a polite note to Lady Spencer requesting leave to visit, but was refused.

The Duke soon gave Bess a taste of what Georgiana had experienced for so many years. Shortly before their marriage, he and Bess made friends with a Mrs Spencer, a young widow who married into the Churchill side of the Spencer family. As she had no money to speak of, and few relatives living in England, the widow was excessively grateful for any show of friendship. Mrs Spencer soon became so attached to the Devonshires that she was one of the few witnesses at their wedding. But afterwards Harryo remarked that her father's phaeton was seen outside Mrs Spencer's door every day, 'sometimes till past 8'.

The Duke did not live long enough for Mrs Spencer to become a serious threat to Bess. He died on 29 July 1811. Bess, however, was not ready to relinquish the fruits of her campaign. She demanded money and jewels from Hart, and even insisted that the Duke had written a secret codicil which gave her Chiswick for life. To support her claims, Bess announced the true paternity of Caroline and Clifford – a shocking act in

*Left: William George Cavendish, Marquess of Hartington, later sixth Duke of Devonshire.* 'I hope to live *to see you not only happy but the cause of happyness to others,' Georgiana wrote to Hart shortly before her death.*

*Above: Chatsworth, 1820. Hart spent hundreds of thousands of pounds altering and improving Chatsworth and Devonshire House.*

eighteenth-century society – and tried to insist that Clifford had the right to use the Cavendish arms. There were ugly rows between herself and the Cavendishes. Finally, at the end of the year Hart bribed Bess to leave in 'a single week' with a generous ex gratia settlement on herself and his two half-siblings. Bess moved out of Chiswick and built a small house in Richmond. After five years of respectable widowhood she packed up her belongings and moved to Rome.

Bess made Italy her permanent home, although she sometimes visited England and eventually regained her former influence with Hart, much to Little G's and Harryo's annoyance. She died in Rome on 30 March 1824, eighteen years to the day after Georgiana's death. A locket carrying one of her friend's reddish-gold curls, and also a hair bracelet of Georgiana's, were next to her bed. Hart was at Bess's side during her last moments, and so, surprisingly, was Georgiana's daughter Eliza Courtney, now Mrs Ellice. Afterwards Hart arranged for Bess's remains to be brought to England and interred alongside those of Harriet, who had died three years previously in 1821, and Georgiana and the Duke.

Georgiana's daughters had mixed feelings when they heard the news of Bess's death. 'It has shocked us very much, she had so much enjoyment of life and I feel so unhappy and anxious about poor Mrs Lamb [Caroline St Jules],' wrote Harryo. 'It also brings past times to one's mind, and many nervous and indefinable feelings. This is a bitter cup, dearest sister.' The eight children belonging to Georgiana and Bess: Hart, Little G, Harryo, Eliza Courtney, Caroline St Jules, [Augustus] Clifford, and Frederick and Augustus Foster remained on good terms with each other all their lives.

Hart took his duties as head of the family very seriously. He looked after all the interests of his siblings; his first act on becoming the sixth Duke was to raise Harryo's marriage portion from £10,000 to £30,000. He also paid Thomas Coutts some of the money that was still outstanding from Georgiana's debts. Through his influence Clifford received the royal appointment of Gentleman Usher of the Black Rod and was eventually made a baronet. Frederick Foster and Augustus were frequent visitors to Chatsworth. Georgiana's two legitimate daughters never achieved, nor sought, the celebrity of their mother. Although Harryo and Leveson Gower presided over the British embassy in Paris with great éclat for almost seventeen years.

Hart did not fulfil Georgiana's expectations; his deafness prevented him from entering politics or playing a significant role in the Whig party. He never married and died childless at the age of sixty-eight in 1858, which meant that the title moved sideways to his second cousin William Cavendish. During his lifetime Hart displayed many of Georgiana's traits. He was a serious collector of minerals, an enthusiastic modernizer who spent hundreds of thousands of pounds altering and improving Chatsworth and Devonshire House, and a famously generous host. As well as enjoying the sisterly adoration of Harryo and Little G, Hart was a popular society figure. He formed a lifelong attachment to the gardener and architect Joseph Paxton, who lived with his wife in a house on the Chatsworth estate. Their relationship provoked comment but not scandal and Hart led a contented if unremarkable life.

It was Louis Dutens in his memoirs who best described Georgiana's effect on her generation. 'Without any intention, she became the directress of the *ton*. She changed the hours, and set the fashions. Everybody endeavoured to imitate her, not only in England, but even at Paris . . . She had an uncommon gracefulness in her air rather than her figure; and appeared always to act entirely from the impression of the moment.'

However, Georgiana was pre-eminently a woman of paradoxes. She once confided to Alexandre Calonne, just before the Regency crisis in 1788, 'I have opened my heart to you and you have seen that despite all my gaiety, it is often quite tormented.' She wrote in a similar vein to Mary Graham in 1778, and to Sir Philip Francis twenty-one years later in 1799. Throughout her adult life Georgiana struggled to reconcile the contradictions that enveloped her. She was an acknowledged beauty yet unappreciated by her husband, a popular leader of the *ton* who saw through its hypocrisy, and a woman whom people loved who was yet so insecure in her ability to command love that she became dependent upon the suspect devotion of Lady Elizabeth Foster. She was a generous contributor to charitable causes who nevertheless stole from her friends, a writer who never published under her own name, a devoted mother who sacrificed one child to save three, a celebrity and patron of the arts in an era when married women had no legal status, a politician without a vote and a skilled tactician a generation before the development of professional party politics.

Georgiana should be credited with being one of the first to refine political messages for mass communication. She was an image-maker who understood the necessity of public relations, and she became adept at the manipulation of political symbols and the dissemination of party propaganda. Georgiana was not alone, however, in the duties she performed as a political wife. Her career exemplifies the political access granted to aristocratic women when politics was still a family enterprise. Georgiana is remarkable for being a successful politician whose actions brought about national events; for attaining great prominence in spite of the fact she was a woman in a society which favoured men; and for achieving these successes while enduring great personal suffering in her search for self-fulfilment.

Long after the scattering of the Whig party and the destruction of Devonshire House Georgiana continues to fascinate because of her single-minded determination to be the heroine of her own story. 'I was but one year older than you when I launched into the vortex of dissipation – a Duchess and a beauty,' Georgiana wrote to Hart three weeks before she died, 'however . . . all that I have seen never weaken'd my principles to devotion to almighty God or took from my love of virtue and my humble wishes to do what is right.'

*A commemorative ring made after Georgiana's death containing a lock of her hair. When Bess died eighteen years after Georgiana, a locket containing one of Georgiana's reddish-gold curls and a hair bracelet of Georgiana's were found next to her bed.*

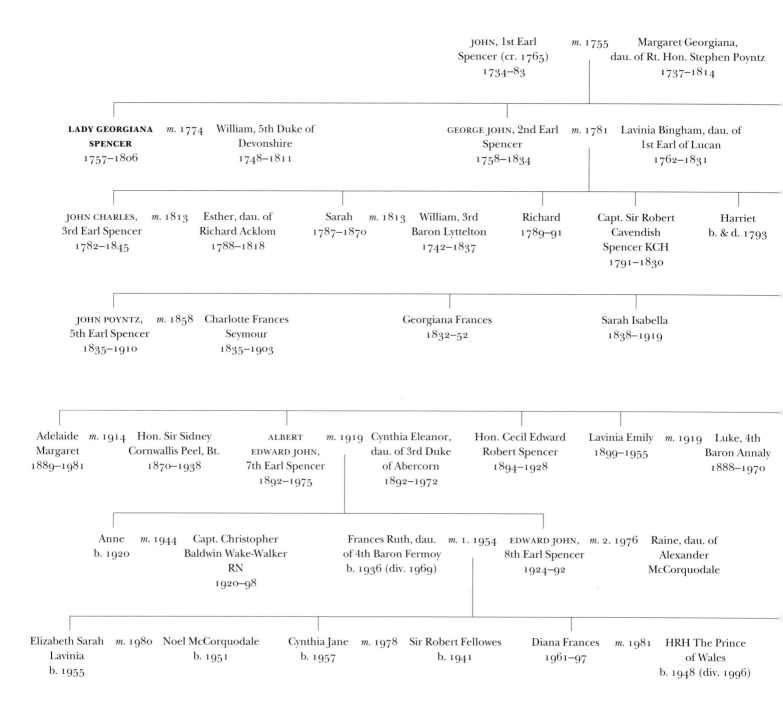

JOHN, 1st Earl Spencer (cr. 1765) 1734–83 *m.* 1755 Margaret Georgiana, dau. of Rt. Hon. Stephen Poyntz 1737–1814

**LADY GEORGIANA SPENCER** 1757–1806 *m.* 1774 William, 5th Duke of Devonshire 1748–1811

GEORGE JOHN, 2nd Earl Spencer 1758–1834 *m.* 1781 Lavinia Bingham, dau. of 1st Earl of Lucan 1762–1831

JOHN CHARLES, 3rd Earl Spencer 1782–1845 *m.* 1813 Esther, dau. of Richard Acklom 1788–1818

Sarah 1787–1870 *m.* 1813 William, 3rd Baron Lyttelton 1742–1837

Richard 1789–91

Capt. Sir Robert Cavendish Spencer KCH 1791–1830

Harriet b. & d. 1793

JOHN POYNTZ, 5th Earl Spencer 1835–1910 *m.* 1858 Charlotte Frances Seymour 1835–1903

Georgiana Frances 1832–52

Sarah Isabella 1838–1919

Adelaide Margaret 1889–1981 *m.* 1914 Hon. Sir Sidney Cornwallis Peel, Bt. 1870–1938

ALBERT EDWARD JOHN, 7th Earl Spencer 1892–1975 *m.* 1919 Cynthia Eleanor, dau. of 3rd Duke of Abercorn 1892–1972

Hon. Cecil Edward Robert Spencer 1894–1928

Lavinia Emily 1899–1955 *m.* 1919 Luke, 4th Baron Annaly 1888–1970

Anne b. 1920 *m.* 1944 Capt. Christopher Baldwin Wake-Walker RN 1920–98

Frances Ruth, dau. of 4th Baron Fermoy b. 1936 (div. 1969) *m.* 1. 1954 EDWARD JOHN, 8th Earl Spencer 1924–92 *m.* 2. 1976 Raine, dau. of Alexander McCorquodale

Elizabeth Sarah Lavinia b. 1955 *m.* 1980 Noel McCorquodale b. 1951

Cynthia Jane b. 1957 *m.* 1978 Sir Robert Fellowes b. 1941

Diana Frances 1961–97 *m.* 1981 HRH The Prince of Wales b. 1948 (div. 1996)

# Spencer Family Tree

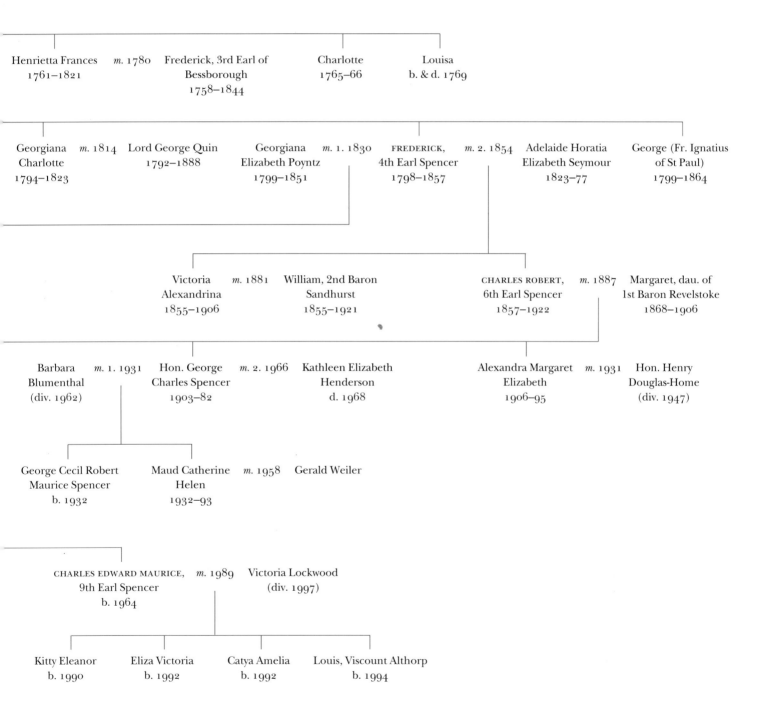

Henrietta Frances
1761–1821
*m.* 1780
Frederick, 3rd Earl of Bessborough
1758–1844

Charlotte
1765–66

Louisa
b. & d. 1769

Georgiana Charlotte
1794–1823
*m.* 1814
Lord George Quin
1792–1888

Georgiana Elizabeth Poyntz
1799–1851
*m.* 1. 1830
FREDERICK, 4th Earl Spencer
1798–1857
*m.* 2. 1854
Adelaide Horatia Elizabeth Seymour
1823–77

George (Fr. Ignatius of St Paul)
1799–1864

Victoria Alexandrina
1855–1906
*m.* 1881
William, 2nd Baron Sandhurst
1855–1921

CHARLES ROBERT, 6th Earl Spencer
1857–1922
*m.* 1887
Margaret, dau. of 1st Baron Revelstoke
1868–1906

Barbara Blumenthal
(div. 1962)
*m.* 1. 1931
Hon. George Charles Spencer
1903–82
*m.* 2. 1966
Kathleen Elizabeth Henderson
d. 1968

Alexandra Margaret Elizabeth
1906–95
*m.* 1931
Hon. Henry Douglas-Home
(div. 1947)

George Cecil Robert Maurice Spencer
b. 1932

Maud Catherine Helen
1932–93
*m.* 1958
Gerald Weiler

CHARLES EDWARD MAURICE, 9th Earl Spencer
b. 1964
*m.* 1989
Victoria Lockwood
(div. 1997)

Kitty Eleanor
b. 1990

Eliza Victoria
b. 1992

Catya Amelia
b. 1992

Louis, Viscount Althorp
b. 1994

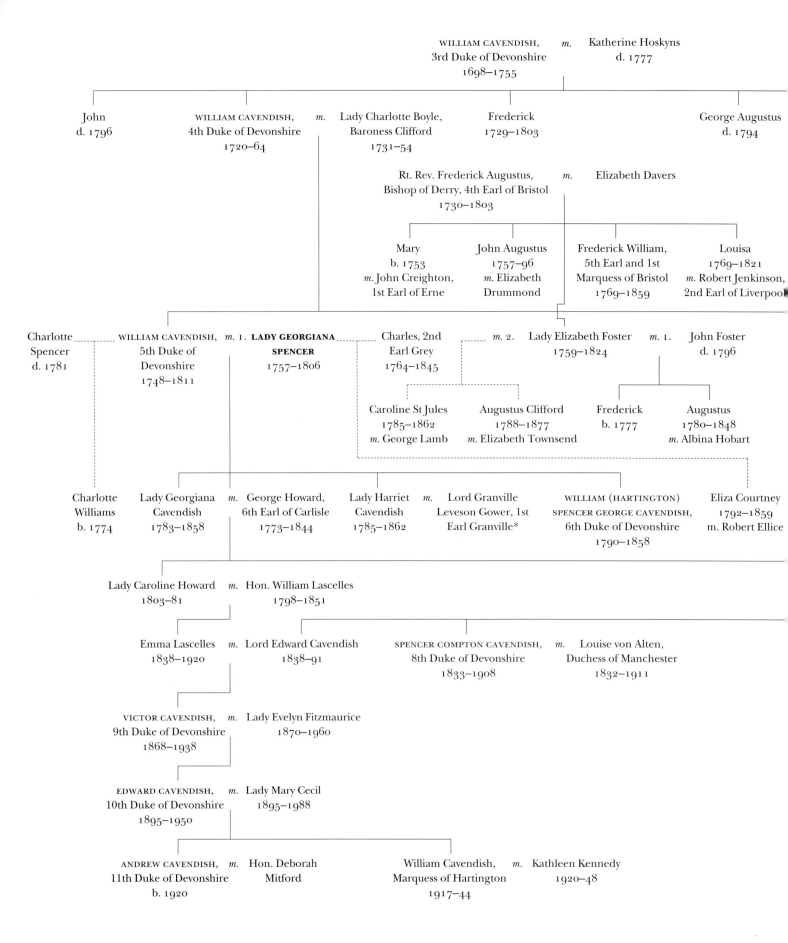

- WILLIAM CAVENDISH, 3rd Duke of Devonshire 1698–1755 *m.* Katherine Hoskyns d. 1777
  - John d. 1796
  - WILLIAM CAVENDISH, 4th Duke of Devonshire 1720–64 *m.* Lady Charlotte Boyle, Baroness Clifford 1731–54
    - Charlotte Spencer d. 1781 ........ WILLIAM CAVENDISH, 5th Duke of Devonshire 1748–1811 *m.* 1. **LADY GEORGIANA SPENCER** 1757–1806 ........ Charles, 2nd Earl Grey 1764–1845
      - Charlotte Williams b. 1774
      - Lady Georgiana Cavendish 1783–1858 *m.* George Howard, 6th Earl of Carlisle 1773–1844
        - Lady Caroline Howard 1803–81 *m.* Hon. William Lascelles 1798–1851
          - Emma Lascelles 1838–1920 *m.* Lord Edward Cavendish 1838–91
            - VICTOR CAVENDISH, 9th Duke of Devonshire 1868–1938 *m.* Lady Evelyn Fitzmaurice 1870–1960
              - EDWARD CAVENDISH, 10th Duke of Devonshire 1895–1950 *m.* Lady Mary Cecil 1895–1988
                - ANDREW CAVENDISH, 11th Duke of Devonshire b. 1920 *m.* Hon. Deborah Mitford
                - William Cavendish, Marquess of Hartington 1917–44 *m.* Kathleen Kennedy 1920–48
          - SPENCER COMPTON CAVENDISH, 8th Duke of Devonshire 1833–1908 *m.* Louise von Alten, Duchess of Manchester 1832–1911
      - Lady Harriet Cavendish 1785–1862 *m.* Lord Granville Leveson Gower, 1st Earl Granville*
      - WILLIAM (HARTINGTON) SPENCER GEORGE CAVENDISH, 6th Duke of Devonshire 1790–1858
      - Eliza Courtney 1792–1859 m. Robert Ellice
    - *m.* 2. Lady Elizabeth Foster 1759–1824 *m.* 1. John Foster d. 1796
      - Caroline St Jules 1785–1862 *m.* George Lamb
      - Augustus Clifford 1788–1877 *m.* Elizabeth Townsend
      - Frederick b. 1777
      - Augustus 1780–1848 *m.* Albina Hobart
  - Frederick 1729–1803
  - George Augustus d. 1794

- Rt. Rev. Frederick Augustus, Bishop of Derry, 4th Earl of Bristol 1730–1803 *m.* Elizabeth Davers
  - Mary b. 1753 *m.* John Creighton, 1st Earl of Erne
  - John Augustus 1757–96 *m.* Elizabeth Drummond
  - Frederick William, 5th Earl and 1st Marquess of Bristol 1769–1859
  - Louisa 1769–1821 *m.* Robert Jenkinson, 2nd Earl of Liverpool
  - Lady Elizabeth Foster 1759–1824

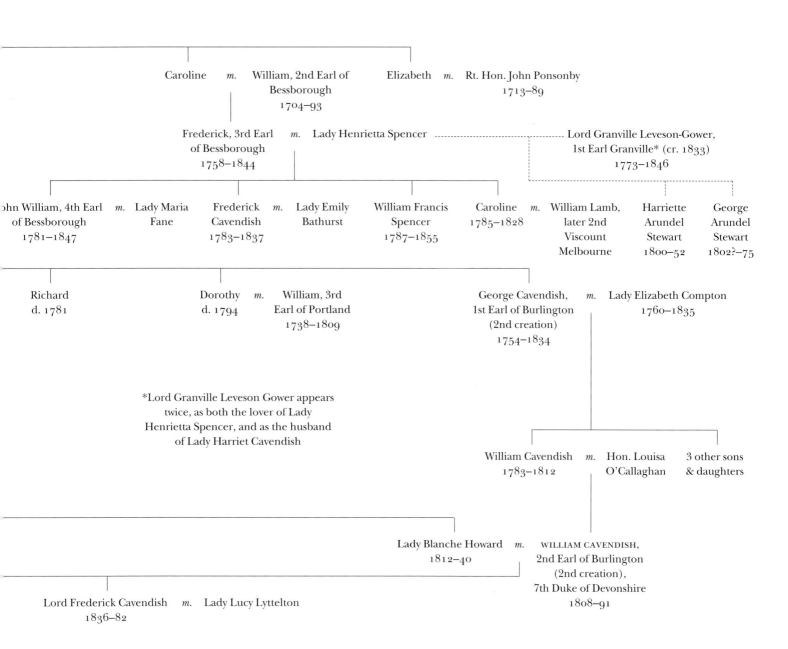

Caroline *m.* William, 2nd Earl of Bessborough 1704–93

Elizabeth *m.* Rt. Hon. John Ponsonby 1713–89

Frederick, 3rd Earl of Bessborough 1758–1844 *m.* Lady Henrietta Spencer ---- Lord Granville Leveson-Gower, 1st Earl Granville* (cr. 1833) 1773–1846

ohn William, 4th Earl of Bessborough 1781–1847 *m.* Lady Maria Fane

Frederick Cavendish 1783–1837 *m.* Lady Emily Bathurst

William Francis Spencer 1787–1855

Caroline 1785–1828 *m.* William Lamb, later 2nd Viscount Melbourne

Harriette Arundel Stewart 1800–52

George Arundel Stewart 1802?–75

Richard d. 1781

Dorothy d. 1794 *m.* William, 3rd Earl of Portland 1738–1809

George Cavendish, 1st Earl of Burlington (2nd creation) 1754–1834 *m.* Lady Elizabeth Compton 1760–1835

*Lord Granville Leveson Gower appears twice, as both the lover of Lady Henrietta Spencer, and as the husband of Lady Harriet Cavendish

William Cavendish 1783–1812 *m.* Hon. Louisa O'Callaghan

3 other sons & daughters

Lady Blanche Howard 1812–40 *m.* WILLIAM CAVENDISH, 2nd Earl of Burlington (2nd creation), 7th Duke of Devonshire 1808–91

Lord Frederick Cavendish 1836–82 *m.* Lady Lucy Lyttelton

# *Cavendish Family Tree*

# Index

# *Bibliography*

Battiscombe, Georgina, *The Spencers of Althorp* (London 1984)

Borer, Mary Cathcart, *An Illustrated Guide to London in 1800* (London 1988)

Cannon, J.A., *Aristocratic Century: The Peerage of Eighteenth Century England* (Cambridge 1984)

Cecil, Lord David, *The Young Melbourne* (London 1939)

Colley, Linda, *Britons, Forging the Nation 1707–1837* (London 1992)

Davidoff, L., *The Best Circles* (London 1986)

Deborah, Duchess of Devonshire, *The House: A Portrait of Chatsworth* (London 1982)

Ehrman, J., *The Younger Pitt* (London 1969–96)

Fraser, Flora, *Beloved Emma* (London 1986)

Friedman, Joseph, *Spencer House: The Chronicle of a Great London Mansion* (London 1993)

George, M.D., *London Life in the Eighteenth Century* (London 1992)

Girouard, Mark, *Life in the English Country House* (London 1978)

Hibbert, Christopher, *George IV, Prince of Wales* (London 1972)

Kelly, Linda, *Richard Brinsley Sheridan: A Life* (London 1997)

Langford, Paul, *A Polite and Commercial People: England 1727–1783* (Oxford 1989)

Mitchell, Leslie, *Charles James Fox* (Oxford 1992)

Pares, Richard, *George III and the Politicians* (London 1953)

Roth, W., *The London Pleasure Gardens of the Eighteenth Century* (London 1986)

Stone, Lawrence, *Road to Divorce: England 1530–1987* (Oxford 1990)

Sykes, Christopher Simon, *Private Palaces: Life in the Great London Houses* (London 1985)

Tillyard, Stella, *Aristocrats* (London 1994)

Tomalin, Claire, *Mrs Jordan's Profession* (London 1995)

# Picture credits

The author and publishers would like to thank the following individuals, collections, galleries and photographic archives for permission to reproduce their material. If we have inadvertently infringed anyone's copyright we will be pleased to rectify the mistake, if notified, in any future edition.

2 Photograph © 2001 Board of Trustees, National Gallery of Art, Washington. Andrew W. Mellon Collection

4 Private Collection (Stapleton Collection, London)

8 From the collection at Althorp

11 From the collection at Althorp

12 *left & right* From the collection at Althorp

13 British Library, London (Bridgeman Art Library, London)

15 Private Collection (Bridgeman Art Library, London)

16 Devonshire Collection, Chatsworth. By permission of the Chatsworth Settlement Trustees

18 *left* Private Collection/The Stapleton Collection (Bridgeman Art Library, London)

18 *right* Guildhall Library, Corporation of London (Bridgeman Art Library, London)

19 Devonshire Collection, Chatsworth. By permission of the Chatsworth Settlement Trustees

21 From the collection at Althorp

23 *above* Private Collection (Stapleton Collection, London)

23 *below* Private Collection (Bridgeman Art Library, London)

24 *above & below* Devonshire Collection, Chatsworth. By permission of the Chatsworth Settlement Trustees

26 Private Collection (Bridgeman Art Library, London)

29 Private Collection (J.B. Archive, London)

30 City of Westminster Archive Centre, London (Bridgeman Art Library, London)

31 Museum of London (Bridgeman Art Library, London)

32 *left* Private Collection (AKG, London)

32 *right* Museum of London

33 *left* Museum of London

33 *right* By courtesy of the National Portrait Gallery, London

34 Private Collection (The Art Archive/Dagli Orti, London)

37 Devonshire Collection, Chatsworth. By permission of the Chatsworth Settlement Trustees

38 Somerset Maugham Theatre Collection, London (Bridgeman Art Library, London)

39 Yale Center for British Art, Paul Mellon Collection/Bequest of Mrs Harry Payne Bingham (Photo: Bridgeman Art Library, London)

41 *above* British Museum, London (Bridgeman Art Library, London)

41 *below* Private Collection (AKG, London)

43 National Gallery of Scotland, Edinburgh (Bridgeman Art Library, London)

44 Collection of the Earl of Leicester, Holkham Hall, Norfolk (Bridgeman Art Library, London)

45 British Library, London (Bridgeman Art Library, London)

46 Private Collection (Bridgeman Art Library, London)

49 Harewood House, Yorkshire (Bridgeman Art Library, London)

51 Private Collection/Giraudon (Bridgeman Art Library, London)

54 Philip Mould, Historical Portraits Ltd., London (Bridgeman Art Library, London)

55 Collection of Earl Spencer, Althorp, Northamptonshire (Bridgeman Art Library, London)

56 Wallace Collection, London (Bridgeman Art Library, London)

57 Wallace Collection, London (Bridgeman Art Library, London)

59 Museum of London

60–1 Yale Center for British Art, Paul Mellon Collection (Bridgeman Art Library, London)

63 Museum of London

64–5 Private Collection (Sotheby's, London)

66–7 Victoria & Albert Museum (Stapleton Collection, London)

69 Scottish National Portrait Gallery, Edinburgh (Bridgeman Art Library, London)

70 Devonshire Collection, Chatsworth. By permission of the Chatsworth Settlement Trustees

73 Ickworth, Suffolk (National Trust Photographic Library, London/Christopher Hurst)

75 Ickworth, Suffolk (National Trust Photographic Library, London/Jeremy Whitaker)

78 Museum of London

79 Wallace Collection, London (Bridgeman Art Library, London)

83 British Museum, London (The Art Archive, London)

84 Private Collection (Stapleton Collection, London)

85 *above* Stansted Park Foundation, Rowlands Castle, Hampshire

85 *below* Devonshire Collection, Chatsworth. By permission of the Chatsworth Settlement Trustees

86 *above* Devonshire Collection, Chatsworth. By permission of the Chatsworth Settlement Trustees

86 *below* The Duke of Buccleuch & Queensberry (The Art Archive/Dagli Orti, London)

92 National Gallery of Scotland, Edinburgh (Bridgeman Art Library, London)

94–5 Museum of London

96 Devonshire Collection, Chatsworth. By permission of the Chatsworth Settlement Trustees

97 City of Westminster Archive Centre, London (Bridgeman Art Library, London)

98 *left* British Museum, London

98 *above & below right* Author's Collection

99 *above left* City of Westminster Archive Centre, London (Bridgeman Art Library, London)

99 *below left* British Museum, London

99 *right* British Museum, London

100 British Museum, London

101 British Library, London (Bridgeman Art Library, London)

102 Private Collection (Bridgeman Art Library, London)

105 Wimpole House, Cambridgeshire (National Trust Photographic Library, London/Roy Fox)

108 Musée Ceramique Sevres (The Art Archive/Dagli Orti, London)

110 Yale Center for British Art, Paul Mellon Collection (Bridgeman Art Library, London)

111 *left* British Museum, London

111 *right* Theatre Museum, London (The Art Archive/Graham Brandon)

112 The Royal Pavilion, Brighton (Angelo Hornak, London)

113 The Royal Pavilion, Brighton (Angelo Hornak, London)

115 Knole, Kent (National Trust Photographic Library, London)

118 *above* Yale Center for British Art, Paul Mellon Collection (Bridgeman Art Library, London)

118 *below* Victoria & Albert Museum, London (Bridgeman Art Library, London)

119 The Directors of Coutts & Co., London

121 *above* Private Collection (AKG, London)

121 *below* O'Shea Gallery, London (Bridgeman Art Library, London)

122 Devonshire Collection, Chatsworth. By permission of the Chatsworth Settlement Trustees

123 *above* New College, Oxford University, Oxford (Bridgeman Art Library, London)

123 *below* O'Shea Gallery, London (Bridgeman Art Library, London)

127 Private Collection (Bridgeman Art Library, London)

128 Devonshire Collection, Chatsworth. By permission of the Chatsworth Settlement Trustees

131 Garrick Club, London (The Art Archive, London)

132 *above* Private Collection (The Art Archive/Eileen Tweedy, London)

132 *below* British Library, London (Bridgeman Art Library, London)

133 By courtesy of the National Portrait Gallery, London

135 National Trust for Scotland, Edinburgh (Bridgeman Art Library, London)

136 Private Collection (AKG, London)

137 National Museum of Art, Havana (AKG, London)

138 Devonshire Collection, Chatsworth. By permission of the Chatsworth Settlement Trustees

140 *left & right* Devonshire Collection, Chatsworth. By permission of the Chatsworth Settlement Trustees

141 Devonshire Collection, Chatsworth. By permission of the Chatsworth Settlement Trustees

144 Devonshire Collection, Chatsworth. By permission of the Chatsworth Settlement Trustees

149 Stansted Park Foundation, Rowlands Castle, Hampshire

150 Private Collection (Stapleton Collection, London)

151 New College, Oxford University, Oxford (Bridgeman Art Library, London)

152 By courtesy of the National Portrait Gallery, London

155 Yale Center for British Art, Paul Mellon Collection (Bridgeman Art Library, London)

156 Trustees of the Glynde Endowment Settlement

158 Fitzwilliam Museum, University of Cambridge (Bridgeman Art Library, London)

159 Yale Center for British Art, Paul Mellon Collection (Bridgeman Art Library, London)

160 By courtesy of the National Portrait Gallery, London

161 Musée Carnavalet, Paris (AKG, London/Erich Lessing)

162 New College, Oxford University, Oxford (Bridgeman Art Library, London)

163 National Maritime Museum, Greenwich

164–5 Attingham Park, Shropshire (National Trust Photographic Library, London)

168 From the collection at Althorp

170 Stansted Park Foundation, Rowlands Castle, Hampshire

171 Yale Center for British Art, Paul Mellon Collection (Bridgeman Art Library, London)

172 New College, Oxford University, Oxford (Bridgeman Art Library, London)

174 *above* Private Collection (AKG, London)

174 *below* Author's Collection

175 British Library, London (Bridgeman Art Library, London)

177 Private Collection (Bridgeman Art Library, London)

180–1 Devonshire Collection, Chatsworth. By permission of the Chatsworth Settlement Trustees

184 Devonshire Collection, Chatsworth. By permission of the Chatsworth Settlement Trustees

185 *above* Devonshire Collection, Chatsworth. By permission of the Chatsworth Settlement Trustees

185 *below* City of Westminster Archive Centre, London (Bridgeman Art Library, London)

187 By courtesy of the National Portrait Gallery, London

188 Private Collection (Christie's Images, London)

190 Stansted Park Foundation, Rowlands Castle, Hampshire

192 By courtesy of the National Portrait Gallery, London

196 *above* Kedleston Hall, Derbyshire (National Trust Photographic Library, London/John Hammond)

196 *below* Royal Institute of British Architects, London

197 Private Collection (The Art Archive/Dagli Orti, London)

198 Archiv fur Kunst & Geschichte, Berlin (AKG, London)

201 Archiv fur Kunst & Geschichte, Berlin (AKG, London)

202–3 Private Collection (The Art Archive/Eileen Tweedy, London)

205 By courtesy of the Trustees of the Goodwood Collection

206–7 Christopher Wood Gallery, London (Bridgeman Art Library, London)

207 From the Castle Howard Collection

209 *above* Private Collection (Bridgeman Art Library, London)

209 *below* Private Collection (Bridgeman Art Library, London)

211 Christie's Images, London (Bridgeman Art Library, London)

212 By Courtesy of the National Gallery of Ireland, Dublin

213 *above* Private Collection (Stapleton Collection, London)

213 *below* Devonshire Collection, Chatsworth. By permission of the Chatsworth Settlement Trustees

216 By courtesy of the National Portrait Gallery, London

218 British Museum, London

221 Private Collection (AKG, London)

224 Devonshire Collection, Chatsworth. By permission of the Chatsworth Settlement Trustees

225 Private Collection (Christie's Images, London)

226 Author's Collection

229 By courtesy of the National Portrait Gallery, London

231 Devonshire Collection, Chatsworth. By permission of the Chatsworth Settlement Trustees

232–3 Private Collection/Phillips, The International Fine Art Auctioneers (Bridgeman Art Library, London)

234 Devonshire Collection, Chatsworth. By permission of the Chatsworth Settlement Trustees

235 Mallett Gallery, London (Bridgeman Art Library, London)

237 Devonshire Collection, Chatsworth. By permission of the Chatsworth Settlement Trustees

252 Devonshire Collection, Chatsworth. By permission of the Chatsworth Settlement Trustees